Re/Constructing "the Adolescent"

Joseph L. DeVitis & Linda Irwin-DeVitis
GENERAL EDITORS

Vol. 33

PETER LANG
New York • Washington, D.C./Baltimore • Bern
Frankfurt am Main • Berlin • Brussels • Vienna • Oxford

Re/Constructing "the Adolescent"

Sign, Symbol, and Body

EDITED BY
Jennifer A. Vadeboncoeur
& Lisa Patel Stevens

PETER LANG
New York • Washington, D.C./Baltimore • Bern
Frankfurt am Main • Berlin • Brussels • Vienna • Oxford

Library of Congress Cataloging-in-Publication Data

Re/constructing "the adolescent": sign, symbol, and body /
edited by Jennifer A. Vadeboncoeur, Lisa Patel Stevens.
p. cm. — (Adolescent cultures, school, and society; vol. 33)
Includes bibliographical references and index.
1. Adolescence. 2. Teenagers. I. Title: Reconstructing "the adolescent".
II. Vadeboncoeur, Jennifer Andrea. III. Stevens, Lisa Patel.
IV. Adolescent cultures, school & society; v. 33.
HQ796.R3736   305.235—dc22   2003027183
ISBN 0-8204-6803-7
ISSN 1091-1464

Bibliographic information published by **Die Deutsche Bibliothek**.
Die Deutsche Bibliothek lists this publication in the "Deutsche
Nationalbibliografie"; detailed bibliographic data is available
on the Internet at http://dnb.ddb.de/.

Cover photos by Kerry A. Collins
Cover design by Lisa Barfield

The paper in this book meets the guidelines for permanence and durability
of the Committee on Production Guidelines for Book Longevity
of the Council of Library Resources.

© 2005 Peter Lang Publishing, Inc., New York
275 Seventh Avenue, 28th Floor, New York, NY 10001
www.peterlangusa.com

Printed in the United States of America

CONTENTS

ACKNOWLEDGMENTS

We acknowledge our high regard for the contributing authors of this book. What began as a shared interest has grown through collaboration into this volume. The authors' dedication and commitment to theoretically grounded and ethical research is evident in their work, and it has been a true pleasure to work with them.

We acknowledge the people whose lives are represented in these chapters. From schools, programs, homes, and other contexts around the world—young people, students, teachers, parents, community members—their words, stories, and practices remind us of the considerable honour and responsibility we have as researchers, educators, and learners.

Finally, we acknowledge the editorial work this volume reflects, and those who made this endeavour possible. We thank Joseph and Linda DeVitis, Series Editors; Bernadette Shade, Production Supervisor; and Dawn Butler, our initial Production Assistant. Our thanks and heartfelt gratitude to Kerry A. Collins, for her ongoing work as Production Assistant and her creative vision for the cover photographs.

Finally, we gratefully acknowledge the copyright holders for permission to use the following copyrighted material:

> The photo and title text from J. Desantis, Unbelievable: We control who you think you are, 2002. Used by permission of the publisher.

INTRODUCTION

"I shall create!" cries the defiant yet propulsive, reaching, stretching, character at the center of Gwendolyn Brooks' touching and gritty homage to adolescents, "Boy Breaking Glass." "If not a note," he continues, "a hole/If not an overture, a desecration." One way or another, I'll invent a life and I'll leave my mark on this earth.

I shall create! It's the radical impulse at the core of our beings, a sweeping gesture, all-out, unreserved. I hesitate to name it universal in these pages and this precinct, but why not? Imaginative power, the creative move, the restless stance is imprinted on our spirits, and is as close to a human signature as we've got. Each of us constructs a life, unique and singular, out of the facticity of our existence. We are thrust into a world not of our choosing; we build what we can, and we make sense as we go, all on that rocky foundation. And while the construction project lasts a lifetime—that is, while we are each a work-in-progress from start to finish—in contemporary Western culture, adolescence is particularly fraught in terms of identity formation.

Re/Constructing "the Adolescent" can help us crack open the common sense assumptions that sit heavy on the body of adolescence. The authors of this volume challenge the taken-for-granted as dogmatic and insistent, rigid and dysfunctional; they note that the social construction of adolescence is unstable, ambiguous, contingent. They invite us to a more hopeful and generative rethinking of the possible meanings and practical implications of adolescence. "What if?" they ask, and in that gesture they ignite the imagination, they "light the slow fuse of possibility."

Puberty is a fact; everything surrounding that fact is fiction. We construct the myths, and just like that, the myths construct us. In "A Winter's Tale" a character explains: "I would that there were no age between ten and three and twenty or that youth would simply sleep out the rest; for there is nothing in the between but getting wenches with child, wronging the ancestry, stealing and fighting." Teenagers are trouble—this is the pervasive and defining myth, the myth that sticks to kids like barnacles, sharp and ugly.

Of course it's true that no one can be mature without being immature, wise without being innocent, experienced before inexperienced, but these categorizations, too, are inventions, precarious and vulnerable. There is no purely stable "experienced," no absolute state called "inexperienced." We are, each of us, on the move and on the make, propelled from yesterday toward tomorrow; we are unruly sparks of meaning-making energy on a voyage through our lives.

For those of us concerned with the situations of childhood, of children and youth, recognizing the vigorous boom and boost of that voyage is important. We note that there are questions that fuel the voyage—Who in the world am I? What in the world are my chances and my choices? These are questions of identity as well as geography—they are personal and idiosyncratic, and, as well, social and cultural, historical and political. Who am I, in this world? What are my choices, given what I find? What can I make out of all that I've been made?

We work in sites of hope and struggle—hope for a future, conflict over the meaning and direction, the scope and size and shape—that that future might take. Schools, for example, might be places of curiosity, imagination, and reflectiveness embodying a passion for the possible, or they might as well be little assembly lines and mini-prison workshops. We might encourage the search for meaning by helping young people develop a capacity to look through a wider range of perspectives—the various disciplines, the array of arts and expressions, a diversity of people as well as one's own experiences—or we might insist on obedience and conformity above all.

This book can help us choose the path of humanization, the direction of enlightenment and liberation. Knowing that we will always fall short, that absolute understanding and once-and-for-all freedom will surely elude us, cannot deter us. We see dehumanization—the reduction of human beings—as both possibility and practice. We seek in contrast the central human project, the task of humanization, without boundaries, without walls. I turn again to the wild and wonderful Chicago poet Gwendolyn Brooks: "This is the urgency. Live! And have your blooming in the noise of the whirlwind."

William Ayers
Distinguished Professor of Education
Director, Center for Youth and Society
University of Illinois, Chicago
Author of *Fugitive Days: A Memoir*
Chicago, Illinois

Youth are heated by Nature as drunken men by wine.

Aristotle

As the roaring of the waves precedes the tempest, so the murmur of rising passions announces this tumultuous change: a suppressed excitement warns us of the approaching danger. A change of temper, frequent outbreaks of anger, a perpetual stirring of the mind, make the child almost ungovernable. He becomes deaf to the voice he used to obey: he is a lion in a fever: he distrusts his keeper and refuses to be controlled. (p. 175)

Rousseau, J. J. (1972/1911). *Emile*. (B. Foxley, Trans.). London: Dent.

To be normal during the adolescent period is by itself abnormal (p. 267).

Freud, A. (1958). Adolescence. *Psychoanalytic Study of the Child*, 15, 255–278.

CHAPTER ONE

Naturalised, Restricted, Packaged, and Sold: Reifying the Fictions of "Adolescent" and "Adolescence"

Jennifer A. Vadeboncoeur

"What do you want to be when you grow up?"

There are several ways to read this question. Perhaps the most common reading is when it is taken to mean, "What career choice have you made?" The notion that careers are singular and that every young person "chooses" his or her career notwithstanding, the question is problematic. It simultaneously implies that who the young person is, at this moment, is not as important as the adult he or she will become. It exemplifies just one of the hegemonic ways that young people are defined and essentialised in western industrial societies today: the "adolescent" as an unfinished product, as undeveloped, as a being whose existence is characterised by exclusion from the dominant child/adult binary.[1] "Adolescence" is often perceived as a wasteland, bordered by "too old for father's lap" and "too young to vote." It is the landscape between the poles of childhood and adulthood, and as such, "adolescents" are frequently marked and categorised as the "ones who don't belong."

For the last century, the social construction of adolescence as a temporary "stage" has been both described and constructed through a theory that emphasises developmental achievements over the course of sequential and cumulative stages. This theory, largely credited to

G. Stanley Hall (1904)—the "father of adolescence"—is so deeply embedded in social discourses about young people that it is taken to be
fact. Occasionally, changes are made to the age brackets and identifying markers of young people, emphasising early adolescence as the
transition beginning with puberty and using late adolescence to describe eighteen year olds and beyond. However, regardless of minor
tinkering with these labels, the dominant view of youth as "unfinished" is remarkably resilient. Such pervasive discourses, and the fictions that coincide with these discourses, simply but effectively serve
to control young people, covertly and overtly restricting their bodies,
relationships, affiliations, and opportunities and ultimately, limiting
their possible life pathways.

    This book provides a forum for the voices and lived experiences of
young people. The researchers who have contributed here willingly
engage with the dilemmas of doing research with youth; some are
more, and others are less, comfortable with this task. Each recognises
that research is fraught with the dangers inherent in translating a
human life into a set of signs. This introductory chapter sets out to
frame the book and to that end I have organised three sections that,
taken together, offer a foundation for each of the forthcoming chapters. First, I begin by introducing the reader to several current discourses regarding young people today that contribute to the
prevailing social "truth" about youth. Next, I discuss some of our
struggles against doing research *on* youth, and attempt to create a
space for young people in this book that allows us to learn from their
experiences, while being ever wary of co-opting them through adult
and research lenses. Finally, I lay out one navigational passage
through the text to serve as a provisional guide for readers. Rather
than organising the text into the common "class, race, gender" triad,
the emphasis here is on speaking across those categories as an alternative to maintaining them. Each chapter is briefly summarised to
allow readers a window into the complexity of the research, while
maintaining the authenticity of the social context (Ochs & Capps,
2001). I turn now to a discussion of discourses about young people.[2]

"ADOLESCENT" DISCOURSES AS FICTIONS

In this section, I highlight several discourses about "adolescents" and "adolescence" as a method of engaging the reader in a discussion about the "truth" of these two categories. The notion of regimes of truth, borrowed from Foucault (1980), is helpful to highlight the powerful way that discourses influence how we see and know young people. Power produces discourses of knowledge, in turn, producing regimes of truth and criteria by which to determine "truthfulness" (e.g., Foucault, 1986). The relations of power that I highlight here reflect the developmental and educational sciences and the media, although the way these relations are played out is locally contextualised. I take as a starting point the notion that power, knowledge, and truth are inexorably entangled, but also that attending to the constructed, contested, and political features of these regimes may open the possibility for alternatives or radical re/constructions.

Constructing a Science that Produces Its Object

While positivism has monopolised western scientific thought since Descartes, challenges have surfaced across disciplinary fields for at least a century, building momentum in the 1970's (e.g., Kuhn, 1962/1970). According to scientific positivism, knowledge of the external world is knowable when rigorous scientific methods are employed that eliminate subjective—emotive, aesthetic, and moral—elements. These elements distort knowledge by tainting research with uncertainty in the form of the hopes, intentions, and/or expectations of the researcher. Once controlled, science, research, and knowledge remain protected from the influence of subjective elements. Without these controls, science is reduced to opinion.

Researchers and theorists within the natural sciences (e.g., Harding, 1991; Kuhn, 1962/1970; Polanyi, 1983), the social sciences (e.g., Bernstein, 1975, 1976; Bourdieu, 1991; Fairclough, 1989, 1992; Foucault, 1975/1995, 1980; Vygotsky, 1978, 1986), and literary theory (e.g., Bakhtin, 1981, 1986; Volosinov, 1929/1986) have created different ways of addressing the limitations of positivism that are based upon a recognition of the sway of social forces.[3] They have also provided both theoretical and empirical maps for the way in which human beings socially construct knowledge and identity through discursive and social practices. This conversation continues with discussions of how

social construction takes place, the extent to which all human experience is mediated by discursive and social practices, and the consequences of multiple, simultaneous, and sometimes conflicting
knowledges and identities within subject positions and social relations.[4] Indeed, the role of science for some has moved from discover-
ing the truth, to constructing good narratives—from uncovering the
world, to creating possible and imaginary worlds. Medawar (1982)
adds that the scientific method itself:

> like any other explanatory process is a dialogue between fact and fancy, the
> actual and the possible, between what could be true and what is in fact the
> case—it is a story of justifiable beliefs about a possible world. (p. 111)

Some conversations move between critiques of positivism and attempts to construct meaningful alternatives, such as recognising par-
tial and positional claims to the "authority of experience" (hooks,
1994) and the radical constructivist shift from truth to "viability" (von
Glasersfeld, 1989). Proponents of this multidisciplinary "interpretivist
turn" have in common a commitment to theorising epistemic claims
embedded within power structures and dialectically constructed
through cultural tools such as speech, written language, sign systems,
gestures, and communicative acts that come into existence by virtue
of the socially negotiated meanings we bestow on them. Indeed, taken
together these mediational means both constitute and are constituted
by the social practices within which they are employed (Wertsch,
1991). Building upon Volosinov's (1929/1986) work, language, as a
system of signs, has both material and ideological properties and effects created through the dialogic link between one consciousness and
another. Signs are material in that they are associated with a particular form, sound, or gesture and they are ideological in that they reflect
alternative "realities," acquiring meanings that move beyond what is
given, or common knowledge, to something that is *new* and extended
in the text (Halliday, 1967; Saussure, 1916/1986; Vygotsky, 1986).

Indeed, once we begin to argue the possibility that humans
socially construct meaning with cultural tools—along with interpretations of social positions, the behaviour of others, and the roles we
perform—we gain access to a new position that allows us to ask the
question: What if? What if this theory is not true? What if this theory

is a fiction? Or in Harding's (1991) famous words, ask "Whose science is this?" Whose knowledge? Who, for instance, writes the discourse of "adolescence"? By whose gaze does the "adolescent" become an object of research? What counts as evidence in this paradigm? Whose perspective and subject position is privileged? Who benefits? Who is silenced? It has become possible to look at disciplinary knowledges as stories, as narratives, as containing a combination of fact and fiction, more or less "truth," and as being motivated by the very perspectives positivism was attempting to control: political, economic, cultural, and religious beliefs and their concomitant value systems.

The work of theorists and researchers, such as Bakhtin, Vygotsky, Bourdieu, and Foucault—to identify a transdisciplinary sample—draws our attention particularly to the use of language and semiotics as a site for the social construction of meaning. One of the quintessential markers of the social construction of adolescents, then, is the language that is used to objectify, refer to, and categorise young people, created and applied in social contexts and exerting an influence between them. The very words used to converse about young people—whether surfacing within disciplinary discourses, such as developmental science, or the everyday talk that saturates many social contexts with mediating discourses—construct restrictive knowledges about possible identities. Unruly. Hormone-crazed. Awkward. Out of control. Risk seekers. This familiar vernacular, invoked from the hegemonic position of the adult or the researcher, carries the same panic, fear, and the need to control as do such institutionally sanctioned versions labelling youth "at risk," "challenging," and "troublesome" (e.g., Moje, 2002).

Narrow and typically negative discourses regarding young people permeate every strata of society, from education to shopping malls to government. Within such limiting discourses, relationships between young people and adults take on the colonial aspects of the dichotomy between the naïve subject and the figure of authority (Bhabha, 1994). Simply put, the "adolescent" is cast as an objectified entity, in need of leadership, guidance, and control from the adult. In this way, the discourse around young people functions ideologically, imparting "shared ideas or beliefs which serve to justify the interests of the dominant group" (Giddens, 1997, p. 583). For adults, and educators in particular, how we regard, talk about, interact with, and structure activities around and with young people is dialectically situated within the dominant, often disabling, discourses surrounding this "difficult stage" of development: a "stage" that is theoretically and ideologically produced.

What if, as Achebe (1988) argues, "theories are no more than fictions which help us to make sense of experience and which are subject to disconfirmation when their explanations are no longer adequate" (p. 98)? What if "the adolescent" is a fiction? What if the uncomfortable stage of "adolescence" is a story made universal, and as such, a time and space that adults impose on and negotiate with young people in western societies? What if what we see and hear and "know" about "adolescents" as a society, or nexus of industrialised societies, is more a function of social discourses, practices, and expectations than a function of the young people to whom we refer? Indeed, less a function of youth and more a function of political, economic, educational, and governmental discourses?

Two issues immediately surface if we consider theoretical "truths" about "adolescents" as possible fictions. The first is that we have to create a space for the possibility that not only are these theories fictions, but also that there is no way to access the "real" behind the "real adolescent" (Walkerdine, 1984). If the "object" or the "subject" of a discipline is constituted discursively, then it may remain more a reflection of the discourses upon which it rests than any external or objective phenomenon "out there." The second issue, addressed in the next section of this chapter, is that the kinds of fictions that we create have ethical and material consequences. Paraphrasing Achebe (1988), perhaps the ultimate judgment on human kind is not whether we acquiesce to a fiction, but rather what kind of fiction will persuade us to comply. A discussion of three discourses, followed by a brief description of youth responses to discourses as calculated interruptions, completes this section.

The Naturalisation of Adolescence

Although a century stands between current research and Hall's (1904) definition of adolescence as a developmental stage marked by "storm and stress," the insertion of this disciplinary knowledge within industrialised social contexts remains a prominent fiction. I would argue that it does so precisely because it aligns and buttresses a theory of adolescence that is based upon the discourses of individuality and natural development that were, and still are, at the forefront of social beliefs. While maintaining that they have uncovered an objective phenomenon—a phenomenon that exists in the real, external world—these discourses actually produce the phenomenon they claim to study and understand.

Walkerdine's (1984) meticulous Foucauldian analysis of the way developmental psychology and child-centred pedagogy were inserted into the existing discourses of twentieth-century economics and education provides an example of this production. At the beginning of the twentieth century, the industrial revolution welcomed young people into factory life in droves, benefiting from inexpensive labour in difficult working conditions. Within a few decades, however, as industrial jobs became more difficult to find, youth were systematically removed from industrial jobs through child welfare laws and compulsory senior schooling. While some young people were able to make the shift from paid work to unpaid school, working-class, immigrant, and marginalised youth were the least welcome and the most likely to be excluded from schools. In addition, the wages earned by many of these working youth contributed to nothing less than the survival of their families.

As a response to fears about poverty and criminal behaviour in youth, the disciplinary knowledge generated from developmental psychology and applied through child-centred pedagogy was an attempt to meet two needs: the social needs of reducing poverty and delinquency,[5] and the needs of the developing child. The "developing child" reflected two Piagetian assumptions about development. First, that development is an individual process, a process propelled by each individual child's own internal drive for equilibration, or cognitive sense making. Second, that development is a natural process, fundamentally based on maturation and biological change. For Piaget (1967), the developmental stages were cumulative and sequential, leading inevitably toward the rational control of emotions in adulthood. All characteristics of the "developing child," the phenomenon under study, were identified as solely individual qualities, arising from a developmental process that was deemed universally human, and therefore, natural.

However, as Walkerdine notes, the developing child as a phenomenon is itself an object that is produced through the discourse of developmental psychology. As such, "the 'real' of child development is not a matter of uncovering a set of empirical facts or epistemological truths which stand outside, or prior to, the conditions of their production" (Walkerdine, 1984, p. 165). Indeed, the developing child does not exist outside of the very discourses and disciplinary knowledges that produce it. Developmental psychology, as just one science within the larger category of natural and social sciences, is centrally implicated in the production of the very object it attempts to study. In addition, when scientific knowledge becomes socially axiomatic and taken for granted, as a society we cease to challenge it. Instead, over time, developmental psychology produces the "real" of development in a fiction about the individual and natural development of all children (see Clark, 1989; Vadeboncoeur, 1997).

Consider the kinds of expectations and self-fulfilling prophecies that are communicated and produced through the implicit agenda and explicit rules used in one type of public space for young people: the middle school. The middle schooling educational movement is predicated upon a developmental rendering of early adolescents as too big for elementary school practices and not quite big enough to survive in the land of high school predators. The result is a call for a unique atmosphere for early adolescents, one that is premised upon the use of pedagogical approaches such as cooperative grouping and peer mediation to deliver educational enrichment (Carnegie Council on Adolescent Development, 1995). While these strategies may well be worthwhile in terms of pedagogy, what the middle school movement fails to do is substantively interrogate how the positioning of early adolescents in society works to cast them in particular roles and pathways (Lesko, 2001). This simultaneously localises the perceived difficulties and overall turbulence of this age group solely within individuals and their physical development. Their difficulties have been "naturalised" and leveraged to argue the "real" of early adolescence, rather than being recognised as experiences that are negotiated within particular social relations and contexts. The controlling and productive role of adults and institutions, along with the way in which structural forces influence opportunity and access, are not questioned and in some cases rendered invisible. The individual success or failure of youth remains centre stage, while a social structural analysis exists outside the realm of consideration. By naturalising the discomforts of adolescents, we come to expect them, and through them, produce the "stage" itself.

Restricting the Adolescent Body and Mind

Society's response to its own assumptions about adolescents is to limit their movement by controlling their time and space, by containing young people in schools and their homes through curfew, and by limiting their access to knowledge and decent jobs. These assumptions lead to practices of control, surveillance, and restriction (Finders, 1998/1999; Lesko, 2001). In this way, the discourses surrounding young people in society relegate them to limited, precarious, and marginalised positions. The fictional assumption here is that it is necessary to do so.

It is interesting to note that Foucault (1975/1995) links the development of "observatories," and methods of training the mind and body through disciplinary power, with the major technological advancements in the sciences, such as telescopes, lenses, and light beams. He argues that while these apparatuses provided the foundation for the new physics and cosmology, social institutions incorporated similar ideas. For example, the spatial structure of hospitals, asylums, prisons, and schools shifted to reflect hierarchical surveillance through "the perfect disciplinary apparatus" which made it "possible for a single gaze to see everything constantly" (p. 173). Sheer geometry supported the model of the central administration desk with patients' or prisoners' rooms surrounding it. But surveillance was extended, like an octopus, through tentacled arms as well. Relay stations were created to further embed the "gaze" through monitors and supervisors, as if by remote control.

The same movement toward hierarchical surveillance was integrated into teaching and the teaching relationship through tutors, assistant teachers, and teachers who tended to spend more time monitoring behaviour than on pedagogical engagement. Discipline, for Foucault (1975/1995), "makes possible the operation of relational power that sustains itself by its own mechanism and which, for the spectacle of public events, substitutes the uninterrupted play of calculated gazes" (p. 177). The teachers supervise the students, and are themselves supervised by the administration. The students, internalising the teacher's gaze, begin to regulate their own behaviour in school, and supervise their siblings (and parents) at home. Hierarchical surveillance is self-reproducing and perhaps one of the most powerful lessons of schooling.

Through the internalisation of systems of surveillance, self-regulated behaviour "contains" differences within people and diversity between people, homogenising the social context. Indeed, "containment" is an arrangement through which all forms of oppression express themselves (Goldenberg, 1978). Whether embodied and/or psychological, containment increasingly restricts and narrows the scope of possibilities for youth, for example, through programs and practices that "quarantine a large percentage of the population" (Goldenberg, 1978, p. 8). Special education programs and tracking or streaming practices are, perhaps, the best known examples of containment, although it is important not to underestimate the kind of containment that is less obvious than physical removal from certain classrooms: the inscription of limited dreams and futures on the habitus of some young people in virtue of their social and symbolic capital (Bourdieu, 1991). Containment is founded on a belief that by separating youth from adults in general—and more specifically, separating youth with "contagious" differences from other "normal" youth—society is protected from youth deviance and diversity, and not "infected" by it.

Goldenberg (1978) asserts that containment operates on three assumptions with regard to young people:

> first, that adolescence (presumably unlike either childhood or adulthood) is a particularly stressful period that is both universal in nature and predictable in onset;
> second, that delinquent, nonconforming, or deviant acts by adolescents are both the result and concrete symptoms of inadequate, incomplete, or pathological socialization; and

third, that existing societal values (particularly as reflected in the practices
and orientations of the institutions charged with their protection, promulga-
tion, and perpetuation) are not only sound, but also supportive of individual
and collective self-determination and self-actualization. (p. 5)

Taken together, these three assumptions provide what appears to be a
valid theory, based upon scientific research and consensus, identifying a specific period of development as adolescence and coupling that
period with delinquent and deviant behaviours. These unfortunate
behaviours are not only a function of this developmental stage, but
are caused by the very developmental "in between-ness" that characterises adolescence: the view of the adolescent as "unfinished" or in-
completely socialised. Finally, these assumptions are self-perpetuated
by providing a rationale for adult-created and controlled interventions for the benefit of young people. The programs and practices initiated tend to segregate youth; perhaps a happy side effect for the
adults and children who are fearful of their contagion.

Secondary schools reflect this controlled partitioning of both body
and mind: a hyper-regulated control of time, from four minutes to
move bodies from classroom to classroom, to forty-six or fifty minute
blocks for Biology, U.S. History, or Algebra II. As Foucault
(1975/1995) noted, the control of time and space, mind and body
movement, reflect hegemony working through powerfully pervasive
techniques subjugating youth as objects in need of control. Surveillance, noted earlier, can be expanded through the organization of
space, perhaps best exemplified in classrooms when teachers lecture
from the front of the room, then move to their desks in the back, while
the students complete desk work. At any moment, from the students'
perspective, the teacher may be watching, observing, taking note of
on-task and off-task behaviours. In the public space of the high
school, work is accomplished "independently," grades are awarded
"individually," and students are ranked according to autonomous capacities and efforts measured by tests that "objectively" assess "natural" ability. Built upon the principles of "social efficiency" and factory
model schooling, any reform of secondary school must examine and
analyse the social and historical rationale for Conant's (1959) original
vision of the comprehensive high school. Reform must engage in

nothing short of a cultural shift in attitudes and beliefs regarding educational opportunities for young people.

Our expectations of youth in general—and more specifically, those we categorise as *particular kinds* of youth based on their appearance and behaviour—influence both the way we see them and the kind of students that they can become. This has profound effects for students when, on the basis of our expectations, we offer different kinds of students access to different kinds of knowledge and pedagogical activities. As noted by Anyon (1980, 1997), Kozol (1991), and Mantsios (1998), for example, working-class students are much more likely to experience direct instruction in school, coupled with rote memorisation. Youth learn through schooling that work entails following the steps of a procedure that was created by someone else, and some teachers control behaviour by controlling access to knowledge. General trends emphasising the control of students in schools are magnified when young people come under the gaze of adults and teachers. Whether through the regimented school day, the separation of subject matter, the physical and psychological containment of youth in schools, or the limited and tightly prescribed right to learn, use, and produce knowledge, young people today find themselves with few options and many restrictions (e.g., Apple, 1993, 1996). That is, until they have access to money.

Adolescent Images: Packaged and Sold

Over the last several decades, an interesting switch has occurred. As some adults seek to limit the range of youth, others seek to construct them through identifiers such as "at risk" and "generation x," and still others seek to describe their experience using "code-switching portfolio people" (Gee, 2002) and "bar-code swipers" (Luke & Luke, 2001). But this naming provides not only a framework by which to deliver social and educational services aimed at remediating or improving conditions for specific groups of children and youth—a process that has its own benefits and costs. It also constructs a new consumer demographic: a new consumer group to target for both image construction and sales. Following Lasn (1999), commodified "fictions grounded in the facts of our life are an easier sell" (p. 38).

In keeping with the general approach of newspapers and news stations to represent the most egregious criminal behaviour and outrageous natural disasters as commonplace, the images of youth and stories about young people offered by the media often reflect the same biases. Not only do we tend not to tell stories that celebrate humanity, we also tend not to celebrate the lives of the many young people who live, and grow, and contribute to our cultures (e.g., Glassner, 1999). The media of industrialised societies provides few alternatives to the hormonal or delinquent image of the adolescent. In addition, the current trend is to exaggerate certain qualities of young people grotesquely, to the point of caricature. Two new representations of adolescents reflecting this trend have been constructed through the media: the "school ground killer" and the "sports star."

Launched into the limelight after the Columbine shootings in Littleton, Colorado, in 1999, the image of the school ground killer became a potent stereotype for adults to use in their argument for more school surveillance and security—though there was little rigorous discussion of gun control, at least in the United States. Rather than examining the possible reasons behind the shootings, along with the question of access to guns and ammunition, federal and state government debate focused on the moral vacuum in schools, the ongoing breakdown of families, and the increasing destructiveness of "today's youth." The conclusion: post the Christian Ten Commandments in schools. Though the number of school shootings has stayed fairly consistent in the United States—four in 1997, five in 1998, four in 1999, four in 2000, and six in 2001—the media causally represents the "individual problems of pathological youth" as a harbinger of social "breakdown": the breakdown of the family, the breakdown of the teaching profession, the breakdown of the neighbourhood, the breakdown of civil society. Highlighting "exceptions" (Tinsley, 1993) and blaming individuals belies the social and political networks within which we all live. It is much easier to fix "individual" problems than structural ones. Systemic social problems are seen through personal or familial reprivatisation discourses that depoliticise (Fraser, 1989), for example, the structural processes of disengagement and general youth alienation.

By contrast, another type of image may be found in sports news reports, where young athletes are held up as deities. The "sports star" image reflects the culminating success of long years of hard work and practice. Following Featherstone (1991), the fit, muscular, youthful, healthy body has "exchange value" over other kinds of bodies in consumer culture. Autobiographical accounts testify to the identification of young people with athletes, and the cultural myth that with commitment and sweat, anyone can become a star. Little mention is made of the sacrifice of all family members, including the athlete, in terms of time, energy, and economic commitments. Still less is known about the group of athletes that did not quite make it. To the extent that these images motivate young people and all of us toward becoming our best selves, they are, perhaps, a success. At the same time, though, sports star images arguably represent one of the most effective vehicles of corporate advertisement: young athletes become walking billboards. Sponsorship is awarded to those who win precisely so that the product becomes associated with the winners. Successful sponsored athletes are "branded" and consumed as celebrities; a useful marketing strategy. The circular irony of this process becomes mind-boggling when one notes the reports of youth tattooing themselves with the Nike Swoosh (Klein, 2000).

Targeting and marketing to young people as potential buyers has increased dramatically since the early 1990's (Klein, 2000). The construction of youth as consumers began earlier, however, with the commercialisation of society as a whole in the 1960's (Wartella, 1995). The end result for youth is a "colonization not of physical space but of mental space" (Klein, 2000, p. 66). Perhaps the best example of this trend is the explosion of Channel One and its contractual purchase of school-based youth audiences in exchange for equipment, news reports, and advertising (see Apple, 1993; Molnar, 1996). Youth participate in consumer consumption as if they were participating in culture, and advertising executives count on peer pressure to ensure the sales of their products. When young people engage in product selection and purchasing, they are negotiating their identity through brand name affiliation. The fiction here is that young people need to consume to be "cool," and it works well for adults who drop off groups of friends at shopping malls as a solution to the sheer absence of after-school activities available to youth. Ironically, shopping is one of the few activities available to young people that provide them with (1) interested adults in the guise of salespeople and (2) what they take to be adult responsibilities, the sense of purpose, for example, that comes from balancing budget concerns with style and the sense of exploration that comes from managing the fashion "jungle." Is it any wonder, then, that some young people fashion themselves both through their language and through their appearance by designing and redesigning their bodies like paint on a canvas?

The concern here is twofold. First, that marketing executives are paid for stalking the minds and bodies of young people. Youth become an important demographic only to the extent that they participate in our economy as consumers (see Wartella, 1995). Second, that young people grow up believing that they will not be fully human without a pair of Tommy Hilfiger jeans. Youth are not valued for what they could contribute in terms of participating in the mode of production. Coupled with the continued exclusion from opportunities to earn a living wage, not to mention the lack of benefits and insurance available for many wage labourers (in the United States), it is virtually impossible for young people to have access to the kind of money required to become the kind of people advertisers are telling them they need to be in order to be successful.

Presenting youth with expectations is one thing, and in schools, high expectations are important. But presenting them with expectations for consumption, with no method of generating the funds needed to reach that level of consumption, is problematic and contradictory. As noted by Klein (2000), relying on data from the Yearbook of Labour Statistics 1980–1997, youth unemployment rates as a percentage of total unemployment in 1997 for sixteen to twenty-four year olds were 35.9% in the United States; 29.9% in the United Kingdom; 20.2% in Sweden; and 30.8% in Spain. Adding one year to the age range reported in 1997, the rates of unemployment for fifteen to twenty-four year olds were 38.6% in Australia; 28.7% in Canada; 30.5% in the Czech Republic; and 21.5% in Finland. Reflecting the ends of the spectrum reported, the lowest rate was 12.2% in Germany for youth fourteen to twenty-four and the highest rate was 72.5% in Indonesia for youth fifteen to twenty-four. How is it that young

people manage the contradiction between increased pressures to consume and decreased job opportunities and living wages?

Interrupting the Story: Generative Youth Cultures

There is no doubt that the discourses of naturalisation, restriction, and
commodification are internalised and utilised by young people today.
In fact, current research, as well as research in this book, highlights
some of the ways in which young people participate in reproducing
the very discourses that we argue reify the fictional "adolescent" and
stage of "adolescence." However, to maintain that youth are simply
willing accomplices in their own oppression is at once reminiscent of
the problematised notion of "false consciousness," and, in addition,
lacks the respect and dignity that agency bestows. Research with
youth does not support the position that young people blindly adopt
and enact the discourses that are transmitted by adults. Rather, given
a dialectical relationship between agent and social structure, youth
culture is itself a heterogeneous and generative social project. While
youth sometimes take up discourses, they also transform, mock, and
parody them, reflecting Halliday's (1978) notion of "anti-languages."

While the language surrounding young people is a set of perva-
sively negative discourses which naturalise deviance, emphasise the
need for control, and encourage the buying and selling of youth images and commodified youth markets, it is also through language we
may better understand the complex social settings within which
young people negotiate space, shift identities, and engage in knowledge construction. Given our changing times, what role can educational researchers play in improving the social and material
conditions of young people? Perhaps by re/constructing the "science"
that constructs the "object" of our gaze, or at least reducing the mis-
conceptions necessitated by working within a positivist framework,
we may create ways to diminish the negative influences of discourses
about youth. We might expand our research lens, recast some adults
as allies, and most importantly, begin to converse with, learn from,
and listen to young people. They might just have strengths about
which we know nothing. They might use resistance as a strategy for
overcoming adult-imposed limitations. Whatever the case, this book

seeks to open that dialogue, to document the contributions of and further create additional spaces for youth to contribute.

THE ROLE OF RESEARCHERS IN THE PRODUCTION OF "BENEFICENT" AND "MALIGNANT" FICTIONS

Returning to Achebe's (1988) notion of scientific and cultural theories as fictions, it is worth taking a moment to mention that not all fictions are the same. This book presents a collection of stories, studies, and approaches to working with young people. The researchers here all share a desire to argue against the essentialist images of young people that depict them as dangerous, at risk, marginal, and menacing members of society. The authors in this book resist binaries of young people that vacillate between miscreants needing control and romanticised notions of wayward in need of safe harbours. As a useful frame, Achebe (1988) distinguishes between "beneficent" and "malignant" fictions. The difference between the two helps to clarify our attempts at countering traditional positivist research.

Quite simply, what distinguishes "beneficent" fictions from "malignant" fictions "is that the first never forgets that it is a fiction and the other never knows that it is" (Achebe, 1988, p. 101). Belief in the superiority of one skin colour over another, or one religion over another, or one gender over another, are for Achebe, all malignant fictions. They are universal, absolutist claims, that appear to communicate a significant message about reality. They are often supported by the assumption, like those highlighted earlier by Goldenberg (1978), that young people need adult control and adult-designed interventions. They surface in well-developed recommendations and seem to make "common sense." Like adding metal detectors and increasing security guards in schools, these responses address symptoms rather than underlying problems. They restrict individuals—control minds, bodies, and relationships—rather than redressing the weight of social inequality and alienation. They poison us and our context with socially constructed limitations, inequities, and material obstacles. One could say that malignant fictions take themselves—their content and meaning—as "truths"—with tragic consequences.

I would like to believe that what the authors offer here is a series of beneficent fictions, though fictions nonetheless. I hope, like Achebe (1988), that readers become active participants in the lives and experiences shared by the authors and young people: that readers use their imagination and join us on a journey to reach a place where events are not merely "happening *before* us; they are happening, by the power and force of imaginative identification, *to* us" (p. 99, italics in the original). It is my hope we become initiates in worlds that we may never know in order to learn about the richness of human experience. To that end, the authors use a variety of standpoints, methodologies, and epistemologies in working with young people. The diversity of approaches reflects the variety of ways that young people live, act, and find their own paths. I expect the ideas in the chapters ahead to overlap and diverge in complex ways and welcome the perspectives they reveal. I encourage our readers to maintain, as always, a critical perspective while applying their imagination to the urgent purpose of developing new ways of seeing, constructing, and making sense of what we learn from and about young people.

NAVIGATING THE TEXT: TEXTUAL FICTIONS
RE/CONSTRUCTING "THE ADOLESCENT"

This final section includes highlights of the chapters that follow. Prior to the highlights, it is important to locate the editors in this book as well. In putting this book together, we have two explicit commitments for our work with young people we want to place in the foreground. First, we are committed to representing the complex lives of young people as a method for contributing to and extending conversations with and about youth and youth cultures. Second, we are committed to finding ways to reflect the richness of young people as thinking, speaking, and acting agents who experience the world through bodies marked by socially constructed meanings. Here then, much of the research discussed includes discursive, performative, and linguistic, analyses of signs, symbols, and bodies.

In particular, this book explores how social languages and discourses about adolescents work in complex ways to both create and constrain possibilities for young people and how those discourses are co-opted, modified, and sometimes abandoned by both youth and adults. Within the constraints and limitations of textual representation, including the linearity imposed on the narratives written here, we attempt to open up spaces for the voices of some young people to resist and contest dominant control over available discourses. Through authentic engagements with young people, we may come to learn about and understand the hybrid ways in which they take up, engage, mimic, challenge, subvert, and alter these available discourses.

Chapter Two, written by Johanna Wyn, draws upon a longitudinal study to explore assumptions about adolescents that have been applied to the lives of older youth. She purposely draws our attention to young people who consider themselves to be in the mainstream in order to challenge the dominant discourses that marginalise young people. Wyn's work disrupts the linear trajectory of developmental models and calls for new approaches that bridge gaps in disciplinary knowledges about young people. In Chapter Three, Lisa Patel Stevens describes the separation between a young girl's school-sanctioned and self-sanctioned literacy practices, and the related subjectivities that arise from these different textual practices. Patel Stevens uses the elisions between these practices as apertures into both the spaces afforded to this young person by adults in schools, and the productively resistant spaces she creates for herself often outside of school.

Jrene Rahm and Karen Tracy, authors of Chapter Four, analyse a youth-initiated discussion in an after-school program, highlighting the ways in which these young people engage in and maintain a rich, responsible dialogue about sexual identity. The authors show that young people are quite capable of sustaining "good" discussion outside of the teacher-regulated classroom setting often assumed to be necessary for successful conversation. Also working outside of traditional school contexts, in Chapter Five, Margaret Finders uses her research and teaching in an alternative program for juvenile youth offenders to highlight questions about the different peer and teacher discourses competing within schools. Finders describes how young people construct among themselves expectations for particular, narrow identity performances. The teachers' normalising gaze, provided as a possible alternative to peer expectations, is not taken up by the youth. In examining how these parallel discourses converge, Finders challenges us to recognise the sheer difficulties of crossing discursive boundaries.

In Chapter Six, Jennifer A. Vadeboncoeur takes up Bakhtin's concept of chronotope to explore an institutional context, including the influence of the physical structuring of time and space on discursive and identity narratives. Mapping chronotopes at both institutional and narrative levels, Vadeboncoeur highlights how one young woman engages a chronotope made available in this alternative school setting to perform a carnivalesque self-narration. Building on the idea of identity construction through self-narration, Judy V. Diamondstone tells the story of Jocelyn in Chapter Seven. She compares an early narrative written by Jocelyn in primary school with a current interview narrative, noting the links between Jocelyn's authorial acts in both written and lived narratives. Diamondstone articulates a theory of development as a grammatical act.

In Chapter Eight, Lisa Hunter explores the social field of a group of young people in health and physical education. Describing the embodied subjectivities afforded to and taken up by four students, Hunter challenges us to reconsider dominant assumptions about mind/body dualisms and the social construction of categories for "good" students, gendered action, and the body. Further complicating our understanding of youth and cultural spaces, in Chapter Nine, Elizabeth Birr Moje and Caspar van Helden destabilise the perception of popular culture as a dangerous threat to, and simultaneously pervasive signifier of, youth cultures. Through their data, the authors provide varying pictures of the semiotic relationships between young people and popular cultural texts. The authors recontextualise popular and youth cultures as connected to larger economic and political systems.

In Chapter Ten, Mollie Blackburn argues that to better teach and learn across differences and ultimately work towards social change, participants need to blur the lines between teacher and student. Blackburn analyses an interaction between inservice teachers and members of a Speakers' Bureau from a centre for gay, lesbian, transgendered, bisexual, and questioning youth. The analysis focuses on the way in which the asking of questions positions the respondent with either more or less authority. The final chapter, Chapter 11 by Lisa Patel Stevens, extends from the contributions of each chapter in this book and draws upon identity politics to theorise subjectivity, offering additional perspectives on re-envisioning young people today. Incorporating complexity theory, Patel Stevens emphasises the importance of rethinking even our own work to ask different and more complex kinds of research questions.

NOTES

1. Following Bakhtin (1993), among others, regardless of our age we are all always becoming; we are never finished beings. So the critique here is not simply a challenge to the way "adolescents" are categorised, but also a critique of the flanking categories of "children" and "adults" as intrinsically more complete, more whole, beings.
2. Special thanks to Carmen Luke for her thoughtful feedback on an earlier draft of this chapter.
3. There are a variety of philosophical positions alluded to here, ranging from critical realism to radical constructivism, to the sociocultural approach, and to social constructionism. My aim is to highlight epistemological perspectives from which theorists and researchers may work that challenge some of the claims of logical positivism, while still respecting the diversity of those perspectives.
4. Though a great deal of work in this area has been completed over the last several decades, more work remains. In addition, it is important to note that these ideas are marginalised by dominant social discourses.
5. Walkerdine (1984) argues that it is during this time that the term "delinquent" came into common use.

REFERENCES

Achebe, C. (1988). The truth of fiction. In *Hopes and impediments: Selected essays 1965–1987*. Oxford: Heinemann.

Anyon, J. (1980). Social class and the hidden curriculum of work. *Journal of Education, 162*(1), 67–92.

Anyon, J. (1997). *Ghetto schooling: A political economy of urban educational reform*. New York: Teachers College Press.

Apple, M. W. (1993). *Official knowledge: Democratic education in a conservative age*. New York: Routledge.

Apple, M. W. (1996). *Cultural politics and education*. New York: Teachers College Press.

Bakhtin, M. M. (1981). *The dialogic imagination: Four essays* (C. Emerson & M. Holquist, Trans.). Austin: University of Texas Press.

Bakhtin, M. M. (1986). *Speech genres and other late essays* (V. W. McGee, Trans.). Austin: University of Texas Press.

Bakhtin, M. M. (1993). *Toward a philosophy of the act* (V. Liapunov, Trans. and V. Liapunov & M. Holquist, Eds.). Austin: University of Texas Press.

Bernstein, B. (1975). *Class and pedagogies: Visible and invisible.* Center for educational research and innovation. Paris: Organization of Economic Cooperation and Development.

Bernstein, B. (1976). *The restructuring of social and political theory.* Philadelphia: University of Pennsylvania Press.

Bhabha, H. (1994). *The location of culture.* New York: Routledge.

Bourdieu, P. (1991). *Language and symbolic power* (G. Raymond & M. Adamson, Trans.). Cambridge, MA: Harvard University Press.

Carnegie Council on Adolescent Development (1995). *Great transitions: Preparing adolescents for a new century.* Washington, DC: Carnegie Corporation of New York.

Clark, M. (1989). Anastasia is a normal developer because she is unique. *Oxford Review of Education, 15*(3), 243–255.

Conant, J. (1959). *The American high school today.* New York: McGraw Hill.

Fairclough, N. (1989). *Language and power.* Singapore: Longman Singapore.

Fairclough, N. (1992). *Discourse and social change.* Cambridge: Polity Press.

Featherstone, M. (1991). *Consumer culture and postmodernism.* London: Sage.

Finders, M. (1998/1999). Raging hormones. *Journal of Adolescent and Adult Literacy, 42,* 252–263.

Foucault, M. (1975/1995). *Discipline and punish: The birth of the prison* (2nd ed.). New York: Vintage Books.

Foucault, M. (1980). *Power/knowledge: Selected interviews and other writings, 1972–1977.* (C. Gordon, Ed., Trans.). New York: Pantheon Books.

Foucault, M. (1986). *The history of sexuality, Vol. 1.* (R. Hurley, Trans.). New York: Vintage.

Fraser, N. (1989). *Unruly practices: Power, discourse, and gender in contemporary social theory.* Minneapolis: University of Minnesota Press.

Gee, J. P. (2002). Millennials and bobos, Blue's Clues and Sesame Street: A story for our times. In D. E. Alvermann (Ed.), *Adolescents and literacies in a digital world.* New York: Peter Lang.

Giddens, H. (1997). *Sociology* (3rd ed.). Cambridge: Polity Press.

Glassner, B. (1999). *The culture of fear: Why Americans are afraid of the wrong things.* New York: Basic Books.

Goldenberg, I. I. (1978). *Oppression and social intervention: Essays on the human condition and the problems of change.* Chicago: Nelson-Hall.

Hall, G. S. (1904). *Adolescence: Its psychology and its relations to psychology, anthropology, sociology, sex, crime, religion, and education.* New York: Appleton-Century-Crofts.

Halliday, M. A. K. (1967). Notes on transitivity and theme in English. *Journal of Linguistics, 3,* 199–244.

Halliday, M. A. K. (1978). *Language as Social Semiotic.* London: Edward Arnold.

Harding, S. (1991). *Whose science? Whose knowledge?: Thinking from women's lives.* Ithaca, NY: Cornell University Press.

hooks, b. (1994). *Teaching to transgress: Education as the practice of freedom*. New York: Routledge.

Klein, N. (2000). *No logo: Taking aim at the brand bullies*. New York: Alfred A. Knopf.

Kozol, J. (1991). *Savage inequalities: Children in America's schools*. New York: Harper Perennial.

Kuhn, T. S. (1962/1970). *The structure of scientific revolutions* (2nd ed.). Chicago: University of Chicago Press.

Lasn, K. (1999). *Culture jam: How to reverse America's suicidal consumer binge—and why we must*. New York: Quill, HarperCollins Publishers.

Lesko, N. (2001). *Act your age!: A cultural construction of adolescence*. New York: Routledge.

Luke, A. & Luke, C. (2001). Adolescence lost/childhood regained: On early intervention and the emergence of the techno-subject. *Journal of Early Childhood Literacy*, 1(1), 93–122.

Mantsios, G. (1998). Rewards and opportunities: The politics and economics of class in the U.S. In G. Colombo, R. Cullen, & B. Lisle (Eds.), *Rereading America: Cultural contexts for critical thinking and writing* (4th ed.). New York: Bedford/St. Martin's.

Medawar, P. (1982). *Pluto's republic*. Oxford: Oxford University Press.

Moje, E. B. (2002). But where are the youth: Integrating youth culture into literacy theory. *Educational Theory, 52*, 97-120.

Molnar, A. (1996). *Giving kids the business: The commercialization of America's schools*. Boulder, CO: Westview Press.

Ochs, E. & Capps, L. (2001). *Living narrative: Creating lives in everyday storytelling*. Cambridge, MA: Harvard University Press.

Piaget, J. (1967). *Six psychological studies*. New York: Random House.

Polanyi, M. (1983). *The tacit dimension*. Gloucester, MA: Peter Smith.

Saussure, F. de (1916/1986). *Course in general linguistics* (R. Harris, Trans. and C. Bally, A. Sechehaye, & A. Riedlinger, Eds.). La Salle, IL: Open Court Press.

Tinsley, M. (1993, February). You and your family. *Daily Telegraph, 26*, p. 3.

Vadeboncoeur, J. A. (1997). Child development and the purpose of education. In V. Richardson (Ed.), *Constructivist teacher education: Building a world of new understandings* (pp. 15-37). Washington, DC: Falmer.

Volosinov, V. N. (1929/1986). *Marxism and the philosophy of language* (L. Matejka & I. R. Titunik, Trans.). Cambridge, MA: Harvard University Press.

von Glasersfeld, E. (1989). Cognition, construction of knowledge, and teaching. *Synthese, 80*, 121–140.

Vygotsky, L. S. (1978). *Mind in society: The development of higher psychological processes*. Cambridge, MA: Harvard University Press.

Vygotsky, L. S. (1986). *Thought and language*. A. Kozulin (Ed.). Cambridge, MA: The MIT Press.

Walkerdine, V. (1984). Developmental psychology and the child-centred pedagogy: The insertion of Piaget into early education. In J. Henriques, W. Hollway, K. Urwin, C. Venn, & V. Walkerdine (Eds.), *Changing the subject: Psychology, social regulation, and subjectivity*. New York: Methuen.

Wartella, E. (1995). The commercialisation of youth: Channel One in context. *Phi Delta Kappan, 76*(6), 448–451.

Wertsch, J. V. (1991). *Voices of the mind: A sociocultural approach to mediated action.* Cambridge, MA: Harvard University Press.

CHAPTER TWO

What Is Happening to "Adolescence"? Growing Up in Changing Times

Johanna Wyn

The starting point for this chapter is the challenge to "rethink youth" in the context of the social and economic changes that have affected so many aspects of social life over the last twenty-five years (Wyn & White, 1997). Elsewhere we argued that:

> Young people in the developed world have been the subjects of an enormous amount of research over the last 40 years. In general, this research assumes that young people constitute a separate and significant category of people: as non-adults. A central and recurring theme in the studies is the problematic nature of being a young person and the even more problematic nature of becoming adult. Much of the literature about youth has inherited assumptions from developmental psychology about universal stages of development, identity formation, normative behaviour and the relationship between social and physical maturation. Yet very little work has been done to clarify the theoretical basis of this categorisation based on age. (Wyn & White, 1997, p. 8)

Other youth researchers have also pointed out that the concepts of adolescence, youth, and adulthood need to be used critically because the meaning of both youth and adulthood has changed over time and according to context. These include, for example, researchers in the United States (Lesko, 1996), in Europe (Wallace & Kovacheva, 1995), in the United Kingdom (Ball, Maguire, & Macrae, 2000), and in New Zealand (Smith et al., 2002). In more recent work based on Australian research, we have examined the distinctive experiences of the post-1970 generation growing up in a world that is very different from that which their parents faced in their youth (Dwyer & Wyn, 2001). Yet, despite this awareness on the part of some researchers, the broader literature reflects a reluctance to let go of conceptions of youth, adolescence, and adulthood that may have outlasted their relevance.

This chapter seeks to problematise the categories we use as the basis for naturalising life stages. The discussion is based on the experiences of growing up for a group of 2,000 young Australians. Their perspectives provide a point of reference against which to assess how the nature of youth and the transition process into adulthood have been conceptualised in academic and policy writing. There, it has become common to argue that the transition into adulthood has been extended, prolonging the period of youth up to the age of thirty years and perhaps beyond. The evidence from my own research does not support this view. Instead, I argue that we need to "rethink" our understandings of youth and adulthood to take account of the extent to which social change has shifted the relationships between adolescence, youth, and adulthood as stages in life.

The need to rethink the use of terms such as adolescence, youth, and adulthood is illustrated by the evident difficulties researchers and policy makers have in finding the right way to characterise the transition from youth to adulthood. Across many different countries, researchers report on findings showing that the normative understandings of growing up no longer fit with the reality. Still there is an apparent reluctance to let go of the idea of normative processes and stages, even as researchers confront the fact that young people follow complex and diverse pathways through education and work and have begun to generate different life priorities than their parents' generation. Faced with the research evidence, we have found that:

> New life stages are being invented (post-adolescence, over-aged young adults) and notions of "extended transitions" and "deferred adulthood" are being explored (Côté & Allahar, 1994; du Bois-Reymond, 1998; Jones & Wallace, 1992). And so, instead of rethinking youth (Lesko, 1996; Wyn & White, 1997) and either questioning its continued usefulness as a simple age category or examining the appropriateness of the established markers of both youth and adulthood, a seeming solution is found by elongating the

> linear sequential model of transition to cover over the inconsistencies that have emerged. (Dwyer & Wyn, 2001, p. 170)

This chapter focuses on the "problem" of conceptualising the processes of growing up. Focusing on the ways in which the transitions through adolescence, youth, and into adulthood have been conceptualised, I argue the case for making stronger links between social change and identity. I argue this, as there are now significant overlaps in the lives of both young and old. The conceptual tools that in the past served to describe life stages are now inadequate for theorising and describing young people's lives.

Drawing on the Life-Patterns Project of the Australian Youth Research Centre, I argue that the legacy of psychological development theories that inform understandings of adolescence continues to have a profound effect on thinking about young people. The two key aspects of this legacy are linearity and futurity. Superficial elements of life that have traditionally been identified with adolescence have been overlaid onto the lives of older youth, to characterise them as "not yet adult," masking real changes that are emerging in the lives of adults. The narrow imagery of linear developmental and transition pathways has continued to dominate thinking about the processes of growing up, despite ample evidence to the contrary (Ball, Maguire, & Macrae, 2000; Chisholm, Buchnen, Kruger, & Brown, 1990; Furlong & Cartmel, 1997; Heinz, 2000; Jones & Wallace, 1992).

This chapter contributes to our understanding of the conceptualisation of adolescence and youth by focusing on ordinary, relatively unproblematic lives. It focuses on young people who would be considered to be "in the mainstream"—rather than those who are labelled "at risk." In doing so, it explicitly challenges the tendency to problematise and even sensationalise specific aspects of young people's lives in isolation from their whole life context. Youth studies, and especially the study of youth subcultures, has tended to ignore "mainstream" youth and to focus instead on generating understandings of youth and adolescence from specific behaviours (e.g., drug-taking, deviance, crime, early school leaving) or on specific identifications (e.g., music, dress, sexuality, lifestyle). I argue that this tendency to focus on the extreme and problematic has, ironically, masked the extent of change to the so-called mainstream.

Secondly, the chapter explores the ways in which assumptions about adolescence have been applied to the lives of older youth in the attempt to hold on to a linear conception of youth development, transitions through youth, and arrival at adult status. I present evidence to support the view that the linear time-line that is implied in these models has been disrupted and that new approaches are needed, bridging the gap between psychology, education and cultural studies literature, as well as from the broader field of youth research. My starting point is the evidence from young people's lives.

In the following section, I describe some of the key features of the experience of growing up for a group of young Australians. In subsequent sections, I draw on this evidence to argue that there is now significant overlap between adolescence, youth, and adulthood. Far from seeing an extension of the period of life characterised as youth, we have evidence that adulthood is being experienced earlier, in incremental and disjointed ways across different life spheres. I argue that we need to rethink the relevance of the terms that we use to describe stages of life, recognising that it is tempting for each generation to see their own life patterns as normative.

TRANSITIONS

The Life-Patterns Project is a longitudinal, panel study of young Australians from the State of Victoria who left secondary school in 1991. In that year, 29,000 young people left school in years ten, eleven and twelve, inclusive. Although the majority left school at the end of year twelve, between seventeen and eighteen years old, the age of compulsory schooling is fifteen years and some students choose not to complete secondary education. These young people were surveyed in 1992 to follow up their progress after leaving school and a representative sample of 11,000 young people was constructed. In 1996, the Youth Research Centre surveyed a smaller, representative sample of this data set of 2,000, maintaining consistency within the sample of gender, socioeconomic background, ethnicity, and geographic location. This sample has formed the basis of our Life-Patterns study, which has followed the progress of this group of young people until the present (Dwyer, Smith, Tyler, & Wyn, 2003). The young people in the Life-Patterns Project were in their last year of secondary school when the project began in 1991. They are now more than ten years out of school. Their experiences and the ways in which they tell their stories provide an insight into the specific experiences of the post-1970 generation.

In previous work, I have pointed out that a person born in the early 1970's in Australia would have come to the end of their compulsory years of schooling in the mid-1980's—a time when the youth labour market was in a state of collapse. The person would have stayed on at school as a member of the very first generation in which the majority actually completed their secondary schooling. At the age of seventeen or eighteen they would have been confronted with a shift in public attitudes and government policy. By the 1980's, there was an expectation that young people needed further education and training to escape continuing high and long-term unemployment rates for young adults with only a high school qualification. Even university graduates with jobs would be experiencing employment uncertainty. By the time they were completing these further studies and juggling a part-time job at the same time, they and their younger siblings would be faced with the prospect of paying increasing university fees (Dwyer & Wyn, 2001).

The Life-Patterns Project has recorded how young people are actively and positively developing their own responses to these circumstances. The use of a participatory methodology has meant that we have been challenged to rethink our assumptions about transitions from youth to adulthood and what it means to grow up today. Through the use of questionnaire surveys and semi-structured interviews throughout the project, we have been able to link broad patterns across the cohort with in-depth studies of individual trajectories. In the following section, I draw on the interviews to introduce the two individual stories of Sue and Frank, before describing the broader patterns. Their stories provide a glimpse of the different ways in which young people in the post-1970 generation are negotiating life.

Two Young People

Sue

Sue described herself as a "very studious" student at school and was captain of the school in her last year. This involved additional duties

that consumed much of her time. She continued to study hard because she wanted to get into a really good course, get a good degree,
and get a good job. She excelled and as a result, gained access to a
competitive course in Manufacturing Management, a scholarship
course that involved a practicum in the United States. She graduated
from this course in three years, and, at the age of twenty-one, was
immediately employed in a role that involved Information Technology management. She took the job because "her degree led her to it,"
and because her parents had pushed her to succeed.

Sue was very motivated to succeed in her job, to save hard, and to
establish a good life for herself. She was earning good money. However, this involved:

> Long hours, the responsibility fell back on me as the consultant. You work in
> a team with their people but they are used to only working nine to five, so
> you'd have to pick up things and work till 9:00 every night.

She said:

> Stressful expectations are put on you. *This* document by *this* time. Continual
> deadlines, non-stop.

Despite this, Sue continued to work hard. In her third year, she was
given a substantial promotion at work. She also began a "serious relationship." At this point, she said:

> I've grown up in the last few years and I've realised that you can do what
> you want in life, but don't get too stressed—life's too short.

To her parents' horror and her partner's disbelief, she made the decision to leave her work and to use her financial reserves to travel. She
saw this decision as one of the things that she was most proud of to
date.

At the age of twenty-four Sue was working for $8.00 an hour in
retail at a snow resort in Canada. She said:

> I am here to ski, to improve my skiing and to relax and have fun. I am much
> more relaxed than I was a few months ago.

This gave her the opportunity to reflect on her life and to consider other options that would allow her to develop other capacities and skills. At the time of her last interview, she was trying to balance the pros and cons of using her remaining funds to travel further or to undertake further education in an entirely different field. Sue felt that at the moment, her priority was to relax. Looking to the future, Heritage Management was something that she could imagine doing in her thirties, and she aimed to get some experience in the field through voluntary work before undertaking a masters program in Heritage Management.

Frank

Frank has never seen further education as a priority. He noted:

> I enjoy writing reports but I have never been much of an academic, I don't seem to retain things very well.

As such he has pursued work rather than study. At first he began working at Pizza Hut as a driver doing deliveries, but "the cost of the fuel meant it just wasn't worth it," so he quit. After leaving Pizza Hut, Frank helped out a friend of a friend who was building a factory. He stayed in this job for eleven months, mainly employed as a light factory-hand with a bit of engineering thrown in. He enjoyed the work but was frustrated by what he saw as poor management and a lack of clear roles of responsibility. However, he did not have to put up with this situation for long. He said:

> For a time there was not much work coming in and we were told we could be laid off, when they ran out of money it was a big relief as it was freezing in winter and sweltering in summer, in other words not a comfortable place to work.

It was after a period of unemployment that Frank came across a bus-driving job.

Frank thinks it is harder today to work out what it is to be an adult than it was in his parent's day. Both of his parents were twenty-one years old when they married, and they worked on a farm. He said:

> Life wasn't so much of a rush then, admittedly you would have your busy times when the crops came in but then there would be a lull and there was real time to spend with your family and friends.

He believes it is "harder now," as the opportunities that existed back then are no longer available.

> I feel I am always on the run, two or three different jobs a day, I don't like it, it takes away from your life and the time you have to think about what you want to do.

Frank describes himself as "a follower, grabbing the tail rather than the horns," explaining that he is "not as forceful or as ambitious" as he would like to be. Frank loves his bus-driving job; he says he loves "the practical jobs which benefit people." He wants to direct more of his energies into truck driving, but admits he only wants to do it for a few more years. There is some impetus, he says, for him to earn a better income, as he has been living with his brother and his brother's girlfriend has just moved in and "you know the story, three's a crowd, so I need to get out and find my own home."

Frank would like to have more time to spend with his family, although he admits that he does enjoy learning from his numerous work places.

> Each job offers something different, and I like becoming more versatile, it helps to also stretch you so you can find your own limits. It's just difficult getting the balance right!

These two short case studies reveal the lives of two very different young people. What their stories have in common with each other—and with the majority of the young people in our study—is an awareness of making the right choices for themselves. They are both aware of the fact that they have to make different decisions from the ones that their parents had available to them (Frank) or that their parents would like them to take now (Sue). Both are concerned to "get the balance right," focusing on their own personal development, finding their own limits, and making the most of their lives.

COMPLEX PATTERNS OF TRANSITION

The experiences of transition among the Life-Patterns cohort reveal the extent to which the post-1970 generation has had to blend new ways of growing up with older, more established patterns. Their patterns of life do appear, at a superficial level, to reflect a generation who refuse to really grow up. The sense that they are trying out different options, reluctant to commit fully to one course of study, one job, one career ladder to climb, or one lifestyle to live, provides the appearance of an "extended adolescence." A closer investigation of the experiences and perspectives of these young people reveals that more fundamental changes to both youth and adulthood are being shaped.

One of the early findings of the Life-Patterns Project was that these patterns of transition are non-linear. Instead, the data reveals complex patterns of transition. Just over half the cohort experienced some sort of change to their academic arrangements during the years after leaving secondary school (from 1992 to 1996). A quarter of the cohort changed courses. A further 20% changed institutions and more than a quarter either had an interruption to their study or discontinued. This suggests that a linear trajectory through education is not the majority experience. Many found that the course of study they entered was not suitable, and others found that other aspects of their life took on a higher priority or influenced their decisions.

These complexities are not surprising, as there was a consistent pattern across both urban and rural areas for combining study and work. Over 30% of young people in both rural and urban settings combined study with work all the time, and a further 25% were studying and working most of the time. We have found that this combination of study and work reflects not only financial necessities, but also a preference among young people to keep their options open. It is interesting to note that this pattern is established in secondary school. Well over half of seventeen year olds held a job at some time, and it is usual for students in Australian secondary schools to work part-time. In this way, these young people are learning to manage multiple and conflicting responsibilities.

NEW MEANINGS OF CAREER

By 1999 and at the age of twenty-four, 51% of the males and 46% of the females had achieved full-time jobs. They are part of the first generation of Australians to be so well educated. They accepted the policy assumption that post-compulsory education was necessary in order to have a career. Yet, our study has found that the jobs they accept either do not fully utilise the skills they have acquired in years of education (and part-time work), or demand very long hours that ultimately undermine job satisfaction. Perhaps it is not surprising, then, that their work is often found to be insufficiently rewarding. Occupational boundaries have become more fluid, and increasingly, jobs are temporary. Many of our participants considered themselves to be over-qualified for their job. Others found the hours too long and, like Sue, felt stressed and that their life lacked balance. This has forced them to reconsider the situations in which they find themselves. Depending on the local circumstances, young people in different locations "make their own assessments of how best to respond to a discernable mismatch between educational levels and job-market realities" (Dwyer & Wyn, 2001, p. 121).

With the participants in their mid-twenties, we observed a change in their thinking as they began to come to terms with labour market uncertainties. While work remained an important element in their lives, other life spheres were emerging as the central focus of their identities, including relationships and leisure. This is evident in what they said about their personal priorities. The top six out of fifteen possible priorities are described in Table 1. These priorities seem reasonably conventional. Having a steady job and placing a high value on family relationships might seem to fit with the priorities of their parents' generation. When asked to elaborate on what they meant by these statements, however, their attitudes diverged from the traditional understandings of these items. While "having a steady job" ranks highest, it does not mean "involvement in work as a career," which ranks seventh, or "making a lot of money," which ranks tenth. Work is seen pragmatically as a means to an end rather than being significant in itself. Similarly, "family relationships," which ranks second, does not mean the traditional nuclear family, marriage, or children. "Marriage or living with a partner" was ranked ninth and "having children" was ranked a low twelfth. This shift in attitudes is already reflected in the Australian statistics, which show lower rates of marriage and fertility for this generation than the previous one (Weston, Stanton, Qu, & Soriano, 2001).

Table 1. *Personal priorities (1996)*

Priority	Rank
Having a steady job	1
Family relationships	2
Developing friendships	3
Involvement in leisure activities	4
Owning your own home	5
Travelling to different places	6

Both Sue's story and Frank's story reflect these broader patterns. Sue's trajectory has shifted her away from "settling down" in a relationship with a partner. She is firmly focused on pursuing other options that will contribute to her own personal development and fulfilment. Frank is also trying to get the balance right, but his situation does not make it likely that he will be in a position to "settle down" either.

By 2002, only 75% were in a full-time job, which is consistent with Australian national figures (Australian Bureau of Statistics, 2002). They experienced a lot of uncertainty and change, with 82% changing jobs since 1996, and nearly a quarter holding five or more jobs since 1996. At the same time, we have seen the emergence of some distinctive attitudes towards the idea of career. The traditional idea that career equates with full-time employment in one occupation—involving upward mobility over time—is not confirmed by their views. Instead, these young people have a subjective assessment of career as a "state of mind" rather than an objective and visible trajectory. Participants emphasised that the meaning of career has shifted. For them, career encompasses a holistic understanding for their orientation in life. For over 80% of the participants, the meanings they attribute to career give highest priority to activities that offer scope for their own *advancement*, an opportunity to show *commitment*, and scope for *fulfilment*. They stated that a career is not a permanent full-time job, it is not necessarily your current job, and does not have to be connected to your source of income. What is striking about their perspectives on career is that they assess career in terms of the potential offered for their own personal experience.

SOCIAL CHANGE

Social and economic change has presented both young and old with new challenges. The young people in our study have responded positively and proactively, and have inevitably shaped identities that allow them to do so. Hence, we have found that flexibility is seen as more important than predictability as a basis for future security in a post-industrial world. In the face of employment insecurity, many young people see that they are more secure if they can achieve "horizontal mobility"—the capacity to move from one job to another, depending on their needs. This skill is valued over the older emphasis on vertical mobility within one occupation.

For these reasons, the life patterns of this generation appear to concern many researchers. Because they do not conform to the patterns of the previous generation, new terms have been coined to describe them. These terms, such as "generation on hold" (Côté & Allahar, 1994), "arrested adulthood" (Côté, 2000), or "youth in crisis" (Lerner, 1995), almost invariably suggest that this generation is undergoing faulty transitions.

I would argue that these terms all miss the point. They elongate a linear trajectory that no longer fits the majority experience of the post-1970 generation. In a recent report on the Life-Patterns study, the researchers reflect on the difficulty of understanding the effects of social change on the time sequence of youth and adulthood.

> There is a strange irony here that is related to the disruptions that have affected the established time-sequence of transition from youth to adulthood. Instead of prolonging the experience of adolescence or postponing the realities of adulthood, those disruptions have caused an overlap in their lives between the two. When they make choices about study, work, relationships, family or lifestyle, the disruptions to the established time-sequence make them feel that they are continually "working against time." The time-line is there, but in terms both of their own parents' experience and of parental expectations for their sons and daughters, there is a constant mismatch between the time-line and life realities. (Dwyer et al., 2003, p. 23)

The disruptions to the time-line tend to be read as disruptions to identity formation. Our evidence suggests young people are not experiencing "extended transitions," but are instead engaging with adult responsibilities and experiences incrementally, early in their lives. They are more likely to be entering a "new adulthood" earlier than the previous generation.

Other researchers too have noted that assumptions about age and stages of life need to be reconsidered (Lesko, 1996). From an early age, school children are encouraged to present a portfolio of their skills and capacities, and to draw on a wide variety of experiences and learning settings to portray themselves. They have engaged very effectively with the "project of the self," displaying a capacity to be reflective about their own lives. This is a necessary skill, because they are required to make active choices about their lives at many points. As Beck and Beck-Gernsheim (2002) have pointed out, in order to survive circumstances that change daily, individuals have to become "stage managers of their own biographies" (p. 24). Their concept of "individualization" captures many elements of the experience and attitudes of the participants in the Life-Patterns study. The way in which they describe their lives, and the decisions that they have to make, is captured by Beck and Beck-Gernsheim's concept of "reflexion." As Lash (2002) explains:

> Reflexes are indeterminate. They are immediate. They do not in any sense subsume. Reflexes cope with a world of speed and quick decision-making. The contemporary individual, Beck never tires of saying, is characterized by choice, where previous generations had no such choices. What Beck often omits to say is that this individual must choose fast, must—as in reflex—make quick decisions...[The individual] puts together networks, constructs alliances, makes deals. He must live, is forced to live in an atmosphere of risk in which knowledge and life-changes are precarious. (p. ix)

The evidence from the Life-Patterns study provides some support for this characterisation, particularly with reference to the approaches young people take to work and employment. Because they have found that employment is precarious, they have had to manage the paradox between the promise of increased levels of education and the uncertainty of labour markets. Their preference to balance a range of commitments has created a trend towards job mobility, to take advantage of better options, or to move horizontally to create space for non-work priorities. In making the necessary choices for themselves, they are weighing up new priorities alongside the established characteristics of adulthood.

Yet there is a reluctance to attribute adult status to older youth. The mismatch between the outmoded time-line and expected "normal" outcomes calls their adult choices into question. As we comment elsewhere "there is a reluctance to let go of established assumptions about what 'ought to be,' and a failure to give due credit to a generation that knows it has grown up in a new kind of social environment and is making the necessary choices of coming to terms with it" (Dwyer et al., 2003, p. 23).

Of necessity, this generation is forging new patterns of life, in response to the paradox of promise and uncertainty. They are developing patterns that will endure into their thirties and possibly beyond, blending and selecting from the old and the new to shape a "new" adulthood.

RECONCEPTUALISING YOUTH AND ADULTHOOD

Beck has used the term "zombie categories" to describe empty categories that have little relevance to the realities to which they are being applied (Beck & Beck-Gernsheim, 2002, p. 203). This is because the nature of the social relationships encapsulated within the concept has changed significantly. The concepts of "family, class, and neighbourhood" are all identified by Beck as categories that have continued to be used in "empirical studies" as though the meanings of these relationships were not problematic. Yet, as Beck and many other theorists have demonstrated, processes of globalisation have brought significant change to the most fundamental institutions in all societies. This challenge to take concepts of analysis critically is relevant for the task of reconceptualising adolescence, youth, and adulthood.

The failure to establish career jobs, to value mobility, and to place a high priority on the capacity to move horizontally across jobs rather than vertically up an occupational career ladder is one of the features of the post-1970 generation that gives the impression of "adolescent patterns" of life. The views of the participants in the Life-Patterns

Project reveal that new concepts of career are being shaped that are far from "adolescent." Their views, described in Dwyer et al. (2003), reveal that they have begun to establish new meanings for "career" and "work." In this section, I describe the choices that inform the decisions of these young people.

The flexibility and mobility that characterises the life patterns of the participants in our study is an effect of a different approach to work and career. They see career as a "mindset," rather than as an objective position.

> A career is a mindset of what I do everyday, not the job I am doing. It's about what I have learned, not what I am being paid for.

> A career is about changing and developing, always extending my skills. (Dwyer et al., 2003, p. 29)

Young people frequently use the word "journey" to depict career as an ongoing process rather than a destination. For them the notion of career has become synonymous with the idea of a journey that enables them to develop themselves and to keep learning, as Frank explains:

> I still think of it (a career) as a full time job, which in reality is rare. It's not for me anyway. I get itchy feet and like learning from one job to another. I just wish I could earn more. Truck driving is still very much part of the journey. (Dwyer et al., 2003, p. 29)

Other participants have said:

> A career is like a journey, it's the chance to sort out what it is which makes me happy. In general the dollars are not the driving force.

> I hated being unemployed but I wanted more than a job, I wanted to do something that added value to the community. I wanted to do something meaningful and important. A career is who you are and what you make of life—who I am personally and professionally and ongoing. (Dwyer et al., 2003, p. 29)

Establishing and maintaining a career was a vital and relatively conscious part of their own personal development and self-discovery process. Careers have an holistic emphasis because they are closely related to individual identity and the development of the self. The participants saw their work as intrinsically linked to their personal relationships, their capacity for self-discovery, and the assistance this provided in working out what they wanted from work. This was understood to be a kind of journey, often a prolonged journey, not always a simple or straightforward process. They said:

> It's not about flicking a switch, it happens over a period of time, you need to stand back and reflect on what's happened—the big picture I mean.

> It's about discovering who you are and developing some confidence along the way to work out what you want and how you are going to get there. (Dwyer et al., 2003, p. 29)

The ways that these young people describe the meaning of career can also be applied to their understandings of becoming adult. Many are aware that they are not following the same pattern as their parents. Some, like the young people in du Bois-Reymond's (1998) study, did not see the "adulthood" of their parents' generation as an attractive goal. But they see many aspects of their lives as "adult"—such as the seriousness with which they take their personal relationships, their commitment to studying, their responsibilities for family, and their engagement with work. Gradually, over time they see their own "adult" patterns of life, patterns which they can see in retrospect as developing even before they left secondary school.

CAREER AND PERMANENCE

It was difficult to establish the difference between a permanent job and a career job for our participants as none of the interviewees were prepared to say that their present job was permanent. The idea of permanence is one of the characteristics of career that is no longer relevant. While some of the participants said they thought their job would be permanent (all being well), they were fully aware that this was unlikely to be the case. As one participant said when asked if her job was permanent: "Permanent? Well, anything can happen really."

All the participants demonstrated an awareness that circumstances can change rapidly. One young man had witnessed his team being made redundant when they arrived for work one Monday morning. Similar to Frank's remarks about being laid off, this young man's response was to hope he might also be given a redundancy as he had lost faith in the institution and wanted to go elsewhere. He felt let down by the situation, saying "You sacrifice, but what do you get back?" When he did not receive a redundancy package, he resigned (after getting another job first). In his new job, he is keeping his options open with the idea that "I will jump if there is a better opportunity." His plan was to set up his own business, a decision which he hopes will protect him from experiencing what he describes as the "total destruction of his work environment in one second" and give him back some sense of having control.

In contrast to the above example, others saw change and uncertainty as just part of the picture. They did not take a shift personally, but rather saw it as "the way it is." They regard change as inevitable and work on skilling themselves both mentally and physically to prepare for the challenges that inevitably lie ahead for them.

In this way, some young people manage better than others. It appears from the interviews that those who approach life strategically generally fare better. As one participant expressed it, "I am strategic, I keep up the contacts, build networks, I need to make sure I am not vulnerable." This young woman has accepted that "living your own life therefore entails taking responsibility for personal misfortunes and unanticipated events" (Beck & Beck-Gernsheim, 2002, p. 24). She has internalised the need to have the capacity to constantly reflect, to reinvent herself, to be flexible, and to remain on alert 100% of the time. It is important to acknowledge that this requires a lot of effort. As this young woman comments: "It's made me tougher, I have had to become harder."

The evidence from our study suggests that, far from living through a prolonged adolescence, they have learned the lessons of making very adult choices early. The diversity of experiences, through secondary school and beyond, reflects a blurring of the boundaries between youth and adulthood. In the following, I describe how participants describe their transitions into adulthood.

Blurred Boundaries

The death of a parent, a serious illness, an understanding that it is up to them and no one else to get good results in years eleven and twelve at school, are all examples which demonstrate that many of the young people have carried adult responsibilities for a significant period of time. They interpret many of their life experiences as "adult," because they did not fit into the "norm." For example, one participant said, "Starting off at TAFE [Technical and Further Education] at age twenty-four when all the other students were seventeen felt like a pretty adult thing to be doing!"

Similarly there are examples of young people engaging positively and confidently with an adult world even when traditionally they are not meant to have arrived there yet.

> I feel I have had a very different life to Dad already, he stayed in the one job till he retired, I have started my own business at twenty-two. I am now responsible for eight men and the quality of what we produce. When I first started out it was difficult to convince clients to take me seriously, they thought I was too young to know what I was doing. (Dwyer et al., 2003, p. 30)

There are also many examples of young people engaging strategically with the world of work in a very "adult way."

> I left the cosmetic industry because it could never provide what I wanted. Starting off as a flight attendant now is definitely a stepping-stone to bigger and better. I have done my homework: I need to do more flying, I need to do a number of short courses, I need to be noticed and I need to keep my eyes open. The goal is to be Qantas' customer service manager in three years.

> I felt frustrated by the team approach, the process took too long and I wanted to work on my own. So with the help of technology I can successfully work from home and everyone is happy. (Dwyer et al., 2003, p. 29)

One of the key elements of making commonly perceived "adult" choices involves balancing commitments in different life spheres and it is clear that for them, managing this complex set of life factors is a key element in their own identity formation. One of the themes that recurs in their narratives about adult choices is the ways in which they shape the sphere of personal autonomy.

Personal Autonomy

When interviewing these young people, it became clear that the interview alone was not the prompt for their thinking on questions of career and maintaining balance in their lives. The interview process provided them with an opportunity to express thoughts and concerns that were already at the forefront of their thinking. Their reflections, and the depth of their narratives, reveal that these issues were regularly discussed with partners, family, friends, and work associates.

These young people were reflective and actively engaged in reaching their life goals. This capacity to reflect, and the tendency to take personal responsibility for their lives, fits closely with the concept of individualisation.

> In order to survive the rat race one has to become active, inventive and resourceful, to develop ideas of one's own, to be faster, nimbler and more creative—constantly, day after day. Individuals become stage managers of their own biographies. (Beck & Beck-Gernsheim, 2002, p. 24)

However, as Bauman in the preface to the same text says, "let there be no mistake: now as before individualization is a fate, not a choice; in the land of the individual freedom of choice, the option to escape individualization and refuse participation in the individualizing game is emphatically *not* on the agenda" (Beck & Beck-Gernsheim, 2002, p. xvi).

The interviewees clearly understand that they have to be active players in planning their own journey, and that this is not a choice. They knew if they did not take on this responsibility, they would be left out—and left behind. As one participant said, "it's up to you to organise your life to work out what you want, no one else."

It may be tempting to typecast this generation as self-obsessed. But further analysis reveals a commitment to contribute to the community through informal processes. What has become clear is that the term community is not used to refer to their "local" community but to their "personal community" (Gilding, 2001). The view expressed by one participant sums this up:

Where we live doesn't feel like our community—more our friends and work become our "local" community.

The greatest challenge, articulated throughout the Life-Patterns Project, has been the struggle to balance priorities and commitments. In general, although a minority of the participants are involved in community, voluntary, and political work, most have found that they do not have the time.

Balancing Commitments

The challenge of balancing commitments runs through each of the different themes to emerge in the interviews. Creating the right balance has become a distinctive activity in itself. This takes the form of daily decisions about their work lives, their personal lives, and the question of their contribution to community and global issues. The result of this is a sense of constant movement, almost like treading water. This momentum involves constantly reviewing where they are in relation to where they want to be, and then determining how satisfied they are with the results of their own personal life "audit." Inevitably, they are faced with planning and implementing forms of change to bring their lives into alignment with their goals. The following extracts from the interviews show how this constant process of assessment and reassessment operates in their lives:

If I continued with the bank it would have meant flying to Sydney three times a week, leaving at six a.m. and returning at midnight, this meant I missed out on seeing my nephew and I missed my footy team play. So I worked out my priorities and work didn't come first.

I have a two year old, even though I loved working in the city, at head office, I wanted to be closer to home and part time. I wanted more time with my family so I'm back in the branches.

I was taking on every shift and my relationship was suffering, so I cut back, I reduced the number of overnighters. (Dwyer et al., 2003, p. 32)

Some young people were more able and effective at this shaping and balancing than others. As one participant stated, "If you have self-doubt in this environment it is very difficult to achieve." Others agreed:

> The juggling is exhausting at times. I have health issues, I am involved in setting up a new business, my wife has just started a new job and we haven't even had a honeymoon yet.

> I often feel really alone; it is difficult to adjust to so many changes, if you drop off the radar screen it is often difficult to get back on. (Dwyer et al., 2003, p. 32)

Many young people had to live through a negative experience at their work place before they knew they had to "shape and balance," and would now describe themselves as disillusioned.

> It sounds awful, that is not committing to the future at my current work but I need to look out myself for—it sounds cut-throat but look at the way the company treated my fellow workers.

> I missed out on a promotion I thought I deserved. It was a political decision, not based on professional competency. I have had to reassess my commitment; I don't think loyalty pays off anymore. If I am this expendable I need to find other things I am interested in. (Dwyer et al., 2003, p. 32)

CONCLUSION

With the benefit of ten years' hindsight after leaving school, the stories of our post-1970 cohort of young people reveal a generation who have made a rapid transition. This transition is not the conventional one, from youth to adulthood, although this has been achieved. They have, of necessity, managed the transition from a school system and social policy framework based firmly on an industrial era to living, working, and studying in a post-industrial era.

In their own words, society and its institutions are seen as relatively fragmented and unreliable. They believe that they have no other option than to rely on themselves to make their lives worthwhile. While relationships with family and friends are very important to them (see Table 1), their statements reveal a strong sense of personal responsibility for their own lives. Rather than focusing on external goals, such as the achievement of a particular status level in an occupation or the success of a political grouping, they focus on very personal goals, such as being healthy, continuing to learn, and personal fulfilment. In one sense, in the course of one generation, they have succeeded in changing the meanings of many of the core elements of life.

Career, for example, is now seen as a personal journey. Young people reflexively construct career narratives that meaningfully link their past, present, and future lives. To the post-1970 generation, the term career is an almost wholly internally referenced concept. This means that it is possible to consider a fragmented, stop-start work life on short-term contracts a career. The idea of permanent work is regarded with suspicion. Instead, a mix of formal and informal learning and mobility across different work settings and experiences are woven together to construct individual "careers" that are far-removed from the upwardly mobile, occupation-based careers of the previous generation.

Drawing on the theoretical ideas of Beck (Beck & Beck-Gernsheim, 2002), this chapter has explored the implications of social change for our conceptualisation of the transition to adulthood. Yet, in focusing on the important elements of change that have affected the experiences of youth and adolescence, it is important to recognise that young people are not a homogeneous group. The social changes that have been referred to here affect all ages in different ways. In this chapter, I have explicitly focused on "mainstream" youth, in order to draw attention to significant social changes. It is important, however, to acknowledge that there is always diversity—social, geographical, and historical.

For example, historians point out that at various times young people from poor families have had to "grow up" quickly in order to contribute to their family's survival by earning a wage or working on the land. In drawing attention to broad patterns of social change, one set of homogeneous categories should not be replaced with another. Rather, the aim of this discussion has been to disrupt the taken-for-granted concept of a linear trajectory that has tended to dominate thinking about youth and adolescence, and to draw attention to the experiences of young people.

In answer to the question posed in the title of this chapter, "adolescence" may be becoming "obsolescent." The life patterns and meanings that young people have generated challenge researchers and policy makers to "rethink" the traditional boundaries around adolescence, youth, and adulthood. Their lives bear witness to the emergence of a new adulthood which, though bearing a superficial resemblance to "adolescence," signals new approaches and values that are reshaping what it means to be adult today.

REFERENCES

Australian Bureau of Statistics. (2002). *Yearbook Australia 2002*. Canberra: Author.

Ball, S. J., Maguire, M., & Macrae, S. (2000). *Choice, pathways and transitions post-16*. London: Routledge/Falmer.

Beck, U. & Beck-Gernsheim, E. (2002). *Individualization*. London: Sage.

Chisholm, L., Buchnen. P., Kruger, H., & Brown, P. (Eds.). (1990). *Childhood, youth and social change: A comparative perspective*. London: Falmer.

Côté, J. (2000). *Arrested adulthood*. New York: New York University Press.

Côté, J. & Allahar, A. (1994). *Generation on hold: Coming of age in the late twentieth century*. Toronto: Stoddart.

du Bois-Reymond, M. (1998). "I don't want to commit myself yet": Young people's life concepts. *Journal of Youth Studies, 1*(1), 63–79.

Dwyer, P., Smith, G., Tyler, D., & Wyn, J. (2003). Life-patterns, career outcomes and adult choices, Research Report 23. Melbourne: Australian Youth Research Centre.

Dwyer, P. & Wyn, J. (2001). *Youth, education and risk: Facing the future*. London: Routledge/Falmer.

Furlong, A. & Cartmel, F. (1997). *Young people and social change: Individualisation and risk in late modernity*. Buckingham, UK: Open University Press.

Gilding, M. (2001). Changing families in Australia, 1901–2001. *Family Matters, 60*, Spring/Winter, 6–11.

Heinz, W. (2000). Youth transitions and employment in Germany. *International Social Science Journal, 164*, 161–170.

Jones, G. & Wallace, C. (1992). *Youth, family and citizenship*. Buckingham, UK: Open University Press.

Lash, S. (2002). Individualization in a non-linear mode. In U. Beck & E. Beck-Gernsheim, *Individualization* (pp. vii–xii). London: Sage.

Lerner, R. M. (1995). *America's youth in crisis*. Thousand Oaks, CA: Sage.

Lesko, N. (1996). Denaturalising adolescence: The politics of contemporary representations. *Youth and Society, 28*(2), 139–161.

Smith, T. L., Smith, G. H., Boler, M., Kempton, M., Ormond, A., Chueh, H., & Waetford, R. (2002). "Do you guys hate Aucklanders too?": Youth voicing differences from the rural heartland. *Journal of Rural Studies, 18*, 179–187.

Wallace, C. & Kovacheva, S. (1995). *Youth and society*. London: Macmillan.

Weston, R., Stanton, D., Qu, L., & Soriano, G. (2001). Australian families in transition: Socio-demographic trends 1901-2002. *Family Matters, 60*, 12 –23.

Wyn, J. & White, R. (1997). *Rethinking youth*. London: Sage.

CHAPTER THREE

Youth, Adults, and Literacies: Texting Subjectivities Within and Outside Schooling

Lisa Patel Stevens

A number of lenses have been used to examine education issues (e.g., curriculum reform, theories of learning, school culture, literacy pedagogy), and it is often through these issues that young people come into view. However, problematic to these frames is the very backgrounding of young people. The depictions of young people through literacy research is no different in this respect. Research into secondary textual practices has tended to centre strongly on those practices around content area texts, readings of canonical literature, and remedial reading pedagogy. Only recently have a small collection of researchers begun to investigate the nature of secondary literacy activities and practices as part of understanding the literate lives of youth and young people (e.g., Finders, 1996; Moje, 2000a; Willis, 1995). Inherent to these studies, and to this one, is an epistemological stance acknowledging the highly constitutive force of language, discourse, and textual practices in the reification of figured worlds of school, home, and beyond. This stance, steeped in Foucault's (1983) ideas about the constitutive force of language in post-modern society, draws attention to the use of literacy and textual practices within schooling contexts as a way of understanding what is possible, but also what is not possible within these social spaces and amid these communicative acts. Also inherent in these studies is the regard for language, embodied discourses, and textual practices engaged by some young people that have little resonance, capital, or relevancy to the traditional print-based literacies privileged within the content area pillars of secondary schools. These studies, along with this one, broaden the academic and educative definitions of literacies, to include those that hold currency, power, and efficacy for contexts and purposes unrelated to school.

This study offers a critical ethnography of one eighth grade female student's evolving and shifting senses of self and, in particular, how her textual practices inside and outside of school offer insight into the social spaces afforded to her subjectivities. While this study is situated in the tradition of others who have investigated the ways in which young people "become somebody" within, against, and astride the context of schooling (e.g., Herr & Anderson, 1997; Moje, 2000b; Suarez-Orozco, 1987; Wexler, 1992), I draw upon post-structural feminism for the concept of subjectivity to talk about Desiree's sense of self.

In contrast to the internal, fixed, and unitary conceptions that mark traditional concepts of identity, subjectivity has been defined by such theorists as Grosz (1994) and Butler (1999). Viewed from Foucauldian lenses, these theorists posit the concept of subjectivity as the cognitive, affective, and imminently embodied characteristics that are numerous, shifting, contested, and fluid. Different from traditional concepts of identity as contained solely within the individual, subjectivity, by name and typical use, casts people as subjects in social, political, and cultural contexts. As such, subjective senses of self are comprised of various culturally constructed and often conflicting discourses, practices, and symbols, and these senses elide fixed markers.

Along with this epistemological stance, my practice of critical ethnography also drew from the agentive aspect of critical inquiry and theory (Popkewitz & Fendler, 1999). Critical theories draw our attention to the ubiquitous and unbalanced dynamics of power, but also compel us to act upon this knowledge and awareness. Critical lenses not only adjust our views of social worlds, but also counteract, transform, and modify the material aspects of these social worlds. In this sense, my practice of critical ethnography coalesced with my recognitive understanding of recognitive social justice, one that privileges the processes of democratic discourse over final outcomes (Gale & Densmore, 2000). This resulted in a research standpoint that used language and literacy to more fully appreciate Desiree's understandings of herself as a capable, sentient, and highly literate young person. As a researcher in both the home and school settings of Desiree's literate contexts, I chose to concentrate my engagement with her in the context of her self-sanctioned literacy practices. In adopting a critical literacy stance toward the texts in her school settings, Desiree was already adopting critical standpoints in relation to her subjectivities. Our conversations centred on raising her awareness of these dynamics and towards increasing her sense of efficacy and empowerment through literacy events.

However, I was also interested in how Desiree navigated the literate terrains of her middle school, and in particular, her physical science classroom. This inquiry was informed by understandings of schooling as reproductive sites of inequity in society, and of students as potentially complicit, subversive, and/or resistant to these patterns. Widely first named and attributed to the large-scale study of the culturally subversive practices of young men in secondary schools in the United Kingdom conducted by Willis (1977), these studies have predominantly focused on the resistance of males, casting their resistance as ultimately detrimental to their lives. This study adds to this conversation by investigating how one young girl creatively, and often generatively, resisted, engaged, subverted, and co-opted the spaces provided by social institutions.

METHODOLOGY

I first came to know Desiree[1] through my work as a consultant to her school in the area of literacy pedagogy. After a small group conversation about students who were struggling with "basic" literacy processes in secondary schools, Sharon, an eighth grade science teacher in the school, approached me and enlisted my help with one of her students, Desiree, whom Sharon suspected to be struggling in literacy. Like many secondary content area teachers, Sharon used print-based texts as a primary pedagogical tool and focal point. Often, when secondary students do not achieve on classroom-based assessments and tasks, they are viewed from a deficit perspective, one that often pinpoints them as struggling readers. Such was the case when Sharon asked me to work with Desiree.

I first began by talking informally with Desiree, thinking that her own accounts of her literacy experiences would shed some light on which literacy skills, practices, and processes were proving to be difficult for her. It soon became apparent that Desiree was far from struggling in a competency-based sense. Instead Desiree was simply but profoundly disengaged from the textual practices sanctioned in school, seeing them as unrelated to her current and future contexts. In fact, after we had been talking for a few minutes, Desiree talked quite openly about the types of highly multiliterate activities that she enjoyed and found relevant outside of schooling contexts. This dichotomy between her performance within school-sanctioned literacy practices and her performance within self-sanctioned practices seemed to result in a particularly salient example of the slippage between Desiree's self-advocated subjectivities and those afforded to her within her secondary school.

To investigate the tensions, patterns, and issues of subjectivity construction within social contexts, I used the approach of critical ethnography. In gathering ethnographic, field-based data from interviews, observations, and artefacts, I was keenly interested in how power differentials come to be realised through the textual practices sanctioned within the schooling spaces and those self-sanctioned by Desiree outside of school contexts. In constructing and representing Desiree's engagement with various textual practices, I paid particular attention to the unequal distributions of power inherent in the social fields comprising Desiree's home, school, and community-based contexts. I observed these contexts as a participant observer, often engaging in, or alongside, Desiree's textual practices and talking to her during those times. She and I also sat down for more formal interviews on about fourteen occasions, and I interviewed her mother, her teachers, and her principal.

I also drew heavily upon the discourses that Desiree used to name and locate her textual practices, and their links to her overlapping subjectivities as a young, female, African American amid a largely Asian American and European American context. As a highly literate fan of particular aspects of mass-mediated popular culture, Desiree's oral and written narratives about her needs, abilities, and strengths bore an interesting contrast to the comments offered about Desiree by her eighth grade science teacher, Sharon. In keeping with a critical ethnographic perspective, I examined Desiree and Sharon's discursive messages using critical discourse analysis (Fairclough, 1989, 1995). This methodology emphasises the social and political groundedness of the language and text segments surrounding Desiree. As such, the methodology drew upon the micro aspects and functions of linguistic markers and their relationship to the larger and hegemonically tinged social, political, and historical fields. Using critical discourse analysis afforded opportunities to examine the relationship between the language and patterns used in relation to Desiree and the possible ways of being afforded therein. This perspective provided the crucial opening to question which aspects of being a student, a teacher, and a literate person are authenticated, silenced, marginalised, and subverted within the spaces of the middle school classroom.

A MIXED REFORM EFFORT: LAURAL MIDDLE SCHOOL

Laural Middle School is located in the inner regions of a large urban area in the western United States. The school has open air hallways, and the sounds of horns and traffic carry easily through the classrooms, where windows are left open in the hopes of catching cooling breezes.

At the time of the study, Laural Middle School had only recently been renamed as a middle school. Almost thirty-six years old, the building and its constitutive practices had been labelled and known as a junior high school, operating along tangible content area divisions and traditional bell schedules. The transition to a middle schooling philosophy was one sanctioned and initiated by the principal of the school, and had been met with mixed responses from the school's faculty. "Teams" of teachers, who shared a common set of students, were to work together to plan and implement interdisciplinary units. While some teams engaged in these practices, other teams of teachers resisted the middle schooling concept of teaming and worked along traditional disciplinary lines for a variety of reasons. Adding to this mixture of implementation, the eighth grade had been designated as a transition year to high school, thus teachers were asked to integrate their pedagogy occasionally but also to work independently. The intention of this approach was for students to be scaffolded from interdisciplinary units to making connections themselves among disparate content area knowledge, skills, and processes.

Desiree's eighth grade team was one of the groups of teachers who made sporadic attempts to engage in team-teaching efforts and make interdisciplinary connections. When they made connections, they often did so through the content area textbooks, with the language arts teachers using the science and social studies texts to model and highlight desired strategic reading behaviours, such as pre-reading and metacognition. However, all of Desiree's teachers expressed frustration at implementing a reform in pedagogy without the benefit of any change in the temporal or content structure to the school day.

Desiree's teachers, and about half of the students in her team, were Asian American. There were a few other African American students in the school, comprising about 1% of the student population. Half of the student population was European American.

DISPARATE LITERATE PERFORMANCES: DESIREE

At the time of the study, Desiree was a fourteen year old African American girl, the daughter of a single mother, who moved to this city about three years ago when her father was transferred to the city's nearby naval station. Since moving, Desiree's father passed away, and her mother has returned to full-time employment as a nurse at the naval station's hospital. On a few different occasions, Desiree's mother told me that she believed that all of these difficult transitions and life events were impacting Desiree negatively in her schoolwork but that she was not sure how to counteract this trend. Desiree, through her own description, had been an excellent student in elementary school, consistently receiving awards for her immaculate work and perfect attendance each year. She expanded on this in a narrative entitled, "The Good Girl I Used to Be":

> I was always the one that the teachers liked. I loved going to school and doing the work exactly how they wanted it done. I would turn in things early, help out after-school and get really excited when the teacher would

thank me or compliment me. What for? Well, I remember that this made Mom and Dad really happy and proud of me. That was even better than the teacher being happy. I felt really confident then, like I belonged in the school and it was my place to be.

Desiree remembered that she began to experience less and less joy from these types of endeavours in sixth grade. She expressed that "other people's comments and compliments" did not motivate her the way they did in her primary school years. She attributed this to school being "boring" and "the same old thing every day." She sometimes remembered to do her assignments and sometimes overlooked them, but did not seem to be too concerned about the consequences of receiving bad grades. As she expressed in one of our conversations, "I just don't get what playing the game gets me. What's the point?" Desiree maintained average grades, occasionally hovering near failing marks and then doing enough work to bring her grades back up to less objectionable thresholds. She expressed several times to me that she no longer felt the strong need to obey the explicit and implicit rules that delimit girls as good students. "It's like, um, they ask the boys to do stuff and the girls just like, um, sit there and supposed to be all nice and sweet," she explained.

In addition to her objections over the implicit rules of obeisance governing the school environment, Desiree was also openly opposed to the dominant European American perspective pervasive in her school textbooks, sometimes referring to it as the reason why she sometimes opted out of school activities. Also underlying Desiree's resistance this perspective was her view of studenting as "acting white." She mentioned an aversion to this performance several times in interviews and often linked this performance with the overrepresentation of European Americans in texts and curricula. In her science classroom, where I observed Desiree, the majority of the pedagogical practices revolved around the content area textbook, a large hardcover textbook with a recent publication date. The most frequent lesson sequence was as follows, as taken from a summary of my ethnographic field notes:

Sharon opened class with lecture about the day's topic. The lecture lasted for approximately twenty-five minutes, in which she used the overhead projector and moved a piece of paper gradually down the overhead to reveal the notes that students were to copy down. During this activity, Desiree copied down the notes but also kept a magazine hidden under her notes that she read when Sharon didn't seem to be looking in her direction. After the lecture and note-taking, Sharon directed the class to read section one of chapter eight in the textbook and to answer the comprehension questions at the end of the section. Sharon instructed the students that what they didn't finish in class would become homework, due the following day in class. The rest of the period was spent in silence, as students worked quietly at their seats on the assigned reading and comprehension questions. During this time, Desiree quickly answered the questions, skimming the text and referring back to the questions frequently. When finished, she tucked the assignment away in her notebook and took out her magazine. [2-22-02]

On other occasions, Desiree often engaged in the superficial and apparent markers of textual activities, such as opening her textbook to the designated page, but then stopped short of completing the written work intended for grading. On the two occasions when I observed Sharon question Desiree about her lack of completed assignments, Desiree simply shrugged and offered no verbal reply. In this way, Desiree offered a partially covert resistance to the textbook-centred literacy events found in Sharon's classroom.

Outside of school, Desiree presented a markedly different set of textual practices, processes, and skills. She engaged in a range of literate practices, spending large amounts of time writing narratives in a notebook she entitled simply, "Me." She also spent quite a bit of time engaged in digitally mediated literacy practices: being online, sending instant messages to friends (IMing), and talking on the phone. She was an avid fan of the R & B group Destiny's Child, and had constructed a fan website devoted to the group. Desiree described her most typical after-school activities:

Desiree: Well, I usually get home around three and go online right away. Because of the time difference [across the United States] there'll be messages on the bulletin board and I like to check those out first. Then, I usually go to my email and then just wherever from there.

Lisa: Is that still on the computer?

Desiree: Um, yeah, well, it like depends on just whatever I feel like doing, ya know? Usually I stay online, but sometimes I just feel like turnin' it all off and goin' to write in my notebook or watching TV or just whatever.

On several afternoons, I observed Desiree as she simultaneously worked on her website, IMed several friends, waited for responses, and talked on the phone to Tonya. Without any doubt, Desiree was a fluid, multiliterate user of various modes, formats, and genres of digital and print-based texts. Furthermore, Desiree not only engaged various aspects of her subjectivities through her textual practices, she also verbalised astute understandings of the relationship between communicative acts and the continual processes of becoming, citing her notebook and its narratives as a key way for her to "understand who I am."

A rich example of Desiree's conscious understanding of her literacy practices as performances of her subjectivities arose about halfway through the study when Desiree and I were talking about possible expansions to her website.

Desiree: You know how I told you 'bout how it's a good idea to have links to other sites and stuff?

Lisa: Yep.

Desiree: Well, I been thinkin' 'bout adding a link to another person but not really sure if I should or not.

Lisa: What's the problem?

Desiree: Well, it'd be to R. Kelly—you know him?

Lisa: Yeah—so what's up with him?

Desiree: Well, I really liked just having women singers on the website—that way it's like about the music but also about girls doin' it, ya know, cuz it's mostly guys in hip hop and R & B, ya know?

Lisa: Yeah, that's a great point, cuz weren't you saying the other day that most of your regular posters [website visitors who post messages to the message board] are other girls?

Desiree: Yeah—like that. Mmhmm.

Lisa: So, you're thinking it'd be good to keep the site as sort of a female space?

Desiree: Yeah—what do you think 'bout that?

Lisa: Well, I think that'd be really good, and I also think it'd be great if you mentioned that specifically in one of your own posts.

Desiree: Um, yeah, like you mean, talk about girls in music?

Lisa: Yeah, and—

Desiree: Like I could talk about how we should spend our money and follow girls because it's harder for them.

Lisa: If that's important to you, then maybe you should make that explicit to your website's visitors.

Desiree: Mmhmm—I just don't want to turn the website into something else, ya know what I mean?

Lisa: Yeah, maybe that's something you could just sort of keep an eye on.

Desiree demonstrated an explicit and thoughtful consideration of the ways in which her textual choices enact, construct, and reveal aspects of her subjectivities. She was able to articulate the voice inside that sees a need to support female artists in a male-dominated aspect of the music industry. But she also recognised how this might overtake the voice that was purely fan-based for that particular group. In this way, Desiree mediated several aspects of her subjectivities amid a social context that also included other young females, most of whom are African American. This conversation led us to examine the ways in which gender is constructed differently and often defined through dichotomous renderings of perceived male to female characteristics.

Desiree and I examined several other artists' lyrics and websites (e.g., Jay-Z, P. Diddy, Lil' Kim, Jennifer Lopez) as inquiries into how the music industry reifies and juxtaposes oppositional stances of gender to appeal to particular demographics. It was within the contexts of this and other conversations that I engaged the transformative purpose of critical ethnography. Increasingly, Desiree and I talked about the raced and gendered practices of certain popular culture texts and her uses of them. Through this and other conversations, Desiree demonstrated purposefully refined and precise literacy practices as well as thoughtfulness about how those literacy practices refracted portrayals of her own subjectivities. Because of this, I saw myself less as someone who was trying to change Desiree's views, as might be assumed from a critical ethnographic perspective, but more as an interlocutor, with a different, but no more privileged, set of languages and concepts around popular culture texts and their potential meanings and functions. In these conversations, Desiree often asked for my perspective—sometimes assumed similar positions and sometimes not—but consistently spoke about her reflections on her practices.

This metacognitive awareness of self and textual practices was also readily apparent in the conversations that Desiree and her mother, Eyvonne, had about her slipping grades. These conversations were consistently civil and thoughtful, with Eyvonne expressing concern for Desiree and her future, and Desiree acknowledging these concerns. But Desiree was also persistent in asking why she should have to participate in activities she viewed as "boring" and "not having to do with anything." Eyvonne frequently expressed to me her frustration at wanting to support Desiree as an independent thinker and wanting her to be successful: "I know full and well what she's talkin' about. I just want her to be successful, and she's thinking for herself, which is great, but she's making it so hard on herself in the meantime. And then she does all these things like the [notebook] and the website, but she keeps making hard choices in school."

Eyvonne's concern was over Desiree's current and future abilities to access the power structure of dominant discourses, practices, and activities that act as currency in the institutional context of schooling and within other domains in society. Eyvonne was caught in the precarious position of wanting to affirm her daughter's critical

perspectives and resistance to dominant discourses but, in a pragmatic sense, did not want Desiree to suffer from being labelled as another minority member who has not succeeded in school, another
"adolescent" inscribed with inabilities. Desiree was clearly capable of
successfully completing her traditional textbook-centred activities
that carry weight in her science classroom, but objected to these due
to their lack of relevancy to her—to her sense of subjectivities within
local and global contexts. In this way, Desiree saw her school as incapable of affirming the subjectivities that she explored through the literacy practices that she chose for herself. She regularly resisted
school-sponsored text-book activities, quite possibly to the benefit of
her own subjectivities.

CONFLICTING DISCOURSES: SHARON AND DESIREE

While Desiree embodied and spoke about her heightened and critical
literacy practices, these enactments of subjectivities also took place
along varied conversations about her literacy abilities within schooling contexts. As noted previously, I first began to know Desiree
through Sharon's concern about her literacy abilities. Sharon had no-
ticed the intermittent consistency in Desiree's work and surmised that
this was due to an inability to contend with the content area and concepts in the text. Sharon was concerned about Desiree "slipping
through the cracks," and sought assistance since this exceeded her
knowledge about literacy skills, practices, and processes, and potential intervention remedies. After I learned about the motivational
basis of Desiree's disengagement with school-based literacy practices,
I shared the information with Sharon. Throughout this and other conversations, Sharon shared her perspectives on Desiree's abilities,
needs, and strengths, but these concerns were narrowly expressed
only through apprehensions over Desiree's ability to succeed in
school. In a Bakhtinian (1981) sense, Desiree and Sharon were engaged in an asynchronous, heteroglossic construction and disjointed
contestation over Desiree's subjectivities as a student and as a literate
person. In what follows, I present several excerpts from interviews
with both characteristics. I offer these in quick succession, to present
them the ways in which Desiree and Sharon offered alternate representations of Desiree's subjectivities. Drawing from both Bakhtin

(1981) and Fairclough (1989), these representations are offered as a source of intertextuality. Bakhtin defines intertextuality as:

> The property texts have of being full of snatches of other texts, which may be explicitly demarcated or merged in, and which the text may assimilate, contradict, ironically echo, and so forth. In terms of production, an intertextual perspective stresses the historicity of texts: how they always constitute additions to existing 'chains of speech communication.' (p. 94)

The exchanges between Desiree and Sharon make up a unique chain of speech communication, one in which what counts as literacy and subjectivity is constructed in complex ways:

> Yeah, well, what I do is use the Internet site to talk about all that stuff [Destiny's Child], but it's also to link to all other sites. You get to know who people are and what they're into that way, and I can tell just by the other websites what we both like. It goes way beyond just the group. [Desiree]

> What I do is email other people, mostly Savannah [an Internet friend of Desiree's, who has more advanced knowledge of HTML and Java coding for the website construction] and ask her how to do stuff. Like here [clicks on the hyperlink for biographies of Destiny Child's members]—she showed me how to make this, um, backdrop, and um, here [clicks on a streaming line of text] how to make this keep going and flashing. [Desiree]

> All that stuff [Desiree's fandom for Destiny's Child and her website construction] doesn't really help her with the curriculum that she needs to get by in school. They need the basic skills of reading and writing and then maybe that other stuff can add to it because books are never going away. [Sharon]

> I don't know—sometimes I'll do the work because it's just easier that way, but most of the time, I just can't see the point and don't get the game. [Desiree]

> This age is going through so much, they need a lot of guidance and support. I'm just having a really hard time getting through to her, and then there are 150 other kids who are in here every day, too. [Sharon]

> If she [Desiree] spent less time listening to those bands and more on her schoolwork, she'd be doing a lot better, but that goes for so many of our

kids. There's just so much other stuff out there that distracts them from their schoolwork. [Sharon]

These speech segments reveal several key aspects about Desiree, about Sharon's positioning of Desiree as a student, and about the significant disconnect between those two perspectives. Using Fairclough's (1989) orders of discourse helps to illuminate the nuances in the particular language choices that relate to the local, institutional, and societal contexts and the ways of being a eighth grade girl within those spaces. The orders of discourse, including genre, discourse, and style, offer ways to situate and locate the relationships between knowledge and power. Fairclough (1989) defines genre as the set of social practices that make up a particular linguistic exchange. This is the textual domain in which we can examine how language is tied together to create certain meanings and silence others. Within these responses, the discourses used enact the interpersonal domain of representing within those genres. Finally, the style, or the way of being within the genre and the discourse, draws attention to relationships of power and knowledge, as certain ideational domains are privileged within the position taken up within semiotic exchanges. A discursive analysis of these responses to open-ended interview questions, along these three orders of discourse, brings to light the particular social, political, and cultural spaces in this middle schooling context.

What is perhaps most striking about these exchanges is, as might be expected, the disconnect between what counts as competency for Desiree's perception of herself as a young person and her teacher's perception of Desiree as a middle school student. Desiree saw herself as a capable and active learner of literacy practices, skills, and processes. She also constructed herself as resistant to particular literacy practices, namely those based in content area texts within school settings.

At the textual level, there is an interesting trend for Desiree to self-name her practices as in, "What I do is..." These phrases evoke a strong picture of metacognition and self-awareness. Desiree would often comment upon the literacy activities she chooses to engage in outside of school, and contrasts these to the lack of choice she is offered at school. She spoke from a position that uses metalanguage to mark explicitly what she likes, does, and deems important.

Sharon, though also commenting upon Desiree's literacy practices and choices, rarely used a personal pronominal textual marker. Instead, she moved quickly to discussions about her students and their needs and activities. This absence of personal pronominal grounding removed Sharon as an agentive force in the literacies that are privileged within the space of her classroom. By backgrounding the choices that were made in her classroom, the preferred literacy activities of copying down lecture notes and answering comprehension questions from the textbook were constructed as the normative centre of classroom textual practices.

Another noteworthy trend in Sharon's responses, particularly those specifically concerning Desiree, was the reference to the age group of middle schoolers. In each of the text segments offered above, Sharon responded to specific queries about Desiree, but was quick to relate these to Desiree's "early adolescent" age group, the term preferred by the National Middle Schooling Association which Sharon had recently joined as a professional member.

In this sense, Sharon spoke consistently from the stance as Desiree's teacher, but more saliently, as a teacher of this age group at large. And though she spoke of Desiree as an individual student, she was more often viewed as one of a collective group, constructed to share the same propensities, interests, and needs. Sharon interpreted Desiree's needs, abilities, and interests within a dominant discourse of the early adolescent, one that draws upon progressivist and romanticized understandings of this age/stage in life as one of turbulence, change, and transition (Finders, 1998/1999). Sharon's words parallel mainstream discourses surrounding young people and represent the pedagogical, curricular, and assessment practices that are implicated in these discourses. By constructing early adolescents as in need of guidance and support, this dually reaffirms their stance as incomplete and therefore eliminates them as a valid source in constructing what might count as a literacy competency. This elimination serves to further instantiate the content area literacy texts and surrounding technicist pedagogical practices as the normative centre of the secondary classroom.

The representation of Desiree as struggling and in need of guidance stands in direct contrast to Desiree's explicit statements about
her quite conscious, confident, and deliberate withdrawals from
school-sanctioned literacy practices. The intertextuality of Sharon and
Desiree's comments point to an ascribed diagnosis of what "early
adolescents" need without a direct inquiry into, and understanding
of, Desiree's needs. In fact, these comments came after Sharon and I
had discussions about Desiree's apparent and precise literacy competencies exhibited outside of school. Sharon's comments point to a
disregard of these competencies, privileging instead those that are
more expository print-based and emphasising the demand that Desiree, and other young people, master "basic" skills first. However,
even a reductionist reading of basic skills would account for the
highly literate activities that Desiree engages in with her print-based
collection of narratives. But Desiree herself resists bringing her own
literacy practices and activities into a school context in open, publicly
performed manners. In this way, Desiree and Sharon trade turns de-
valuing the preferred literacy practices of the other. They dispute
what sorts of textual events count as literacies, and in a broader sense,
what aspects of Desiree's subjectivities count.

DISCUSSION

The ethnographic and discourse data in this study point to a significant disconnect in two areas of Desiree's life, particularly as enacted
in relation to schooling contexts. First, the discourses about young
people present alternative and incongruent views of Desiree when
juxtaposed against Desiree's views of herself. Second, the textual
practices enacted in various settings differ widely and are saturated
with power-tinged readings of what counts as a legitimate literate
practice. These two areas of disconnect have parallels with each other,
as literacy and literate practices are key mechanisms by which educators often name some students and work to construct them as successful, skilled, and proficient while others are seen as struggling and
incompetent. In short, the literate practices that are valued differently
by Sharon and Desiree serve to represent conflicting voices that result
in a heteroglossic and contested view of Desiree's subjectivities.

The dominant discourse of young people occurs through the pastoral talk about "adolescents." Steeped in developmentalist epistemologies and understandings of human beings as individuals, the naming and defining of the stage of adolescence is widely attributed to G. Stanley Hall (1904). Hall's theory draws upon biological underpinnings to cast this age span as a time of storm and stress. The discourses stemming from this theory have developed into a dominant view of "adolescents" as unruly, rebellious, and in need of guidance (Lesko, 2001). This societal Discourse (Gee, 1996) is mirrored closely in Sharon's talk not only about Desiree, but also in her sweeping conflation of Desiree's educational needs with the needs ascribed to young people at large. This discursive move from the individual to the group's image alone shows how dominant, pervasive discourses can sweep over the individual variations presented within a segment of the population.

This sweeping negation undervalues many of the highly literate and metacognitive ways that Desiree negotiates her literate performances in two very distinct realms: the institutional school setting where she sees little relevance in the textbook-centred activities versus the open-textured context of home, where she is more successful at mediating and negotiating the connections between more generative and more congruent performances of her subjectivities. Ironically, while Desiree is labelled as a struggling reader, she engages in deep reflection and engagement with literacy practices that she thinks best reflect her subjectivities as a young African American woman. And while she is resistant to the traditional textual practices of her school and often withdraws from these, this act can also be viewed as a productive performance of her own subjectivities. In this way, what is missing from her literacy practices counts, as communicative and performative acts, as much to Desiree as what she chooses for herself. The salient rift over the social construction of her subjectivities is underscored by the conflicting conceptions held by Desiree and Sharon. The disconnect between their two textual practices serves as an enactment of the opportunities, closures, and slippage stemming from the discourses about "adolescents" and how Desiree, as a young person, interacts with, against, and alongside those discourses in forming her own subjectivities.

What may be particularly and historically unique about the inconsistency between Desiree and Sharon's accounts of preferred literacy
skills is the apparent offset between traditional print-based literacies
and more contemporary digitally mediated literacies. Sharon's views
of multimediated literacies as ancillary to the true business of schooling echo a current and tangible rupture between the lived experiences
of an aging teacher workforce and that of millennial generations
weaned on Short Message Service (SMS) messaging, hypertext, email,
and digital music (Hagood, Stevens, & Reinking, 2002). Sharon's
comments point to a hierarchical classification of digital literacies as
secondary to the "basics" of print-based literacies. While Desiree's literacy development over time was not a focus of this study, the ethnographic data point strongly to her abilities to increasingly engage
with, develop within, and manipulate print-based and digitally mediated literacies in complex, concurrent fashions, for different purposes
and for different reasons. In essence, she transformed and augmented
her practices based on the technologies and purposes at hand. Yet, the
infusion of technology into schools has not resulted in a similar transformation of institutional literate practices. Rather, the technology has
largely been appropriated as tools to fit within the accepted curricula
and pedagogies (Luke, 2002). As Sharon enacts dominant discourses
about adolescents and clings to traditional notions of literacy, reading,
and textbook-centred practices, Desiree seeks and engages with public pedagogies to provide her with the multimediated literacies she
deems as important, relevant, and engaging.

Consideration of this dichotomy against the social backdrop of
fast capitalist and globalised economies based on semiotic signs
(Habermas, 1979) points out an ironic and substantial crevice between
Sharon's technicist practices in school and the highly variant practices
engaged by Desiree outside of school (Luke, 2002). The fact that this
discrepancy occurs within the scope of whole-school pedagogy, curriculum, and assessment reform points to a strong need to reconsider
the underpinnings of these reforms.

Educational reforms often draw their data and theoretically justify
their conclusions from analyses of teachers, institutional constructs,
and the officially sanctioned spaces of schools. By and large, they
have not been informed by the literate, embodied, and performed

lives of young people within and outside those spaces. For example, how might the reform of middle schooling, in its third or fourth decade in the United States—and now gaining fervent momentum in Australia—be shaped differently if the biological and developmental underpinnings of the stage of adolescence were interrogated with both quantitative and qualitative research about the lived worlds, both material and figured, of young people outside of schooling contexts? In the past, educational reforms have suffered equally and failed predictably due, at least in part, to insufficient theorisation of the purposes of secondary schools and lack of full consideration of young people, in their variant and diverse subjectivities.

NOTE

1. All identifying names have been replaced with pseudonyms.

REFERENCES

Bakhtin, M. M. (1981). *The dialogic imagination: Four essays* (C. Emerson & M. Holquist, Trans.). Austin: University of Texas Press.

Butler, J. (1999). *Gender trouble: Feminism and the subversion of identity* (Rev. ed.). New York: Routledge.

Fairclough, N. (1989). *Language and power*. London: Longman.

Fairclough, N. (1995). *Critical discourse analysis: The critical study of language*. New York: Longman.

Finders, M. (1996). "Just girls": Literacy and allegiance in junior high school. *Written Communication, 13*, 93–129.

Finders, M. (1998/1999). Raging hormones: Stories of adolescence and implications for teacher education. *Journal of Adolescent and Adult Literacy, 42*, 252–263.

Foucault, M. (1983). Afterword: The subject and power. In G. Burchell, C. Godon, & P. Miller (Eds.), *Michel Foucault: Beyond structuralism and hermeneutics* (pp. 148–156). Chicago: University of Chicago Press.

Gale, T. & Densmore, K. (2000). *Just schooling: Explorations into the cultural politics of teaching*. Philadelphia: Open University Press.

Gee, J. (1996). *Sociolinguistics and literacies: Ideology in discourses* (2nd ed.). New York: Falmer.

Grosz, E. (1994). *Volatile bodies: Toward a corporeal feminism*. Sydney: Allen & Unwin.

Habermas, J. (1979). *Communication and the evolution of society*. Boston: Beacon Press.

Hagood, M. C., Stevens, L. P., & Reinking, D. (2002). What do *they* have to teach *us*? Talkin' cross generations! In D. E. Alvermann (Ed.), *Adolescents and literacies in a digital world* (pp. 68–83). New York: Peter Lang.

Hall, G. S. (1904). *Adolescence: Its psychology and its relations to physiology, anthropology, sociology, sex, crime, religion and education.* New York: Appleton.

Herr, K., & Anderson, G. L. (1997). The cultural politics of identity: Student narratives from two Mexican secondary schools. *Qualitative Studies in Education, 10*(1), 45–61.

Lesko, N. (2001). *Act your age!: A cultural construction of adolescence.* New York: Routledge/Falmer.

Luke, C. (2002). Recrafting media and ICT literacies. In D. E. Alvermann (Ed.), *Adolescents and literacies in a digital world* (pp. 95–108). New York: Peter Lang.

Moje, E. B. (2000a). To be part of the story: The literacy practices of gangsta adolescents. *Teachers College Record, 102,* 652–690.

Moje, E. B. (2000b). *All the stories we have: Adolescents' insights on literacy and learning in secondary school.* Newark, DE: International Reading Association.

Popkewitz, T. S. & Fendler, L. (Eds.). (1999). *Critical theories in education: Changing terrains of knowledge and politics.* New York: Routledge.

Suarez-Orozco, M. (1987). "Becoming somebody": Central American immigrants in U.S. inner city schools. *Anthropology and Education Quarterly, 18*(1), 287–299.

Wexler, P. (1992). *Becoming somebody: Toward a social psychology of school.* London: Falmer.

Willis, A. I. (1995). Reading the world of school literacy: Contextualizing the experience of a young African American male. *Harvard Educational Review, 65,* 30–49.

Willis, P. (1977). *Learning to labour: How working class kids get working class jobs.* Farnborough, UK: Saxon House.

CHAPTER FOUR

Doing "Good" Discussion: Young People Engaged in Politically Messy, yet Compelling Conversation

Jrene Rahm & Karen Tracy

Across a number of disciplinary traditions, there is consensus about what counts as features of a "good discussion." One especially comprehensive model is seen in the work of the philosopher Bridges (1979, 1988, 1990), whose ideas have been adopted and adapted by educational researchers interested in fostering good discussion in classrooms (e.g., Dillon, 1994; Preskill, 1997). As Bridges (1988) notes, "discussion is always discussion of, about or on something. There is always a subject, question, matter or issue which is 'under discussion'" (p. 16). In Bridges' model of good discussion, definitional criteria for discussion are specified and intermingled with normative features of the good. For instance, he describes a good discussion as one in which people talk, listen, and respond to one another and where participants explore multiple perspectives on a topic with the goal of developing new levels of understandings. Descriptors such as "reasonable," "orderly," "peaceful," and "truthful" are attributes of good discussions. Participants in a "good" discussion bring to these events respect for the opinions of others and for the sharing of different perspectives coupled with a concern that evidence is taken into account and that it is presented with clarity and conciseness. Openness is a quality that is given attention and usually has multiple referents: that the topic is open for the development of understanding, that the discussion space is open to all who wish to participate, and that participants are "open-minded." Finally, phenomenological elements are specified. Speakers need to feel free to raise issues and address any other person involved. All participants are expected to be committed to engaging in a common search for meaning (Bridges, 1979).

Good discussion is seen as entailing cognitive qualities (interest in pursuing a topic), affective qualities (concern and commitment among participants), and as having the potential to involve speakers carrying them beyond their intentions (Burbules, 1993). Currently still unaddressed, however, is a particularly important question: What might a good discussion look like at the level of discourse particulars? What conversational practices occur in or, conversely, are noticeably absent from discussions that would be evaluated as good?

When identifying discourse markers of good discussions, it seems important to distinguish among discussion genres or topics. It is unlikely that a good discussion of a science problem (e.g., O'Connor, 1996) would display the same features as a discussion of a sensitive or socially controversial issue (Tracy & Ashcraft, 2001). Exemplary discussion of controversial topics, such as abortion, English Language Amendment initiatives, or sexual orientation,[1] are likely to exhibit different discursive features than other genres of discussion. In addition, if the discussion is conducted in a site that is linked to action, for example, making policies or changing rules, laws, or practices, we would expect it to be conducted differently than if the discussion purpose is solely for the edification or enjoyment of its participants, or for encouraging deeper understanding.

Key to assessing a particular discussion as good, we suggest, is that the participants avoid pitfalls common in that particular category of discussion. Put another way, a discussion ideal is most helpful if it is anchored by an understanding of its dangers. In advancing criteria for effective discussion of math problems in a middle school classroom, for instance, it would be surprising to hear someone advocating the importance of avoiding heated emotional expression. Although it is possible to imagine students getting emotional discussing a math problem, this is not a typical difficulty. This is not the case with discussions of controversial values. Intense and inappropriate emotional expressions are routine problems. At the same time, another difficulty is equally common: no emotion in the participants' conversation, or worse, no conversation at all. Helping people feel comfortable speaking about controversial values is difficult. Yet the particularities of a discussion's topic or site are rarely addressed in models of discussion ideals (Bridges, 1990; Hyman & Whitford, 1990). In the classroom context, Dillon (1994) does allude to subject matter, but only to emphasize that both "hard" subject matters (i.e., mathematics and science) and "soft" subject matters (i.e., literature and social studies) are suitable for discussion.

In sum, many models of good discussion omit treatment of issues that are crucial. They are detached from the demands of actual discussion and are stripped of the particulars of context that would make a more grounded understanding of good discussion features possible. In this chapter, we pursue an analysis of the discursive particulars of one youth-initiated discussion about sexual orientation. In doing so, we intend to offer an example of a more grounded analysis of discussion particulars. What makes the chosen case particularly interesting is the way it also highlights the ability of three young people to initiate, develop, and sustain a compelling and politically messy discussion. Working with content that is not likely to be fostered in schools, they keep the conversation going despite interruptions by peers and instructors, and manage to engage in a discussion of many related topics with depth and competence. In fact, their discussion is an illustration of a conversation that might never surface, much less develop, within the confines of a classroom. Hence, the analysis offers insights into the discourse skills of this group of young people in non-school settings, adding to a growing literature that challenges the often negative representation of adolescent talk grounded in the work of intergenerational communication and the work on communicative competence (Goodwin, 1990; Heath, 1998, 2000; Maybin, 1993, 1994; Tannock, 1998, 1999; Williams et al., 2002).

The focal discussion occurred in City Farmers, a summer gardening program in the United States that offers youth from ethnically diverse inner-city neighborhoods the opportunity to learn more about plant science, work ethics, and life skills. In large measure, the program is an embodiment of a philosophy prevalent in many education and training programs where it is assumed that "young people's 'unstructured free time' is a breeding ground for 'social problems,' especially among young working-class people and or young people of colour"(Griffin, 1993, p. 88). The goal of the City Farmers program is to produce marketable crops while assisting youth from "disadvantaged backgrounds" to learn a range of practical and communicative skills. Youth participated voluntarily in the program and received an educational stipend. Actually "doing" gardening work—rather than merely "talking about" gardening work—was emphasized. Indeed, many of the young people perceived their participation in this program as their first summer job (see Rahm 1998 for details). The dialogue examined here occurred as the youth harvested basil for an upcoming event. Since harvesting basil leaves is a rather repetitious activity, it was an activity particularly conducive to a complex discussion.

The remainder of this chapter is organized as follows. We begin with a presentation of some of the relevant literature regarding "adolescent" talk and topic sensitivity. We then offer some information about the setting and the speakers. In turn, we describe discourse features of the actual discussion. We conclude by considering the implications of this case for understanding models of good discussion, promoting good discussion in a variety of sites, and for future studies of the communication of young people.

"ADOLESCENT" TALK AND TOPIC SENSITIVITY

Historically speaking, if one were trying to find a discussion worth examining in greater detail, researchers would typically *not* start with a group of young people (thirteen to fifteen years old). This can, in part, be explained by the widespread view of "adolescence" as a time of storm and stress (Hall, 1904) and the negative connotations of "adolescents" as hormone-raging, identity-seeking, and peer-conforming (Lesko, 1996). In fact, a recent study of intergenerational communication showed that adults from twenty to sixty years of age see adolescents as non-communicative, less accommodative, and more self-promotional than adults (Williams & Garrett, 2002). Community adults who have a lot of contact with teens (e.g., police, social security, and benefit officers) also believe that teenagers lack communication skills (Drury & Dennison, 1999, 2000). Furthermore, research on adolescent-parent and adolescent-sibling interactions highlights the pervasiveness of conflict in this age group and the need for interventions to enhance communication skills of young people (Drury, Catan, Dennison, & Brody, 1998). Although a counter-trend that seeks to develop a more nuanced view of adolescence is beginning—exemplified in the recent Report of the Task Force on Language, Social Psychology and Adolescence (Williams et al., 2002)—youth are routinely treated as communicatively challenged, conversational victims to the expertise of others, as well as due to their own discourse limitations (Griffin, 1993).

Moreover, if one were to single out a particular topic worth examining in greater detail, a discussion of sexual orientation among a group of young people would *not* be expected to be a prime candidate. Sexual orientation is a difficult topic for discussants of any age as it invariably involves a range of moral issues and participants' own sexual orientation (e.g., Lemke, 1995; Tracy & Ashcraft, 2001). Given the potentially new and fragile quality of a young person's sexual orientation, finding a high-quality discussion of this topic would seem unlikely. The fact that the conversation took place in a youth program may explain in part why exploration of such a topic was possible. As noted by Whitehead (1932), "the habit of active thought, with freshness, can only be generated by adequate freedom" (cited in Coles, 1995, p. 162). Such a spirit is typical of youth organizations and programs like City Farmers in that such places frequently become powerful resources for youth to openly explore issues of diversity (Fine, Weis, Centrie, & Roberts, 2000).

Given the homophobic climate of schools and sometimes families, informal settings are often the only place where a safe space is provided for the emergence of "constructive" dialogues about sexual orientation (Friend, 1991; Heath & McLaughlin, 1993; Uribe, 1995). Furthermore, discussions of sexual orientation and other issues linked to multiculturalism in schools often fail to engage with the conservative arguments that are taken seriously by the larger society (D'Souza, 1997; Willet, 1998). This is evidenced by the frequent accusation that public education is "PC." In not allowing, or discouraging, conservative arguments to be voiced, there is no serious engagement with "the controversy" of sexual orientation. Instead, the discussion situation becomes one in which conservative opinions are treated as errors to be corrected, or participants (given past experiences in such discussions) self-censor, suppressing what they think is taboo and unsuitable for the occasion. For a discussion of a contentious issue to be of high quality, there needs to be exploration of different sides of the controversy. Undoubtedly this criterion poses a problem for some controversial topics in certain settings. If a university or school district, for instance, has an official institutional position on a controversy that weighs in on one of the societal "sides," then achieving a good discussion seems unlikely. Nevertheless, the possibility of quality discussion of a politically sensitive topic is not simply a question of location (formal versus informal educational setting) as Fine et al. (2000) emphasize. Instead, how the program itself is perceived in the eyes of youth and the kinds of possibilities for constructive discourse it supports are also relevant.

In this case, just as the youth voluntarily sought out participation in the gardening program, they also voluntarily pursued sexual orientation as a topic worth discussing. The gardening program emphasized respect for each person; this respect in turn encouraged the youth to respect each others' arguments and positions throughout their discussions. Authentic, hands-on learning was also emphasized, which came to define the learning opportunities the conversation brought about. Accordingly, the setting and its ethos made possible the kind of talk we observed while also marking it in important ways. The fact that the topic was initiated by youth also cannot be overlooked. It made the topic particularly important and authentic to them, as was apparent by Marvin's[2] discursive work to both sustain the conversation and redirect it when it was "off track." As noted by Gadamer (1989), "to conduct a conversation means to allow oneself to be conducted by the subject matter to which the partners in the dialogue are oriented" (p. 367). As will become clear, this was the case in the discussion examined here and may in part be due to the fact that the youth themselves initiated and sustained the topic.

BACKGROUND

The Discussion Context

All of the youth in the City Farmer program were waiting to be assigned tasks for the day by their team leader, Bill. During that time, one person wanted to know how Bill's roommate was doing. There were comments among the larger group that Bill, a male in his thirties pursuing an elementary teaching degree at a local university, might be gay since he was living with another male. To find out, Sula, one of the key discussion participants, asked him whether he supported alternative lifestyles. Bill responded, "I guess you could say yes, I support, I don't encourage them, but I support them." A twenty-six minute discussion about sexual orientation ensued among Andrew, Marvin, and Sula (the main participants), with the first author (Rahm) and several other members of the program as minor contributors.

Key Participants

The first discussant, Andrew, was a thirteen year old white[3] male described by the team leaders as someone who "daydreamed" and "drifted," never completing tasks he was assigned. Andrew was participating in the program for the second consecutive summer. He lived in a single-parent home with his mother and attended a local public school. His home neighborhood, surrounding the garden, was composed primarily of black families.

Marvin, the second participant, was a fourteen year old black male also described as struggling to stay on task. According to a staff member, if Marvin was not supervised he "showed initiative in finding other things to do besides work." Marvin was participating in the program for the first time together with his sister. His mother worked in one of the offices providing administrative support for the program. Marvin lived in a single-parent home in a black neighborhood. He was enrolled in a Catholic school in which he interacted primarily with white middle-class children.

The third participant, Sula, was a fifteen year old black female who was always busy talking about issues in her life with team leaders and friends. Staff regarded her talking as a way to get away with as little gardening work as possible. One team leader's evaluation, quite similar to the ones noted for the other speakers, was also negative. Sula was described as someone who "show[ed] no desire to be anything but a body taking up space, showed no willingness to work at any time at any task in the garden and showed no concern for others, is not polite nor considerate." Another team leader explained that she was not invested in gardening per se, but in forming friendships with the adults in the program and thereby finding people she could talk to and confide in. Sula was the oldest in a family of six and was also participating in the program for the second time. Sula's father volunteered time as a bus driver for the program.

As these descriptions make apparent, these participants were not regarded as model youth by the program staff. In fact, the three youth were discussed numerous times during staff meetings as "problem cases." Nevertheless, the program director dismissed such markers repeatedly and demanded the staff give these youth a chance to grow, be responsible, and take ownership of their work. Tensions like these are not atypical of youth programs nor, for that matter, within any context where youth spend time with each other and supervising adults in positions of power (Lesko, 2001). Often the youth become scapegoats for problems and their contributions remain unnoticed. They are seen as trouble rather than as resources (Heath, 2000; Heath & McLaughlin, 1993). So while the adults of the program generally stressed an overall positive view of the participants, an appreciation for their efforts, and a commitment to "making the program work," this vision was not uniformly expressed by all staff members or consistently offered to students.

An Overview of the Twenty-Six Minute Discussion

The discussion about sexual orientation was carried on in the context of harvesting herbs. At two points the leader Bill intervened, first, to give instructions about how to harvest basil, and later, to reprimand the boys for doing too much talking and not enough harvesting. There were several comments about the videotaping and whether "cussin" was appropriate. In addition to discussing what were reasonable expectations of women in the areas of work, family, and military duty, the discussion of sexual orientation involved back-and-forth exchanges about: (a) Jewish and gay people during the holocaust; (b) how gay people the youth knew had been treated, or what gay people they knew had done; (c) how participants would react if their own child were gay; (d) similarities and differences in the treatment of gay people versus African Americans or women; (e) affirmative action and fairness; (f) the likely sexual orientation of each discussant; (g) what God and the Bible say about sexuality; (h) the normalcy of homosexuality compared to crime; and (i) differences in male and female responses to gay individuals.

The discussion was transcribed in its entirety. In transcribing, we attended to all words, vocalized sounds (uh, um, uh huh), and restarts and repairs; only occasionally did we attend to particulars of intonation or utterance timing.[4] As discourse analysts have repeatedly noted, there is no single "right" level of transcription detail (Craig & Tracy, 1983; Jaworski & Coupland, 1999; Ochs, 1979). Rather the best level is one suited to the theoretical aims of the researcher. Our aim was to identify discourse moves that discussants might be able to consciously monitor. For this reason, an intermediate level of transcription detail seemed most appropriate.

FEATURES OF THE DISCUSSION

Features that made this discussion noteworthy can be related to the group's activities with regard to three areas: (1) the actual content of the discussion in terms of the arguments considered; (2) how the group developed ownership of the discussion; and (3) how group members used and responded to personal disclosures in the discussion.

The Group Engaged Arguments for Different Sides of the Controversy

In an analysis of adults' written statements, to illustrate heteroglossia, Lemke (1995) identifies and contrasts two of several discourses on homosexuality that have been articulated in the United States. Each of these discourses is taken up by distinct communities. For instance, one community, the Christian fundamentalist group, argues that homosexuality is sinful and abnormal. From this view—a Christian Fundamentalist View—sexual intercourse is conceptualized as an act expressly for reproduction; any other purposes are going against God. Another visible community involves gay activists who oppose this Christian Fundamentalist View and laws, for example, prohibiting gays from marrying or dismissing gays from the military who publicly announce their sexual orientation. This position—a Gay Activist

Position—treats differences in sexual orientation as one among many biologically linked, natural, individual differences among humans. To discriminate against persons in terms of sexual orientation is seen as morally wrong. As emphasized by Lemke (1995), these are "only two of many social discourse voices on the subject of homosexuality and gay rights" (p. 44). Wary of oversimplifying or subscribing to a binary world view, we have chosen to focus on these two voices in an effort to make visible positions in the dialogue.

The central themes of the conversation included an examination of whether homosexuality is normal and what fair treatment of homosexuals may entail. Their talk reflected many of the main arguments (pro and con) that have occurred in public discourses on sexual orientation. For instance, there was evidence of the Christian Fundamentalist voice throughout the transcript:

Excerpt 1

(a)   You're not born gay though, it is a choice in a way. (ln. 59)

(b)   Well, it says, it says in the Bible. (ln. 77)

(c)   Well I am just saying, it's out of the norm. (ln. 146)

Similarly, a more liberal view with traces of a Gay Activist voice surfaced numerous times as well:

Excerpt 2

(a)   But God teaches to accept everyone. (ln. 83)

(b)   NO. I am not saying they should be treated better than anyone else (pause) they should be ACCEPTED. (lns. 543–545)

(c)   I think it's just some ( ) you're born with, accept that other people are gonna be like this. (lns. 318–319)

Moreover, there was direct engagement of one position with the other:

Excerpt 3 (lns. 109–120)

Marvin: Well you have to at least admit it's not natural.

Andrew: How is it not natural?

?:   Cause it ain't.

Marvin: I mean, well, seriously, look at it this way, I mean if it if it was natural//

Andrew: //Well then who made them to be that way?

Marvin: No, just listen, if it was natural for people to be gay then there would be a lot more bisexual people around, if it was natural to be gay, seriously, I mean think about it.

Andrew: NO It's, I bet there are a lot more bisexual people than you know, but they hide in the closet. They say I am gonna pretend (.) to be straight so I don't get into trouble.

Here, Marvin invokes a Christian Fundamentalist voice to question the implications of sexual orientation for reproduction. His remark is challenged by Andrew, who seems to be voicing a liberal view, revealing traces of a gay activist stance. Andrew reminds Marvin that gay people routinely have to "hide in the closet" to stay out of trouble. By invoking these oppositional voices, the youth were able to explore the issue in some depth. In essence, the boys brought to the foreground an important social dispute between Christian Fundamentalists and Gay Activists, namely whether it is "natural" to be gay. Andrew and Marvin's comments engage several of the most serious points of difference on this issue.

"Owning" a Discussion: Discourse Moves

Topical Pursuit Moves

As noted by Almasi, O'Flahavan, and Arya (2001), topical pursuit moves are essential for coherence and proficient discussions. Such moves also characterized the discussion explored here. For instance, there were numerous interruptions throughout the twenty-six minute dialogue that could have halted the discussion. Yet, the youth kept the discussion going. Some interruptions had to do with the assigned task of the young people to harvest herbs. For instance, after the team leader had explained to them how to pull herbs, he left. Afterwards, Marvin brought the talk back with the topic resumption marker, "Well anyway, I was saying..." (ln. 164). Whenever their discussion wandered to another topic—the camera and "cussing," whether women should stay at home with their kids—one of the youth introduces another facet of controversy about sexual orientation to continue the conversation.

Following a reprimand from the leader for talking too much and not pulling herbs fast enough, we see another instance of topical pursuit.

Excerpt 4 (lns. 374–385)

Andrew:	OK. But

Marvin: No, but you CAN'T be guaranteed to win!

Leader: OK. Less talk—more work.

Marvin: We ARE working. Look we have the whole bag full ((lifts up garbage bag full of basil)).

Leader: OK. That's great. But the last two minutes I was watching you, you were just sitting there talking doing NOTHING.

((Sula defends herself, to which Bob reports)): I am not including you in this one...these two gentlemen right here...((he talks on while the boys start working and try to get their conversation going again))

Marvin: But anyway, but ((Leader still talking in back)) (pause)

Andrew: But then affirmative action isn't fair either.

Marvin: Yeah it is!

In response to Marvin's argument that gay people have special rights on the job and can bring lawsuits, Andrew responds that the situation for gay people is no different than affirmative action for African

Americans. Note how the conversation seamlessly continues despite interruptions by the team leader who challenges them to be more task-focused. The group's investment in the topic, then, is made visible by their willingness to pursue it. In other words, motivation to sustain a topic is discursively displayed by markers such as "but anyway" and "well anyway." In this exchange "anyway" was used nine times, demonstrating their commitment to the topic.

Besides the group leader's comments, peers also tried to derail these three youth from their discussion, questioning if they were "still" talking about *that* topic. The group's continued focus on the topic in the context of peers' attempts to get them to another topic highlight the group's involvement in what they were discussing. Moreover, because no authority had instructed them "to discuss" this topic—instead discouraging it as disruptive of harvesting—the discussion is visibly owned by the participants. Topic ownership, then, is made most visible when others seek to halt, derail, or change a topical focus. The pursuit and development of an issue in the face of challenges is part of the way a group displays involvement in a topic.

Meta-talk About Discussion Sensitivity

Along with topical pursuit, another indicator of participant involvement in controversial discussions is meta-talk. Meta-talk consists of utterances that reference how participants are talking to each other and what it means for a person to talk in a particular way. Discussion topics are sensitive by virtue of the fact that espousing a position may be taken as evidence that the speaker is a certain kind of person or has a certain attitude (Bergmann, 1998). When the ascribed position or attitude is not one that applies to the speaker, a person may be reluctant to express his or her views. In a good discussion, then, explicit acknowledgment of this discussion challenge is a way to keep a sensitive discussion going. Let's consider how this dynamic played out in the discussion.

In the opening of this discussion, when the youth are giggling and raising questions about Bill's sexual orientation, one youth, Andrew, repeatedly asserts "I just don't think there is anything wrong with it" (lns. 15, 25). In response to his comment, others in the garden attempt to accommodate Andrew's remarks by retorting: that's "because you (pause) you experienced it, man" (lns. 16, 17). Throughout the discussion, Andrew espouses a Gay Activist Position to his two peers. Midway through the discussion, he comments about the expressive difficulties he is facing.

Excerpt 5 (lns. 164–172)

Marvin:	Well Anyway well like I was saying, I mean, you know, if, if you wouldn't be gay then that means you don't condone it.
Andrew:	It's (pause) either way, Okay if I said either No I'm not gay, I won't do that, then you are homophobic, but //but
Marvin:	//you're not homophobic.
Andrew:	if you say, if you say, well I'm( )people will say you're homophobic. And then if you say yeah well, I accept these people, then they say you're gay ( ) So either way, you're screwed.

Meta-talk about discussion sensitivity is a way to build space between an argumentative position and the other attitudes and identities presumed to be entailed by advocating a particular position. Hence, meta-talk makes the discussion of a morally charged issue possible. It also highlights the discussants' investment and willingness to persist, even in the face of others potentially arriving at negative judgments about a speaker. The following comment (Excerpt 6) from Sula illustrates a different kind of meta-talk move.

Excerpt 6 (lns. 433–447)

Sula:	But mmh, like I was saying, you know what I am saying, its—I'm not actually gonna say I am normal because who knows what normal is.
?:	//well no
Marvin:	//There, there is no such thing as normal.
Andrew:	Yeah. So how come you're saying these people are wrong 'cause they're not normal?
Marvin:	Well, I mean they're not//

Andrew:	//you don't know what normal is?
Sula:	I was not saying that they're wrong, I was just saying that it is not right=//
Marvin:	//Yeah//
Sula:	=because of what the Bible says.
Andrew:	NO //you
Sula:	So //I guess I guess I am saying that it is wrong.

Sula is charged with referring to gayness as wrong, something she then rewords as "not right" given what the Bible says. Sula's meta-statement at the end—"I guess I am saying that it is wrong"—is reformulating the meaning of her past utterance. It reveals how difficult it was for her to defend her position and how challenging the discussion was. This exchange also shows the participants' commitment to discussing the topic and their investment in understanding the issues. Hence, meta-talk makes possible the public acknowledgment of topic sensitivity. In sum, through topical pursuit moves and meta-talk the youth enacted their commitment to a serious exchange about the topic.

Management of Personal Connections with the Discussion Topic

One way of ensuring that a discussion of a controversial topic does not get overly heated is for discussants to stay abstract and distanced from the topic, for example, using platitudes. If participants make no links with concrete persons and life choices, the discussion is unlikely to get heated. It is also likely to be one in which no one oversteps the line or shows "disrespect." Discussions of controversies that implicate one or another feature of discussants are likely to challenge participants' communicative skills. At the same time, a discussion in which no personal connections are explored is likely to be superficial and not especially thoughtful. Controversies about people and lifestyles, by their very essence, are morally implicative (Bergmann, 1998). To discuss a contentious issue as if it involved no more than figuring out how to plant a row of beans is as inappropriate as discussing the topic in a disrespectful manner, for example using personal attacks rather than challenging the content of the argument. In addition, discussions of controversies that involve personal disclosure and storytelling can all too easily become a rambling conversation that lacks a sustained intellectual focus (Knoblauch, 1991). Good discussion, then, requires talk that emotionally engages aspects of the issue—and the topical digressions that such talk often involves—without crossing into disrespectful expression, or losing grasp of the thematic thread of the argument. How did Sula, Andrew, and Marvin attend to both of these concerns?

Emotional involvement with the issue was displayed through the use of personal stories, a discussion practice that analysts of academic colloquia (Tracy, 1997), political policy issues (Gamson, 1992), and everyday exchanges (Tannen, 1989, 1998) have argued is important. For instance Sula, whose standpoint was largely consistent with a Christian Fundamentalist view, nonetheless told a story about how she and other girls at her school had "no problem" with a gay boy that the other boys would not accept. Marvin, who also spoke mostly from a conservative position, told about a gay friend of his mother who had recently died of AIDS, but who was "a really nice guy" and was "really manly." While such comments do portray notions of gayness that are stereotypical, the way in which the youth managed to interweave personal material with the topic of the conversation is notable.

In addition to telling stories about their personal experiences, these young people also made use of identity-implicative hypotheticals. Identity-implicative hypotheticals position one's self, or others, into a different category than the one that is the focus of a discussion to explore a facet of an issue's meaning. For instance, after announcing that "There is no way I am gonna be gay," "no way," (lns. 121–122), an assertion difficult to interpret as other than against gays, Sula nevertheless proceeds to speculate how she would feel if she were the mother of a gay child.

Excerpt 7 (lns. 126–129)

> Okay if I was to have a child and that child had that kind of lifestyle, I
> would be against it. But I am not just gonna say so okay you're gay (pause)
> treat them differently but I am, I am gonna disapprove of it. And I am not
> gonna like it.

Sula's position may not be entirely internally consistent, for example
how is she going to "disapprove" and "not like it" but nonetheless
treat her gay child "no differently"? However, the identity-implicative
hypothetical does mark her emotional investment in thinking through
the issue. Putting herself in the position of the mother of a gay child
leads her to adopt a more nuanced position; one that is less ada-
mantly homophobic.

At several points, and in different ways, Andrew, who is white,
and Marvin, who is black, address each other's whiteness and black-
ness to further the discussion about what counts as reasonable treatment of gay people. Following a story, which Marvin tells about a
Caribbean man who had been raped by the police and then began to
identify as gay, he asserts that being gay is a choice and is not normal.

Excerpt 8 (lns. 336–351)

Marvin:	…gayness, it's not normal. Let's think about it, I mean, put yourself into a position where, you're, you're, you're—
Andrew:	Well, then whiteness isn't normal either.
Marvin:	Yes it is.
Andrew:	I mean, how is it different than, well, I mean, it's just a sexual choice, it's not gonna affect you.

Andrew counters Marvin's assertion that being gay is not normal by
invoking what Andrew believes is an analogous category, whiteness,
which describes himself. In the debate over what constitutes "normal," this comparison of race with sexual orientation leads to a discussion of whether gay people receive "special treatment," which in
turn leads to an examination of the reasonableness of affirmative action and whether whites are better treated.

Related to the use of identity-implicative hypotheticals is a practice in which speakers refer to different facets of their identity to make a point. For instance, Marvin and Sula used their own experiences as black youth to suggest parallels in oppression and suffering between gay people and themselves. A reference to Andrew's white racial identity was also used by them to position Andrew as a certain kind of person. It is quite easy to imagine contexts in which this move would have halted the discussion, but in this case, to the credit of the participants, it did not.

Excerpt 9 (lns. 508–519)

Sula: So, you know what I'm saying, if you think about it, it is really a privilege to you to be white!

Marvin: //Yeah, that's right!//

Andrew: //No//

Andrew: Well it is kind of not a privilege because I live in a black neighborhood.

Sula: No, but I'm saying, if you were to walk into, if you were to walk into Dillards or something, just because that is a high priced store, you would no matter what, you better, no matter, if I had more money than you

Marvin: you still would be better treated

Sula: you would still be better—

Andrew's remark that "it is kind of not a privilege because I live in a black neighborhood" serves as a means to reposition his opponents. It also led to a more extensive discussion about what better treatment means within their community. For example, Sula continues with a poignant case of what privilege means to her through an instance of racism she observed on television. In response, Andrew offers a counter-example: "If I walked into the hairdresser over there (gesturing to the immediate largely black neighborhood), she would not even look at me, would she?" Sula responds by narrating a scenario of what would most likely happen, which seems to exhaust this train of thought. Marvin then brings the conversation "back on track" by introducing the issue of how blacks have been treated in the past, something Andrew immediately picks up on by emphasizing how gay people have been treated in the past. Explicit shifting among identities allowed the participants to see the issue in more complex ways.

The participants were able to have a discussion in an animated, passionate manner that did not spill over into disrespectful expression. This was clearly an impressive achievement. Their ability to do so, we suggest, flowed not only from the context of their talk and how they expressed themselves, but also from the content of their relationships. The young people had been with each other daily for several weeks as they worked together. Extended participation in a joint activity, while performing concrete tasks, seemed to be an especially good environment for fostering interpersonal communication among group members, and this generated the conditions necessary to build the participant's abilities to disagree without the use of personal attacks.

DISCUSSION

In this chapter, we pointed to ways a youth-initiated discussion developed and was managed over time through an exploration of its constitutive features and their juxtaposition. In essence, through analysis of discourse markers, we have shown what it means for the discussants to "collaborate in the joint authoring of multivoiced texts about discussion topics" (Patthey-Chavez & Goldenberg, 1995, p. 109). Most important, the multivoiced nature of the discussion made it dialogic rather than simply a debate. Indeed, the discussion involved creative, constructive exploration and the expression of oppositions and disagreements—an astonishing accomplishment given the sensitivity of the discussion topic. We illustrated the manner whereby youth engaged arguments of both sides of the controversy, explored markers such as topical pursuit moves and meta-talk about discussion sensitivity. These features illustrate how the youth owned their discussion and reveal how they managed personal connections to the discussion topic through emotionally charged comments, stories of personal relevance, and identity-implicative hypotheticals. These characteristics are taken as supportive of our claim that this dialogue is illustrative of a good discussion while also making visible youths' communicative competence. To further substantiate this claim we now integrate our findings with some of the relevant literature.

Why a "Good" Discussion?

We begin with a reexamination of the theoretical notions of good discussions put forth by Bridges (1979, 1988, 1990), Dillon (1994), and Burbules (1993). Most important, the discussion we examined was clearly "reasonable" and "orderly" as shown by the turn-taking behavior among the speakers and the serious consideration given to each others' arguments. The dialogue was also "peaceful" in that speakers maintained respect for each other even during times of disagreement and potential attack (e.g., when Sula remarked that being white is a privilege for Andrew, and Andrew initially disagreed, then clarified why). To what extent the dialogue was "truthful" is somewhat more difficult to assess. Clearly, the youth were willing to share personal experiences and their own stances toward an emotionally laden topic. When considering the notion of "openness" the analysis suggests that the topic was developed over time and explored in a variety of ways, through reference to personal as well as historical contexts, and from different perspectives (e.g., Christian Fundamentalist and Gay Activist perspectives). Finally, the topics that were pursued over time and some of the emotionally laden issues raised, the privilege of whiteness, for example, indicate that the speakers felt free to raise issues deemed important and valuable to them. The participants felt comfortable to address each other in ways they considered useful for the pursuit of the argument. Hence, the kinds of cognitive and affective qualities outlined by Burbules (1993) were clearly visible and led to the involvement of speakers in a dialogue over an extended period of time. These qualities carried the discussion far beyond what they might have initially anticipated when asking for the team leader's position on alternative lifestyles.

The dialogue analyzed here can also be taken as an instance of a good discussion given its avoidance of pitfalls common to discourse about sexual orientation. For instance, there were no signs of verbal harassment, which tends to characterize much talk in school hallways

(Lovell, 1998). Furthermore, the three youth explored sexual orientation from more than one perspective, suggesting an openness to different opinions often lacking in talk in either school contexts (Lovell, 1998; Reiss, 1997) or at home (O'Conor, 1995). It was not a discussion that was counter-productive to the understanding of the lives of gay people, a worry often raised in opposition to teaching about homosexuality in schools (Reiss, 1997). It is also widely recognized that youth are interested in talking about sex, "just not *their* sex or sexual orientation" (Farr, 2000, p. 205). In fact, talk about sex among peers may be most productive since peer groups offer acceptance of arguments and positions that other discursive contexts would not (O'Conor, 1995; Williams et al., 2002). Peer groups also tend to be more open to contemporary views and less judgmental than family members and hence, often become contexts for the disclosure of intimate information (Youniss & Yates, 2000; Zamanou, 1985). For these reasons, it might not be surprising that this group of youth decided to pursue the topic of sexual orientation, and did so with sophistication.

Deconstructing and Reconstructing Reality: The Conversations of Youth

The talk of young people has often been taken as something to be corrected or ignored (Daiute, 1997). Our analysis seriously challenges such assumptions. The youth managed and engaged in a compelling discussion. They listened to each others' ideas, voiced their opinions, and worked with content that is politically charged and often avoided or suppressed as a topic of conversation in other contexts where they spend time. Unfortunately, the content of their discussion reified and left unquestioned many stereotypes and preconceived notions of sexual orientation. However, the form the discussion took over time, for example, respectful turn taking and challenging ideas rather than people, made it evident that for these youth, language was a tool to deconstruct, construct, and reconstruct reality. In fact, one could argue that talk of this nature is the beginning of an openness to morally charged topics generally. For instance, Andrew's level of expertise challenged the stereotyping the others engaged in to some degree and, in turn, offered them tools, such as vocabulary and perspective, to talk about sexual identity in less homophobic ways. Similarly,

Sula's understanding of white privilege provided both conceptual tools and the depth of lived experience to develop the analogy between the oppression of people who are black and people who are gay. As noted by Leap (1999), youth need opportunities to acquire both the language and perspective of gay culture. Maybe the discussion explored here was just such an opportunity.

Like others, we examined what youth can, and actually do, achieve with language (Goodwin, 1990; Heath, 1998, 2000; Maybin, 1993, 1994). And as shown by studies of youths' identity work and peer relationship building (Brown, Mory, & Kinney, 1994; Eckert, 1989; Eder, 1995; Gee, Allen, & Clinton, 2001; Williams et al., 2002), our analysis further highlights how language and communication are central to the lives of young people. As noted by Fortman (in Williams et al., 2002), "teens learn to define themselves through verbal interaction with others" (p. 72). Studies like these challenge stereotypes of young people as superficial and their peer groups as potentially negative sources of social influence (Brown et al., 1994; Williams et al., 2002).

Our study also adds to an evolving literature on the language use of young people outside of school, a literature that has brought to the foreground youths' incredible linguistic, social, and cultural competence (Goodwin, 1990; Heath, 1998, 2000; Hoyle & Adger, 1998; Tannock, 1998, 1999). As noted in the Task Force Report (Williams et al., 2002), however, more studies of the communication experiences of youth in diverse settings are needed. In addition, we need to move beyond mere documentation of youth talk to an understanding of how young people use talk and manage the many genres of talk in their everyday lives. Most important according to Williams (2003), we need to listen "to the voices of young people themselves in our research—too much research is conducted by adults for adolescents without ever listening to adolescents themselves" (p. 48). While having attempted to make audible the voices of three youth for a wider research audience, it would be equally interesting and worthwhile to explore the speakers' own perceptions of their discussion and integrate such an interpretation with the one presented here.

CONCLUSION

The dialogue presented in this paper can be best thought of as an "opportunity space" (Diamondstone, 1999). The discussion offered these young people a context in which to explore alternative perspectives regarding sexual orientation and to develop their own opinions, beliefs, and identities in relation to the arguments put forth. In essence, the youth made use of language to connect with each other, to understand the world they live in, and to reveal themselves in it (Lindfors, 1999).

Clearly, our analysis helps put forth realistic notions of good discussion by underscoring its inherent processes. Yet, we wonder whether treatment of the content of a discussion—in addition to the conduct of a discussion—needs to be considered in greater detail in future attempts to evaluate discussions as good. Here, we only focused on discursive particulars, pointing to the "possible" when dealing with a highly emotionally and politically charged subject—ideas that now need to be explored further and extended, we hope, to other contexts and situations. Such work could also further contribute to the development of a counter-discourse to the stories told of the "communicatively incapable and incompetent adolescent."

NOTES

1. In this paper we use the terms "gayness" (as used by the youth in the dialogue examined), sexual orientation, and sexual identity interchangeably when addressing the topic of the conversation. In doing so, we are cautious to distance ourselves from what these terms have been taken to mean through various epistemological lenses. We simply use them to identify the topic of the conversation, but do not intend to subscribe to the biological view such terms often appear to represent or, for that matter, any other binary views of sexual identity. Instead, we want to show how these youth had an "open dialogue about sexual orientation" (Leck, 1995, p. 198), a dialogue that was at times problematic, but nevertheless appeared to matter greatly to these youth and was, for that reason, important for us as researchers and advocates of youth to listen to.
2. All identifying names have been replaced by pseudonyms.
3. We use the labels white and black to denote youths' ethnicities, terms they invoked themselves in self-descriptions.
4. The transcript uses the symbols of the conversation analytic system in a simplified form (see Atkinson & Heritage, 1984; Psathas, 1995). Double backslashes indicate where overlapping speech began and ended. Words or phrases in caps indicate

loud speech. Pairs of equal signs indicate latched speech with no audible pause. Colons indicate speech cutoffs. Commas, question marks, and periods were added to aid readability. In many cases these symbols correspond to falling (period), rising (question marks), or continuing (comma) intonation (though the tapes were not checked for this level of transcript accuracy). Descriptions of stretches of talk between focal excerpts are indicated by double parentheses.

REFERENCES

Almasi, J. F., O'Flahavan, J. F., & Arya, P. (2001). A comparative analysis of student and teacher development in more and less proficient discussions of literature. *Reading Research Quarterly, 36*(2), 96–120.

Atkinson, J. M. & Heritage, J. (Eds.). (1984). *Structures of social action: Studies in conversation analysis.* Cambridge: Cambridge University Press.

Bergmann, J. R. (1998). Introduction: Morality in discourse. *Research on Language and Social Interaction, 31,* 279–294.

Bridges, D. (1979). *Education, democracy, and discussion.* New York: Lanham.

Bridges, D. (1988). A philosophical analysis of discussion. In J. T. Dillon (Ed.), *Questioning and discussion: A multidisciplinary study* (pp. 15–28). Norwood, NJ: Ablex Publishing.

Bridges, D. (1990). The character of discussion: A focus on students. In W. W. Wilen (Ed.), *Teaching and learning through discussion* (pp. 97–112). Springfield, IL: Charles Thomas Publisher.

Brown, B. B., Mory, M. S., & Kinney, D. (1994). Casting adolescent crowds in a relational perspective: Caricature, channel, and context. In R. Montemayor, G. Adams, & T. Gullotta (Eds.), *Personal relationships during adolescence* (pp. 123–167). Thousand Oaks, CA: Sage.

Burbules, N. C. (1993). *Dialogue in teaching: Theory and practice.* New York: Teachers College Press.

Coles, M. J. (1995). Critical thinking, talk and a community of enquiry in the primary school. *Language and Education, 9*(3), 161–177.

Craig, R. T. & Tracy, K. (Eds.). (1983). *Conversational coherence: Form, structure and strategy.* Beverly Hills, CA: Sage.

Daiute, C. (1997). Youth genre in the classroom: Can children's and teachers' cultures meet? In J. Flood, S. B. Heath, & D. Lapp (Eds.), *Handbook of research on teaching literacy through the communicative and visual arts* (pp. 323–333). New York: Macmillan.

Diamondstone, J. V. (1999). Tactics of resistance in student-student interaction. *Linguistics and Education, 10*(1), 107–137.

Dillon, J. T. (1994). *Using discussion in classrooms.* Buckingham, UK: Open University Press.

Drury, J. & Dennison, C. (1999). Individual responsibility versus social category problems: Benefit officers' perceptions of communication with young people. *Journal of Youth Studies, 2,* 171–192.

Drury, J. & Dennison, C. (2000). Representations of teenagers among police officers: Some implications for their communication with young people. *Youth and Policy, 66,* 35–46.

Drury, J., Catan, L., Dennison, C., & Brody, R. (1998). Exploring teenagers' accounts of bad communication: A new basis for intervention. *Journal of Adolescence, 21,* 177–196.

D'Souza, D. (1997). Foreword. In A. J. Schmidt, *The menace of multiculturalism* (pp. ix–x). Westport, CT: Praeger Press.

Eckert, P. (1989). *Jocks and burnouts: Social categories and identity in the high school.* New York: Teachers College Press.

Eder, D. (1995). *School talk: Gender and adolescent culture.* New Brunswick, NJ: Rutgers University Press.

Farr, M. T. (2000). "Everything I didn't want to know I learned in lit class": Sex, sexual orientation, and student identity. *International Journal of Sexuality and Gender Studies, 5*(2), 205–213.

Fine, M., Weis, L., Centrie, C., & Roberts, R. (2000). Educating beyond the borders of schooling. *Anthropology and Education Quarterly, 31*(2), 131–151.

Friend, R. A. (1991). Choices, not closets: Heterosexism and homophobia in school. In L. Weis & M. Fine (Eds.), *Beyond silenced voices: Class, race, and gender in United States Schools* (pp. 209–235). Albany: The State University of New York Press.

Gadamer, H. (1989). *Truth and method.* New York: Crossroad.

Gamson, W. A. (1992). *Talking politics.* Cambridge: Cambridge University Press.

Gee, P. J., Allen, A.-R., & Clinton, K. (2001). Language, class, and identity: Teenagers fashioning themselves through language. *Linguistics and Education, 12*(2), 175–194.

Goodwin, M. H. (1990). *He-said-she-said: Talk as social organization among black children.* Bloomington: Indiana University Press.

Griffin, C. (1993). *Representations of youth: The study of youth and adolescence in Britain and America.* Cambridge: Polity.

Hall, G. S. (1904). *Adolescence: Its psychology and its relations to psychology, anthropology, sociology, sex, crime, religion, and education.* New York: Appleton-Century-Crofts.

Heath, S. B. (1998). Working through language. In S. M. Hoyle & C. T. Adger (Eds.), *Kids talk: Strategic language use in later childhood* (pp. 217–240). New York: Oxford University Press.

Heath, S. B. (2000). Linguistics in the study of language in education. *Harvard Educational Review, 70*(1), 49–59.

Heath, S. B. & McLaughlin, M. W. (Eds.). (1993). *Identity and inner-city youth: Beyond ethnicity and gender.* New York: Teachers College Press.

Hoyle, M. & Adger, C. T. (1998). *Kids talk: Strategic language use in later childhood.* New York: Oxford University Press.

Hyman, R. T. & Whitford, E. V. (1990). Strategic discussion for content area teaching. In W. W. Wilen (Ed.), *Teaching and learning through discussion* (pp. 127–146). Springfield, IL: Charles Thomas Publisher.

Jaworski, A. & Coupland, N. (Eds.). (1999). *The discourse reader.* London: Routledge.

Knoblauch, H. (1991). The taming of foes: The avoidance of asymmetry in informal discussions. In I. Marková & K. Foppa (Eds.), *Asymmetries in dialogue* (pp. 166–194). Savage, MA: Barnes & Noble.

Leap, W. (1999). Language, socialization, and silence in gay adolescence. In M. Bucholtz, C. A. Liang, & L. A. Sutton (Eds.), *Reinventing identities: The gendered self in discourse* (pp. 259–272). New York: Oxford University Press.

Leck, G. M. (1995). The politics of adolescent sexual identity and queer responses. In G. Unks (Ed.), *The gay teen: Educational practice and theory for lesbian, gay, and bisexual adolescents* (pp. 189–200). New York: Routledge.

Lemke, J. L. (1995). *Textual politics: Discourse and social dynamics.* Bristol, PA: Taylor & Francis.

Lesko, N. (1996). Past, present, and future conceptions of adolescence. *Educational Theory, 46*(4), 453–472.

Lesko, N. (2001). *Act your age!: A cultural construction of adolescence.* New York: Routledge.

Lindfors, J. W. (1999). *Children's inquiry.* New York: Teachers College Press.

Lovell, A. (1998). "Other students always used to say, 'look at the dykes'": Protecting students from peer sexual orientation harassment. *California Law Review, 86,* 617–654.

Maybin J. (1993). Dialogic relationships and the construction of knowledge in children's informal talk. In D. Graddol, L. Thompson, & M. Byram (Eds.), *Language and culture* (pp. 142–152). Clevedon, UK: Multilingual Matters.

Maybin, J. (1994). Children's voices: Talk, knowledge and identity. In D. Graddol, J. Maybin, & B. Stierer (Eds.), *Researching language and literacy in social context* (pp. 131–150). Philadelphia: The Open University.

O'Connor, M. C. (1996). Managing the intermental classroom group discussion and the social context of learning. In D. I. Slobin, J. Gerhardt, A. Kyratzis, & J. Guo (Eds.), *Social interaction, social context, and language* (pp. 495–509). Hillsdale, NJ: Lawrence Erlbaum.

O'Conor, A. (1995). Who gets called queer in high school? Lesbian, gay, and bisexual teenagers, homophobia and high school. In G. Unks (Ed.), *The gay teen: Educational practice and theory for lesbian, gay, and bisexual adolescents* (pp. 95–101). New York: Routledge.

Ochs, E. (1979). Transcription as theory. In E. Ochs & B. B. Schieffelin (Eds.), *Developmental pragmatics* (pp. 43–72). New York: Academic Press.

Patthey-Chavez, G. G. & Goldenberg, C. (1995). Changing instructional discourse for changing students: The instructional conversation. In R. F. Macías & R. R. Garcías Ramos (Eds.), *Changing schools for changing students* (pp. 107–134). Santa Barbara: University of California Linguistic Minority Research Institute.

Preskill, S. (1997). Discussion, schooling, and the struggle for democracy. *Theory and Research in Social Education, 25*(3), 316–345.

Psathas, G. (1995). *Conversation analysis: The study of talk-in-interaction.* Thousand Oaks, CA: Sage.

Rahm, J. (1998). *Growing, harvesting, and marketing herbs: Ways of talking and thinking about science in a garden.* Unpublished dissertation, University of Colorado at Boulder.

Reiss, M. J. (1997). Teaching about homosexuality and heterosexuality. *Journal of Moral Education, 26*(3), 343–352.

Tannen, D. (1989*). Talking voices: Repetition, dialogue, and imagery in conversational discourse.* New York: Cambridge University Press.

Tannen, D. (1998). *The argument culture.* New York: Ballantine Books.

Tannock, S. (1998). Noisy talk: Conversation and collaboration in a youth writing group. In S. Hoyle & C. Adger (Eds.), *Kids talk: Strategic language use in later childhood* (pp. 241–65). Oxford: Oxford University Press.

Tannock, S. (1999). Working with insults: Discourse and difference in an inner-city youth organization. *Discourse and Society, 10*(3), 317–350.

Tracy, K. (1997). *Colloquium: Dilemmas of academic discourse.* Norwood, NJ: Ablex.

Tracy, K. & Ashcraft, C. (2001). Crafting polices about controversial values: How wording disputes manage a group dilemma. *Journal of Applied Communication Research, 29*, 297–316.

Uribe, V. (1995). A school-based outreach to gay and lesbian youth. In G. Unks (Ed.), *The gay teen: Educational practice and theory for lesbian, gay, and bisexual adolescents* (pp. 203–210). New York: Routledge.

Willet, C. (Ed.). (1998). *Theorizing multiculturalism: The current debate.* Malden, MA: Blackwell.

Williams, A. (2003). Introduction to the colloquy. *Journal of Language and Social Psychology, 22*(1), 47–49.

Williams, A. & Garrett, P. (2002). Communication evaluations across the life span: From adolescent storm and stress to elder aches and pains. *Journal of Language and Social Psychology, 21*(2), 101–126.

Williams, A., Thurlow, C., Drury, J., McKay, S., Forman, J., Eckert, P., & Mastronardi, M. (2002). *Report of the Task Force on Language, Social Psychology and Adolescence.* International Association of Language and Social Psychology. Available: http://www.ialsp.org.

Youniss, J. & Yates, M. (2000). Adolescents' public discussion and collective identity. In N. Budwig & I. Uzgiris (Eds.), *Communication: An arena of development: Advances in applied developmental psychology* (pp. 215–233). Stamford, CT: Ablex.

Zamanou, S. (1985, November). *A study of teenagers' perceptions of topic appropriateness for discussion with parents.* Paper presented at the annual Speech Communication Association Convention, Denver, CO.

CHAPTER FIVE

"Gotta Be Worse": Literacy, Schooling, and Adolescent Youth Offenders

Margaret Finders

In education circles, one can hardly talk about discourses without invoking James Gee. In 1990, he explained how a discourse community works like an identity kit that comes pre-equipped with ways of seeing, acting, thinking, and talking in the world (Gee, 1990). In addition, he has more recently unpacked the rhetoric of New Capitalist workplaces, which he says "require empowered employees who can think for themselves and who think of themselves as smart and creative people. They require employees who are good at problem solving and who can use various tools and technologies to solve problems" (Gee, 2002, p. 58). This essay concludes by noting "It has not been my intention here to make recommendations for the future, but only to look into the future—there are two possible courses of action (not necessarily mutually exclusive)" (Gee, 2002, p. 66). According to Gee, one course is to give up on public schools, accept their neo-liberal function of delivering "the basics" accountably, and work to provide activities and experiences, as well as politically critical capacities, for children who are disadvantaged outside of school. The other is to fight the neo-liberal agenda and make schools sites for creativity, deep thinking, and the formation of whole people, schools where all children can gain success defined in multiple ways and the ability to critique and transform social formations in the service of creating better worlds for all. While Gee's hopes are on the latter, he places his bet on the former.

Like some of the students described by Gee, the students that I work with have mostly given up on public schools and believe that schools have given up on them. One student, Angel,[1] a fifteen year old European American mother of a two year old, described herself through the eyes of adults in the following manner:

> The biggest thing is slut 'cause I had a baby. No teacher called it to my face. But they looked upon me like that. They looked at me like I was nothin' at all 'cause I had a baby when I was thirteen.

Angel, expelled from a mainstream middle school and on probation, said, "You know, we did a lot of things to prove we were the way we were. We were *juvenile delinquents*. And so we gotta be worse." In a private discussion about doing school work, another fifteen year old, Diego, told me, "It's like you gotta be bad. Like prove somethin'. Like in front of Tara, it's okay maybe, but now with Lopez around, no way." These fifteen year olds, expelled from school, vehemently denied literacy engagement and enacted a rigid set of rituals performed to preserve a sense of self. It was their acts of resistance to school experiences that made them think of themselves as smart and creative people.

The alternative education offered at the Teen Learning Center (TLC) represents an effort to prevent some of these youth from being removed from the community and placed in costly out-of-county residential treatment programs. Sponsored by three school corporations and the judicial system, this alternative middle school provides an education program to students in the county who have been expelled from school and who, as wards of the court, are ordered to attend. Students attend TLC in the basement of a local community center from 9:00 a.m. to 3:00 p.m. five days each week. The classroom, a large open recreation room, was not designed for schooling. At one end of the room are overstuffed couches and a TV. There are no desks, and students work at tables shoved together at the other end of the room. School materials consist of a mismatch of discarded and borrowed textbooks, two donated outdated computers, and whatever supplies the teachers and I can scrap together. Progress reports are sent weekly to probation officers documenting each student's academic and social performance. Everything about the material conditions of the school sends messages about the value of education for these particular students. Yet, as both a school and a non-school—a liminal state between official school where students are cast as deviants and recreational center where students often demonstrate physical and linguistic prowess—TLC is renowned. This dynamic sets the stage for redefining an "adolescent" identity kit, for reconfiguring ways of seeing, acting, thinking, and talking in the world.

A number of scholars have recently argued that the significance of peer dynamics is grossly underestimated in classroom life (Finders, 1997; Lensmire, 1994; Lewis, 1997). To more fully understand the dynamics of literary learning, I undertook a year-long ethnographic study at the Teen Learning Center. Through support from a National Council of Teachers of English research foundation grant, I served as the language arts teacher at TLC for one academic year.

Studies suggest that school failure for working-class kids may be based on the fact that the only available role models for these students are victims or rebels (Eckert, 1989; Everhart, 1983; Griffin, 1985; Lareau, 1987; MacLeod, 1987; Willis, 1977). Available roles for girls are often presented in similar dichotomies: selfish or selfless (Gilligan, 1988), good girls or bad girls (Fine & Macpherson, 1993; Walkerdine, 1990). Walkerdine (1990) writes, "in a recent study an overwhelming number of girls of all ages gave descriptions of their ideal girls which included the terms 'nice, kind, and helpful'" (p. 51). This notion of the ideal, Walkerdine argues, connects good performance with docility and positions girls in roles that privilege helpfulness as the highest level of attainment. Coming from low-income, single-parent homes, the middle school females at TLC are far less willing to embrace the role of the "nice, kind, and helpful" girl. While the original design for this study was to study girls exclusively, as the study evolved, it became increasingly clear that what West and Zimmerman (1987) call the "doing of gender" at TLC demanded that I include both males and females. In order to examine how enacted gender identities governed the social practices and literate engagement of the focal students, both male and female students were included in the study.

THEORETICAL PERSPECTIVES

Drawing from post-structuralist feminist theory (Davies, 1993; Luke & Gore, 1992), I set out to explore the dynamics of literacy experiences at TLC, a transitional middle school for youth offenders. My theoretical perspective derives from the notion that discursive practices hold constitutive forces that shape experience. Subjectivity is not an essence but a set of relationships, and discourse is the agency through which the subject is produced (Davies, 1993). Biklen (1995), for example, explains, "Discourses are institutionalized ways of understanding relationships, activities, and meanings that emerge through language [talk, rules, thoughts, writing] and influence what people in specific institutions take to be true" (p. 81). Discourses enable and constrain particular subject positions and relationships available within them. They shape how people come to understand the world in which they live, how they judge the worth and actions of self and others. Discourses, however, should not be viewed as simply constraining. Weiler (1998) explains, "People are not simply defined by ideological constructs of what they should be, but negotiate expectations, both external and internalized in their own consciousness, in the context of material need and desire through competing discourses" (p. 353). Likewise, Biklen (1995) argues:

> Discourses are central in producing shared meanings in institutions, but people negotiate the meanings they make. People are not automatons who are simply obedient to the perceived shared rules that guide the institutions in which they work and live. Discourses must be continually shaped and are renegotiated by how people live and act in their daily lives. (p. 81)

From this perspective, discursive understandings shape experiences; yet the relation between discourse and experience is dialectical rather than hierarchical. Lu and Horner (1998) hold that critical ethnographers must sustain the tension between experience and discursive understanding. They caution critical ethnographers to acknowledge the dangers of one discourse speaking for another and argue that "an ethnography of these experiences would have to ask how they are experienced by people in different material social locations and in terms of the particular discursive understandings they give to them" (p. 259).

In this chapter, I examine schooling as it is experienced by unsuccessful middle school students. I turn now to the study designed to examine the available discourses circulating at TLC.

THE STUDY

The goal of this study was to examine within the institution of a school, the available discourses and the construction of gendered subjectivities through which students named themselves. Drawing upon post-structuralist theory, I set out to look at the available discourses circulating at TLC. Yet post-structuralism is not so much a position from which to view the data, but a way of approaching data, evidence, knowledge, and their construction. As Davies (1993) writes, "The theory does not provide a frame or lens through which to look at the data (nor is the data a lens on a world which is thought to exist independent of that data), but a way of drawing attention to aspects of text and talk otherwise not visible" (p. 14).

In order to look at the array of discourses, I analyzed the data from the perspective of each participant in the following manner: what is taken as true, what is regarded as desirable, what are the expectations for how individuals should act, and when and with whom do these assumptions and expectations shift? I was interested to learn what discourses were taken up and how both adults and students spoke themselves into existence. I hypothesized that if one could gain access to the multiple discourses, then one could begin to articulate a set of pedagogical moves to support the literacy development of youthful offenders, something that to date has not been accomplished.

As noted earlier, the main goal in conducting this study was to gain an understanding of the multiple discourses circulating at TLC and to examine how TLC students positioned themselves within these discourses. As an "identity kit," discourse communities are always multiple. Cintron (1991) problematizes the notion of community identity. He writes:

> As Bakhtin (1981) suggests, communities that are in contact interanimate each other. They infect, disrupt, and even discharge their differences during their interaction such that each community's beliefs, values, and language

system (including its way of speaking) are exchanged, resulting in ephemeral identities. (p. 24)

In this chapter, I examine such competing discourses and such ephemeral identities. I argue that the invisibility of the conflicts within them serves to further disenfranchise young women from low socioeconomic status (SES) backgrounds in public school settings. Butler (1993) emphasizes the ways in which repeated performances of gender can be transgressed within the very discourses that produce them. As will become evident, Angel was quite competent reconfiguring her place in the school and in the world by using the tools within the discourses that set out to control her. For the purpose of analysis, I present these discourses as distinct; in daily life these discourses are of course multiple, complex, and interrelated. I now turn to the discourses that shape lives in the wider public school system—the competing discourses dictating who and what TLC students should aspire to be. I then turn to TLC and focus upon the ways in which the students and teachers create meaning through those discourses.

RIVAL RHETORICS: PREDOMINANT DISCOURSES CIRCULATING IN PUBLIC SCHOOL SETTINGS

TLC students came to school with a keen sense of identity, a well-articulated construction of desire and a rigid set of rituals performed to preserve a sense of self. They brought to the school context certain expectations for how individuals must act and judged the value of individuals in relation to these expectations. Theories of resistance point out that students who are either unwilling or unable to meet compliance standards of school are labeled as deficient or deviant and destined by those labels for school failure (D'Amato, 1987; McDermott, 1987). Erickson (1987) argues that high school diplomas serve for low SES students primarily as "docility certificates" (p. 208). TLC students, all low SES, earned reputations for not being docile. Angel explained it this way:

We're not afraid. We don't care if we get expelled. We don't care at all. We're careless. And that's the big bad thing. We can do what we want. I don't care. It's just the way we are.

In this chapter, I argue that "just the way we are" is not governed by peer pressure, as is so often characterized in discussions of adolescents. Rather participation is governed within particular discourse communities that demand rigid adherence to particular performances. As I will show, gender and class scripts received from the larger culture define and constrain particular behaviors. Circulating within public school settings are competing discourses that inform individuals how to go about their daily rituals. Through school discourses, particular "resistant" students were subjected to what Foucault (1980) would call "normalizing judgments"—judgments that landed them at TLC. At TLC, adolescents negotiated their memberships in multiple, competing discourse communities, often using resources from competing discourses to transgress the dominant school culture. The discourses of teaching, the discourses of adolescence, and the discourses of female sexuality all facilitate a particular way of enacting and understanding daily life at TLC.

Women's Work: The Discourses of Teaching

Gendered enactments are at the center of school work. Teaching is an occupation that has remained overwhelmingly female (Apple, 1986; Biklen, 1995; Walkerdine, 1990). Biklen (1995) identifies prevailing competing discourses of teaching: discourses of domesticity and discourses of professionalism aligned with clinical discourses compete within the school to covertly authorize a teacher's actions and beliefs, thereby setting normative modes of appropriate pedagogical practice. In the *discourse of domesticity*, the position of the teacher is most often constructed as that of a nurturer, providing service to others. This discourse situates schooling in the domain of family life and positions teachers in roles that closely match the traditional position assigned to adult women, privileging helpfulness as the highest level of attainment. Such a construction positions the teacher as "nice, kind, and helpful," as Walkerdine (1990) argues, connecting good performance with docility.

The *discourse of professionalism*, notes Biklen (1995), is represented as disinterested and supported by clinical discourses emphasizing the objective technologies, for example, of testing, assessment, and clinical evaluation. Here, work life is distinct from family life. Wage

earnings, social status, and a professional body of knowledge construct teaching as an occupation.

At TLC, tensions between the head teacher, Jennie Carter, and the
teaching assistant, Jerry Brown, were clearly based on these competing discourses. Jennie, forty-eight years old, constructed her position
at TLC through the discourse of domesticity. For Jerry, on the other
hand, testing and clinical evaluation were central to his position as a
teacher. Perhaps to distinguish his position from "women's work,"
Jerry regularly used the metaphor of a business to teach at TLC. Often
he said so explicitly, as in "Would you wear those clothes to work?"
"You can't have your pants saggin', and your underwear showing
and maintain any kind of a job" he would tell Wayne and the other
TLC students on many occasions. Jerry and Jennie's differing stances
were clearly visible to TLC students. Angel described their positions
in the following manner:

> Well with Jerry, it was that he's doing all this, trying to be a hard front and
> show us he's the boss. He's in charge. And I've been here three years, and
> here comes Jerry waltzing in and trying to take over. I didn't like it. It was
> our school, you know. And here comes in this stranger from California or
> wherever he's from and tries to take over, you know, and it's like he goes,
> "You need to walk this way and talk this way and dress this way. You can't
> write this or that or say that or this." I told him if I wasn't pregnant I'd get
> up and knock him on his blank-blank-blank. Ms. Carter said that if you get
> frustrated and angry, and there's nothing you can do about it, write it down.
> Get it all out on paper or whatever. I was doing that, and I didn't want him
> to see because it wasn't for his eyes. It was only for Ms. Carter. That's it.

For Jennie, school competence included caring about others and
developing strong social relationships. Literacy, for Jennie, was a tool
in which to learn to express the self: "Get it all out on paper." For
Jerry, school competence included developing a respect for authority,
punctuality, and a work ethic. Literacy, for Jerry, was functional:
completing job applications, writing resumes.

Raging Hormones: The Discourses of Adolescence

Elsewhere, I have documented a normalizing discourse that serves to
regulate adolescent behavior through the sociocultural invention of
adolescence as a life stage (Finders, 1997, 1998/1999). Adolescence as

a "life stage" emerged from a particular set of sociopolitical conditions. Yet adolescence is generally regarded as part of a "natural" life cycle that is biologically determined. The discourse of adolescence holds that (1) adolescents sever ties with adults; (2) peer groups become increasingly influential social networks; (3) resistance is a sign of normalcy for the adolescent; and (4) romance and sexual drive govern interests and relationships. According to this discourse, adolescent meanness and conflict—driven by uncontrollable hormonal surging—are interpreted as signs of "normal" adolescent development. "It's like you gotta be bad. Like prove somethin," as Diego told me. Taking up a discourse of adolescence that dictates that "normal" adolescents must display conflict, TLC students enacted particular behaviors. Tagged as juvenile delinquents furthered the need to display resistant behaviors. Angel characterized it this way: "You know we did a lot of things to prove we were the way we were. We were *juvenile delinquents*. And so we gotta be worse."

Both males and females enacted their identities through displays of "being worse," but "badness" at TLC was distinctly gendered. Males at TLC displayed their prowess through their criminal offenses. Girls, on the other hand, displayed their prowess through their sexuality. Note in the following transcript how presentations of self are clearly gendered and distinctly delinquent. Boys identified themselves through their criminal acts. Girls identified themselves through their bodies. When a guest arrived at TLC, Jennie asked each student to introduce him or herself.

Ricky: I'm Ricky. I've been here since the beginning of the year. I got arrested for paraphernalia [possessing drug paraphernalia] and driving without a license.

Wayne: Wayne. I'm in eighth grade. I threw a punch at Ferguson [middle school principal].

Angel: Uh. [Appearing to wake up] Oh I'm tired. I was out all night with my boyfriend if you know what I mean. I didn't get any sleep. Ha. You know what I mean.

As these pieces of transcript illustrate, boys in general constructed their identities through their actions—possessing paraphernalia, driving without a license, punching a principal. For the young men at TLC, identity status came from physical prowess and action. Young women, on the other hand, identified themselves through their embodied sexual activity. This brings us to a third discourse circulating at TLC.

The Public and the Private: The Discourses of Female Sexuality

The discourse of sexuality is most often taken as more or less "natural" and denies its location within social relations of power. Drawing on Foucault, Haug (1987) argues that "sexuality should be viewed as ideology, in other words, as a complex system of norms and values, through which individuals socialize themselves from top to bottom" (p. 207). Fine (1992) identifies the prevailing discourses of female sexuality inside the public schools. First is the *discourse of sexuality* which equates adolescent heterosexuality with violence. The second discourse identified by Fine is *sexuality as victimization*. She writes, "To avoid being victimized, females learn to defend themselves against disease, pregnancy, and 'being used'" (p. 34). Fine argues that these two discourses position females as victims and males as potential predators. *Sexuality as individual morality* is the third discourse. "This discourse," writes Fine, "values women's sexual decision making as long as the decisions made are for premarital abstinence" (p. 35). This discourse is built upon a language of self-control and self-respect. All of these discourses position the early adolescent female as a passive recipient of male yearning and deny the existence of a *discourse of desire*, the fourth discourse identified by Fine. She acknowledges that a discourse that names desire, pleasure, or sexual entitlement for females barely exists within the public school if at all. And it certainly was not evident at TLC.

For fifteen year old Angel, pregnant for the second time, the discourse of female sexuality circulating at TLC positioned her as incompetent, immoral, and as she said, as "Nothin' at all."

The Pressures of Competing Discourses

Angel drew from each of these discourses: the discourse of teaching, the discourse of adolescence, and the discourse of female sexuality. Her sexual desires and sense of entitlement were interwoven with her multiple identities as juvenile delinquent, mother, and student. Angel embraced a subject position as a highly sexualized being. In a private interview she reported:

> Yeah, they thought, "You're no good. You'll never amount to anything." The sheriff, the teachers, and they kept saying it, "You're no good." That's what they think, but I take care of myself. I take care of my son. I take care of him when he's sick. I make sure he's got what he needs. I'm a good mom to Tyler.

Central to the construction of identity for Angel was a home and family identity. Yet within the home and family identity, as Angel embraced this domestic code, she began to challenge it and redefined her place in a public and powerful sphere. In the following transcript, the now sixteen year old Angel (She-Ra Mom, as she calls herself) discusses her decision to return to school after dropping out for four months.

> It'll be tough. Sherry's like, "You're going back to school? Don't you like to sit at home?" And it's like, "Well, yeah. But I don't want to be doing that the rest of my life, living in a cardboard box," and especially now I have to think about Tyler and my future kids and marriage and everything like that. I want a good job and hopefully going to college, but I don't know if that's gonna happen. I just might be a manager somewhere.

While she is planning for marriage and her children, Angel begins to challenge the domestic code: "I want a good job and hopefully going to college." "Domestic" and "docile" were by no means synonymous for Angel. Good performance for Angel was not perceived as being "nice, kind, and helpful." In contrast, she called herself "She-Ra Mom" and perceived her status as "mother" to give her power over, and responsibility for, her peers. She-Ra Mom physically and verbally whipped the younger boys into shape:

> I'm the mom. They were my kids. She-Ra Mom is what they called me. I kept everybody in line. There wasn't a moment that anything happened there that I wasn't there, that I wasn't in the middle of. You know, everybody came to me with problems. It's like I was there. You know. I was their mom. I kept everybody in place and it worked.

One can sense tensions in Angel's conflicting perceptions of her position as "mother." While she felt competent as mother ("You know, everybody came to me with problems. It's like I was there. You know. I was their mom"), she also felt her two pregnancies had cast her as incompetent as a student ("You're no good. You'll never amount to anything"). Her powerful identity as She-Ra Mom was perhaps a means to transgress the identity of "mother" available in the discourse of domesticity. "Mother," as performed by Angel in the context of this alternative school, illustrates Butler's (1993) views that performances of identity which come already inscribed within a discourse can be destabilized, as in this case, reconfigured into She-Ra Mom, powerful physically and mentally. Claiming pride within the discourse of domesticity, which positioned her as a competent and fully functioning female member of the community, Angel reconfigured power from a discourse that cast her sexuality as deviant.

FAMILY MEETING TIME: THE MAKING OF MEANINGS THROUGH MULTIPLE DISCOURSES

In order to understand the social and cultural interplay in the construction of meaning, I turn now to the morning ritual of TLC to demonstrate how multiple discourses were enacted at the school. Multiple sets of rules, those defined by school authorities and those controlled by the peer dynamic operating within the classroom, demand adherence to competing expectations.

Drawing from the discourse of domesticity, Jennie, the head TLC teacher, started each morning talking about TLC as a community. In what was called Family Meeting Time (FMT), she focused discussions on the importance of shared vision, goal setting, and positive attitudes. She initiated a reward system to recognize positive behaviors and academic success at school. During FMT, she might ask particular students to come forward to be recognized for earning 100% on an exam or perfect attendance for a two week period. This Family Meeting Time was also used to discuss issues and problems that emerged at TLC or were found in the media. Students were asked to discuss such things as racial tensions and age-specific smoking laws at a national and local level.

Family Meeting Time was set up by Jennie to create a space for democratic interactions. Students were invited to freely share their views on issues. Most often, Jennie, or the teaching assistant, Jerry, proposed a conversation about legal and moral behaviors and consequences for particular choices and actions. As you might guess, these conversations never became lively debates or heartfelt sharing times. Only when an issue hit too close to home, such as Jerry's insistence at imposing a dress code, did conversations take off and most often resulted in yelling, fighting, or even calling the police. At the end of the year, these meetings were still never lively debates. Jerry and Jennie struggled to create this sharing time, which never played out as they had hoped. Conversations did not evolve into lively engaged interactions. The exchanges were always forced and slow. While Jerry and Jennie constructed the family meeting as a sharing of the authority within the classroom context, TLC students did not recognize this talk time as any real opportunity for power. As Diego said, "If you talk about it, they'll use it against you."

Resonant with Foucault's (1980) notion of a normalizing gaze, in which surveillance becomes an internal overseer, TLC students self-monitored their interactions. While they all reported a strong affection, trust, and deep respect for Jennie, their own history as students encouraged them to approach Family Meeting Time as "school time" which in turn carried certain expectations of how one must act. FMT sessions also carried certain consequences ("If you talk about it, they'll use it against you").

In a private interview, Jennie described her philosophy of Family Meeting Time in the following manner:

> My position is to go into their world to try to meet them at their world. To try to show them what is takes to go in the route they want to go. So I guess I want to create a spot where the respect is there. To me there are bigger issues in life like honesty, integrity, and persistence and I'm not denying the academic preparation. It's just that there is more to education than that. It's more and more complete, isn't it? But I'm not sure that forcing them academically is gonna make it happen anyway. And so I would rather work on this complete acceptance and meeting them where they see their vision taking them and assisting them along the way. They need to feel a part of it. Because I'm afraid otherwise they'll just drop out. I think about how hard we worked toward building the rapport, building that community with the

kids. Building a family so we could weather the negative stuff. And it does drain the people doing it. And you work through that and hopefully get past the negative to where you can make meaningful progress. But we could just never get past that.

Acknowledging that with all her efforts, "we could just never get past that," Jennie continued to orchestrate Family Meeting Time each morning in which students were asked to consider actions and consequences. She recognized the "drain" it put on the adults. Yet she was compelled to hold tightly to the discourse of domesticity, engaging the students in family meetings that cast her in the role of nurturing, "assisting them along the way," as she said.

Each student had another community, more permanent and more powerful than the one at TLC. Here is C. J.'s philosophy of Family Meeting Time:

C. J.:   That didn't do nothin' for me. Talkin' about these bullies going around and beatin' up on kids. For Christ's sake. I don't need that.

M. F.:   Do you think that it helps others?

C. J.:   No. I think it's retarded. We sit in there, and we're supposed to talk, but he [Jerry] just keeps going on talking on and on about bullies, you know. And then every time something would happen and someone would get pulled out and he's say how you know you need to control your anger and all this and you don't. And all the time because in terms of helping if somebody comes up and says on you don't want to fight and blah blah blah. You know you're sittin' there mad and already you're saying. "What are you doing coming up to me?" And if I'm gonna fight, I am, and if I'm not, I'm not.

M. F.:   Anything that Jennie did in the family meeting that was useful? In terms of helping people to get along.

C. J.:   It was all retarded. It was a good idea. But nobody in there looked at that as a Family. Maybe Marvin did. Because pretty much that was Marvin's family, but I didn't look at it as a family, you know. I'm just there. I'm at school. And they kept trying to do these different things. Like don't look at it as school. Look at is as a community and a family. I'd always

> agree with it, [as his public performance] but I couldn't ever. I
> have a real strong family. This is just a school.

Like C. J., Angel viewed Family Meeting Time very differently from the TLC adults. Unlike C. J., though, she did not put up a public performance. During FMT, Angel often swore at Jerry or some of the boys. Interestingly, Angel chose curse words for her school public performances, but in private interviews, she replaced them with space holders: "I told him if I wasn't pregnant I'd get up and knock him on his blank-blank-blank."

As is evident, participation in the public arena of Family Meeting Time had very different meanings for the TLC students and for their teachers. For Jennie and for Jerry, communicative competence in FMT meant a movement toward successful rehabilitation for these juvenile offenders. But both boys and girls at TLC earned symbolic capital through another discourse community. TLC students constructed symbolic capital in terms of "badness." Most powerful were those who possessed the most physical and verbal prowess, money, and court records. Those with the least amount of economic capital relied on symbolic capital to create an individual sense of standing within a community of performative competence. Following Bourdieu (1977), low SES creates a greater dependence on the accumulation of symbolic capital. While C. J. may, in his words, "always agree with it" in his public performance enacted to be recognized as a competent participant in Jerry and Jennie's world, he reported privately that "I couldn't ever." Such participation would demand a denial of his competence in what was for C. J. a more powerful discourse community of juvenile offenders. For TLC students, the meanings most often attached to participation in Family Meeting Time denied one's status as a competent member in a more powerful discourse community. For them, participation in Family Meeting Time meant deference and docility. Participation as a youthful offender meant prowess and performative prestige.

FAMILY MEETING TIME AND THE ARRIVAL RITUAL

TLC was designed as a transitional school. Students came and went as deemed appropriate by the judge and probation officers. School officials expected that students would benefit from the attention provided in a small group atmosphere and viewed the goal of TLC as ameliorating delinquent behavior. The court system and school officials envisioned this through a system of punishments; Jennie had a vision of reform through a system of care and reward. Neither worked.

The temporary community at TLC had its norms called into question every time a new student arrived. And this occurred sixteen times. On days in which a new student arrived, Jennie set in motion a ritualized performance by asking students to discuss their academic success with the newcomer. She worried to me privately each time a new student arrived that there would likely be a fight. In order to reduce the threat of violence, Jennie set the tone for first day initiation by making public the standards of acceptable performance and showcasing particular students who were doing very well at TLC. Ironically, new students often came to TLC with the symbolic power of recently being arrested, and in a sense, challenged the more successful students to re-create the community as a community of juvenile offenders. What was valued by new members was the opportunity to display status and position—not in terms of how far one had come, but by how bad one had been. Conflict was one of the ways these students could get their norms "on the table." During morning break, right after community-building exercises, the students went beyond the eyes and ears of the teachers in order to re-establish their positions as powerful. This norm-checking most often resulted in physical fighting.

Clearly the system of rewards and punishments did little to modify the behavior of these juvenile offenders. On the contrary, it became a means to confirm them. Here is the bind: each of these students had a much more powerful status outside of school within a community that constructed them as competent members. So every time a new student came, and Jennie led them in another discussion on the philosophy and vision of TLC, the current students were quite literally positioned in dual, competing memberships.

As noted earlier, Erickson (1987) argues that for low SES students a high school diploma is nothing more than a docility certificate. TLC students would agree. Positioned as competent members of a community of youthful offenders on the one hand, but deemed failures in their schooling on the other, the performative choice was clear: their identity as resistant students had to be preserved. In private interviews, I asked students why there was a fight each time a new student arrived. Bret reported, "Just gotta happen that way," and Diego explained, "That's because you know, we don't know them so we try to start something. Like at break, Tom had his first day and Sherry was getting in his face and later on somebody asked, 'Tom, hey what's you think of Sherry?' and he goes, 'I think she's a slut.'"

C. J. explained it this way:

> Everybody gets adjusted to the way it was before they came and they have to readjust when they come. Like Wayne when Ricky came, he had to show he was the big tough guy and Ricky didn't take it. So see when Jade came Chenelle had to do the same thing. And before when Angel was there and before Jade came, Angel said she had to take care of Jade. LeeAnne said that about Tara and then Tara said that about Sherry. So it sort of like girls have to prove themselves to girls and guys have to prove themselves to guys.

At TLC physical conflict and verbal abuse were ways of getting norms on the table, of establishing and maintaining hierarchical rankings. Physical prowess for both boys and girls was called into question every time a new student arrived. Ms. Carter set out her version of the school norms explicitly on the first day. This arrival ritual created a crisis of identities, a confrontation of rival rhetorics. Situated within competing discourse demands, TLC students had to reestablish themselves as competent and powerful.

The juxtaposition of discourses is evident as each new student arrived with symbolic power as a youthful offender. Successful TLC students carried symbolic power, earned through the court systems. Yet, TLC students who were succeeding within the school structure were unable to "school" new students into their established norms because that would have challenged the identity of the new students as competent juvenile offenders. Instead, new students actually "schooled" the veteran students by virtue of carrying the most currency in "being bad." They held the most recent arrest record, granting them the most power.

Students who were becoming successful in the school structure at TLC were trapped in competing discourses. Since their identities were defined through their deviant behavior, the reward system and emphasis on conformist standards of success worked against positive change. Students did not want to be singled out and recognized as doing well in school. Jennie's overt requests to reform could not compete with covert demands to be bad.

Drawing from a discourse that normalized resistance, both male and female TLC students enacted a competitive presentation of "you gotta be worse." Goffman (1959) describes such group negotiations as performance teams defined as "any set of individuals who co-operate in staging a single routine" (p. 79). In this way, membership in a particular "performance team" may demand the staging of particular routines. Davies (1993) created the term "category maintenance" to describe actions "whereby children ensure that the categories of person, as they are coming to understand them, are maintained as meaningful categories in their own actions and the actions of those around them" (p. 18). As a performance team of juvenile offenders, TLC students orchestrated actions for the purpose of category maintenance. They felt constrained to operate within that role and were explicitly schooled by peers in behaviors to maintain the category of "juvenile offender." Surveillance and protection demanded a very narrow band of appropriate behaviors within the school context.

CATEGORY MAINTENANCE: GENDER ENFORCEMENT AND LITERACY LEARNING

The "doing of gender" was also played out in school performances and specifically governed literacy learning in distinct ways. For male TLC students, "literate learner" and "juvenile offender" were constructed as mutually exclusive categories. With so much riding on the norm of the latter, success with the former threatened to re-categorize them. Recall Diego's statement: "It's like you gotta be bad. Like prove somethin'. Like in front of Tara, it's okay maybe, but now with Lopez around, no way." Category maintenance worked to constrain literate engagement in this court-ordered transitional school for youthful offenders. Yet the dominant discourse of adolescence that views resistance as "normal" adolescent behavior made these boys' performances somewhat acceptable and made them seem reachable to the TLC teachers, including me. We operated from a "boys will be boys" perspective, if you will.

For female TLC students, "you gotta be bad" came with a very different set of expectations and consequences. The discourses of female sexuality underscore many traditional elements of a woman's place, particularly that she must be controlled. Determined to establish an identity as powerful, females at TLC enacted behaviors as highly sexualized beings—as out of control. But the girls at TLC engaged freely in literate activities. For them, literate learner and youthful offender were not mutually exclusive categories. They read and wrote regularly. They were, in fact, competent readers and writers. They used reading and writing to prove they were bad, and they proved it through their bodies: they spoke, read, and wrote about their sexuality.

Classroom teachers bring certain expectations for how individuals should act and judge the value of individuals in relation to these expectations. The construction of the female self as a highly sexualized being created great boundaries for the middle-class TLC teachers, especially me. I preferred girls to be "nice, kind, and helpful," but found these girls to be "mean, obscene, and disgusting." For the adults, literate learner and sexualized adolescent female were much more mutually exclusive categories than convergent categories. Clearly, category maintenance was in operation for the teachers and the youth at TLC. These attitudes undermined the girls' positions as competent communicative members of the classroom. Denying these young women positions as competent members left them little possibility to move beyond a defensive position.

As noted throughout, the connection between good performance and docility puts girls, along with their nurturing teachers, in positions that privilege helpfulness as the highest level of attainment. This notion of "good performance" is based on middle-class, white cultural views. Fordham's (1993) research documents the diversity of gender constructions. She writes, "Because womanhood or femaleness is norm referenced to one group—white middle-class Americans—women from social groups who do not share this racial, ethnic, or cultural legacy are compelled to silence or gender 'passing'" (p. 8). The denial of the diversity of gender roles serves to marginalize working-class girls whose actions do not match their middle-class teachers' view of what constitutes "nice" performances and "private" sexuality.

For me, a self-monitoring system was in operation that regularly and systematically re-established a traditional view of literacy and a middle-class view of female sexuality, both of which denied the female TLC students status as competent members of the classroom. I came to TLC with what I thought was a broad definition of literacy. But my field notes chronicle a constant struggle to push the TLC students closer to a traditional definition of literacy. For example, while I was willing to work with popular magazines, I viewed them as a *bridge* to more "appropriate reading materials." Category maintenance was, for me, a self-monitoring system by which I regularly re-established a traditional view of literature. Applebee's (1974, 1981, 1990) historical studies of the teaching of writing and literature reveal that while there is no nationally mandated curriculum for high school English, there is a homogeneity in the English curriculum across the nation. While innovative practices are abundant in professional literature, the maintenance of a rigidly and narrowly defined category for what counts as English is certainly at work in many public school English departments across the nation. Such norms clearly had an influence on me at TLC.

The gender and class politics at work in constructing female youth offenders raises important issues about the stigma attached to female youthful offenders in schools. The specific discourses operating were fundamental in maintaining tacit gender and class distinctions. By design, TLC was a transitional middle school for both males and females. In actual practice, however, the girls were more quickly integrated back into mainstream schools while boys remained at TLC for extended periods of time. Twice as many boys as girls were ordered to attend school at TLC, and on average, the judge ordered boys to be in attendance twice as long as girls. During my year at TLC, no boy was returned to his public school. These discrepancies cannot be fully understood without recognizing the multiple and complex relationships among discourses, especially regarding gender and class among TLC students and society at large. The discourse of adolescence, which situates resistance and conflict as developmentally "normal," serves to privilege male offenders. While the girls may have been perceived as immoral, lacking both self-respect and self-control, female deviance was less threatening to others. Yet while more boys spend more time in the TLC program than girls, none of the girls who returned to their mainstream school completed the academic year. Unlike the six male students who successfully completed the academic year at TLC, all the female students who returned to their schools either dropped out or were placed later in residential treatment programs.

Undeniably, more work needs to be done on the effects of normalizing discourses on schooling. Our institutions have a responsibility to respond to the needs of these students rather than to continue to construct them as incompetent. Docility can no longer be the means by which we teach our students—young women or men—to succeed in school. So what might all of this mean to a literacy educator? Can we begin to make schools deep thinking places where all children can gain success defined in multiple ways?

RECATEGORIZING LITERACY: IMPLICATIONS FOR PEDAGOGY

To achieve a vision of education where schools are deep thinking, creative places, educators must address the ethical and intellectual habits of students, and help students to recognize and respect the diversity of discourses that exist within multiple communities. Schools must become sites where children can gain success defined in multiple ways and the ability to critique and transform social formations in the service of creating better worlds for all. Recategorizing literacy education becomes one means by which we can help students to gain deeper understandings of how discourses operate in order for them to use and transform the various tools available within the discourses to pose and solve problems. Luke (2003) and others have argued for an expanded definition of literacies, a definition that allows us to make visible the ways in which discourses situate us and shift from traditional literacy practices to critical literacy and critical language awareness. Luke (2003) writes:

> Our aim is to shape literacy practices that are about engaging and managing the images, representation and texts that constitute identity, work and

ideology, and, finally, those that engage with other cultures and sensibilities. The shift here is one of recognizing the difference between information and knowledge, and perhaps subtler and more important, the difference between knowledge and its ethical applications in social and cultural action. (p. 21)

Scholars are calling for a literacy pedagogy that builds from an awareness of the influence of both language and culture upon our lives (Cherland, 1994; Lewis, 1997; Moss, 1995). Cherland (1994), for example, calls for a critical pedagogy that explores vested interests in texts and examines the ways in which individuals are positioned to read and respond in certain ways. This presents a new agenda for literacy programs. As literacy educators, we must provide opportunities and models for examining what counts as competence in our literacy programs. Literacy educators must take up a critical stance that deepens understandings of the influence of both language and culture upon lives and classrooms.

As my aim, I wanted to provide TLC students with strategies to make discourses visible and new discourses available. During language arts time, TLC students and I brought in texts and began reading as ethnographers, looking at how the characters were constructed in particular texts and contexts. We focused on uncovering the implicit values and assumptions that governed the actions and judgments of particular characters. In other words, we examined the discursive positioning at work within the texts. Angel's critical commentary served as a springboard for a literacy program in which we took a critical stance toward what we were reading. We read for assumptions, attitudes, and values implicit in various texts—the local newspaper, *Low Rider Magazine*, court documents, *The Outsiders*. During our literacy class, I began asking students to look at how the text constructed individuals and events. Together we began examining the social, historical, and cultural constructions of particular positions available in texts, the classroom, and the larger culture.

While we were exploring how young people were represented in magazines and music videos, a series of articles about the possibility of relocating TLC was published in the local newspaper. Community members wrote letters expressing their concerns with placing a school for juvenile offenders in their neighborhood. Drawing on her critical skills, Angel reflected on the local newspaper's construction of herself and her peers: "So they've constructed us as juvenile delinquents. They make it look like we are all in trouble or on welfare or something like that. They try to make it look like we are all wards of the court. That's BS." Her work as an novice ethnographic reader led her to organize classmates to write the following letter, which was published in the newspaper:

> We the students of TLC would like to speak out on our own behalf and rights. We are not all troubled kids or wards of the welfare system and most of us asked to return to TLC. It is true that we have had trouble in the past, but we are taking positive actions to change our behaviors so we can be respected, trusted, and looked upon as young adults rather than juvenile delinquents. We have a 95% attendance rate at TLC. We earn A's and B's. If we earn lower than a B, we redo our work until we are successful. The atmosphere at TLC supports our learning. We feel respected as people. We take responsibilities for ourselves and each other. No one here laughs at others. We respect our differences and learning needs. TLC is a school for second chances. Everyone deserves a second chance. We are proud to be TLC students.

The new approach to literacy was not undertaken without adversity and controversy. The guiding "You gotta be bad" mantra for the students at TLC created obstacles for this approach to literacy. Internet access to pornography and to the lyrics of well-liked groups such as the Wu Tang Clan created roadblocks. Although I banned these particular materials after discussing the limits of "academically appropriate materials" as defined by school and judicial authorities, similar genre material, such as gangsta rap music, was incorporated. Yet the very act of appropriating content such as gangsta rap music into a curriculum changes perceived boundaries. The very appeal of gangsta rap diminishes once incorporated into the context of the classroom and its ownership co-opted. If "you gotta be bad" can be enacted through one's choice in music—music that advocates sexual and physical violence, for example—how are these discourses affected when they become at least nominally endorsed by authorities within the school context? But regardless of text content, the dynamics of literacy experiences—whether at TLC or any school—demand particular performances, and classroom-based examinations will, of course, create a social space in which students stand to gain or lose status among their peer groups. At TLC, surveillance of this status was both external and internal. TLC students self-monitored their own actions and monitored the interactions of others. Their parallel histories as competent juvenile offenders and incompetent students carried certain expectations of how they must act. And they carried certain consequences: "It's like you gotta be bad. Like prove somethin'."

Rather than giving up on the Angels in school or giving up on public schools in general, we need to think together about how we might make schools places where all students can gain success defined in multiple ways. After teaching language arts at TLC for one year, I would argue that our first move is to disrupt the dominant discourses that position some students as non-competent members of the classroom. Angel, for example, was a highly competent reader and writer. Yet the discourse of female sexuality prevented even me from viewing her as competent. Clearly, Angel did not neatly fit my category of the middle school literacy learner; nor did I fit her categories either. She constructed me as someone who, as she said, "You have no clue, do you, Peg? You don't understand anything about me. You think that reading some book is going to make some big difference. You think you are better than me. You think I'm a little slut, don't you?"

She was right. Even in this chapter, I hear myself casting her behaviors as deviant, in need of remediation or control. Maybe I am guilty of allowing one discourse to speak for another, still trapped in my discursive readings of her actions. Perhaps her enacted sexuality is not, as I have argued from a middle-class, middle-aged discursive position, an attempt to maintain her position as "being bad."

NOTE

1. All identifying names have been replaced by pseudonyms.

REFERENCES

Apple, M. (1986). *Teachers and texts: A political economy of class and gender relations in education*. New York: Routledge.

Applebee, A. (1974). *Traditional and reform in the teaching of English: A history*. Urbana, IL: National Council of Teachers of English.

Applebee, A. (1981). *Writing in the secondary school*. Urbana, IL: National Council of Teachers of English.

Applebee, A. (1990). *Literature instruction in American schools*. Report Series 1.4. Albany, NY: Center for the Study and Teaching of Literature.

Bakhtin, M. M. (1981). *The dialogic imagination*. Austin: University of Texas Press.

Biklen, S. (1995). *School work: Gender and the cultural construction of teaching*. New York: Teachers College Press.

Bourdieu, P. (1977). *Outline of a theory of practice*. Cambridge, MA: Harvard University Press.

Butler, J. (1993). *Bodies that matter*. New York: Routledge.

Cherland, M. (1994). *Private practices: Girls reading fiction and constructing identity*. London: Taylor and Francis.

Cintron, R. (1991). Reading and writing graffiti: A reading. *The Quarterly Newsletter of the Laboratory of Comparative Human Cognition, 13*, 21–24.

D'Amato, J. (1987). The belly of the beast: On cultural differences, castelike status, and the politics of school. *Anthropology and Education Quarterly, 18*, 357–360.

Davies, B. (1993). *Shards of glass*. Cresskill, NJ: Hampton Press.

Eckert, P. (1989). *Jocks and burnouts: Social categories and identity in the high school*. New York: Teachers College Press.

Erickson, F. (1987). Transformation and school success: The politics and culture of educational achievement. *Anthropology and Educational Quarterly, 18*, 335–356.

Everhart, R. (1983). *Reading, writing and resistance: Adolescence and labor in a junior high school*. Boston: Routledge.

Finders, M. (1997). *Just girls: Hidden literacies and life in junior high*. New York: Teachers College Press.

Finders, M. (1998/1999). Raging hormones: Stories of adolescence and implications for teacher preparation. *Journal of Adolescent and Adult Literacy, 42*, 2–13.

Fine, M. (1992). Sexuality, schooling, and adolescent females: The missing discourse of desire. In L. Brodkey & M. Fine (Eds.), *Disruptive voices: The possibilities of feminist research* (pp. 31–59). Ann Arbor: University of Michigan Press.

Fine, M. & Macpherson, P. (1993). Over dinner: Feminism and adolescent female bodies. In S. Biklen & D. Pollard (Eds.), *Gender and education: Ninety-second yearbook of the National Society for the Study of Education* (pp. 126–154). Chicago: The University of Chicago Press.

Fordham. S. (1993). Those loud Black girls: (Black) women, silence and gender "passing" in the academy. *Anthropology and Education Quarterly, 24*, 3–32.

Foucault, M. (1980). *Power/knowledge: Selected interviews and other writing 1972–1977*. New York: Pantheon.

Gee, J. (1990). *Social linguistics and literacies: Ideology in discourses*. London: The Falmer Press.

Gee, J. (2002). Millennials and Bobos, Blue's Clues and Sesame Street: A story for our times. In D. Alvermann (Ed.), *New literacies and digital technologies: A focus on adolescent learners in new times* (pp. 51–67). New York: Peter Lang.

Gilligan, C. (1988). *Moral voice: Adolescent development and secondary education.* Cambridge, MA: Harvard University Graduate School of Education.

Goffman, E. (1959). *The presentation of self in everyday life.* New York: Doubleday.

Griffin, C. (1985). *Typical girls: Young women from school to the job market.* New York: Routledge and Kegan Paul Methuen.

Haug, F. (1987). *Female sexualization: A collective work of memory.* London: Verso.

Lareau, A. (1987). Social class differences in family-school relationships: The importance of cultural capital. *Sociology of Education, 60,* 73–84.

Lensmire, T. (1994). *When children write: Critical re-visions of the writing workshop.* New York: Teachers College Press.

Lewis, C. (1997). The social drama of literature discussions in a fifth/sixth-grade classroom. *Research in the Teaching of English, 31,* 163–204.

Lu, M. & Horner, B. (1998). The problematic of experience: Redefining critical work in ethnography and pedagogy. *College English, 60,* 257–277.

Luke, A. (2003). Literacy education for a new ethics of global community. *Language Arts, 81(1),* 20–22.

Luke, C. & Gore, J. (1992). *Feminisms and critical pedagogy.* London: Routledge.

MacLeod, J. (1987). *Ain't no makin' it: Leveled aspirations in a low-income neighborhood.* Boulder, CO: Westview Press.

McDermott, R. P. (1987). The explanation of minority school failure, again. *Anthropology and Education Quarterly, 18,* 361–364.

Moss, G. (1995). Rewriting reading. In J. Holland & M. Blair (Eds.), *Debates and issues in feminist research and pedagogy* (pp. 157–168). Clevedon: The Open University.

Walkerdine, V. (1990). *Schoolgirl fictions.* New York: Verso.

Weiler, K. (1998). Reflections on writing a history of women teachers. In C. Woyshner & H. Gelfond (Eds.), *Minding women: Reshaping the educational realm* (pp. 347–369). Cambridge, MA: Harvard Educational Review.

West, C. & Zimmerman, D. H. (1987). Doing gender. *Gender and Society, 1(2),* 125–151.

Willis, P. (1977). *Learning to labor: How working class kids get working class jobs.* New York: Columbia University Press.

CHAPTER SIX

The Difference That Time and Space Make: An Analysis of Institutional and Narrative Landscapes[1]

Jennifer A. Vadeboncoeur

Time and space are central to human experience. And whether we follow Kant's (1848/1999) view that time and space are forms of intuition that exist *a priori*, prior to experience as an imposition of our mind, or work from Bakhtin's (1981) position that, rather than being transcendental, time and space are lived within the immediate world, the influence of these two aspects of experience is profound. Bakhtin's (1981, 1986) concept of *chronotope*, initially applied to literary theory, is a tool for exploring the ways in which both time and space are experienced by characters in literature. In this study, I employ Bakhtin's concept of chronotope to map both the institutional and narrative landscapes of students in an alternative[2] high school program.

The sociocultural approach (Wertsch, 1991) provides the foundation for my framework, with a particular emphasis on Vygotsky's (1978, 1986) theory and methodology extended through the work of Bakhtin (1981, 1986). Using this approach, I emphasise cultural tools, such as speech genres and social languages, and other discursive practices, as mediational means through which human relationships, and features of those relationships like identity and alterity, are constructed. The focus of this chapter is twofold. I am interested in the application of the chronotope as an analytical tool for understanding the co-constitutive process of institutional and narrative practices in an alternative high school program. In addition, I am interested in thinking through, in a small way, Soja's (1989) call for a historical and geographical materialism by re-emphasising an analysis of space. The structure of an alternative high school program in the United States and the way in which time and space are lived in the social geography of the school setting are discussed as dialectical reflections of, and contributions to, the identity narratives of the students.

I have organised this chapter into four sections. In the first section, I describe Bakhtin's (1981, 1986) chronotope as an analytical tool for literary comparison, as well as a tool for comparing and analysing institutional settings and identity narratives. Here, I focus on the ways in which the experience of time and space are foundational to the construction of identity and alterity. Next, I compare the *official school chronotope* with the institutional chronotope of an alternative high school program. Similarities and differences are discussed related to both time and space. In the third section, I analyse identity narratives of one female student within the program, using formal and informal texts gathered between August 1999 and June 2000. I conclude, in the fourth and final section, with a summary and a discussion highlighting the complex benefits and limitations of alternative high school programs.[3]

CHRONOTOPE AND IDENTITY

This section includes a brief discussion of chronotope as a literary tool, along with its application as an analytical tool for comparing institutional contexts and identity narratives. In narrative discourse (Bloome, 2003; Ochs & Capps, 2001), an analysis of chronotopes makes possible comparisons within social contexts and across the lived experience of time and space.

Time and Space in Literary Texts: Chronotope as an Analytical Tool

Chronotope is a concept that Bakhtin borrowed from Einstein's Theory of Relativity (Bakhtin, 1981). Through chronotope, "spatial and temporal indicators are fused into one carefully thought-out, concrete whole. Time, as it were, thickens, takes on flesh, becomes artistically visible; likewise, space becomes charged and responsive to the movement of time, plot and history" (p. 84). The chronotope defines genre and generic distinctions, and determines, to a significant degree, the image of human characters in literature as well. To explore how time and space are lived in works of literature, perhaps the most straightforward example is from Bakhtin's analysis of *adventure time* found in Greek romances, such as *An Ethiopian Tale* by Heliodorus written between 220–250 A.D. In general, this kind of text, "the adventure novel of ordeal," tells about the suffering of young lovers and was typically written between the second and sixth century A.D. (Bakhtin, 1981, p. 86). It reflects the stereotypical narrative formula:

> a young boy and girl of marriageable age, beautiful and chaste, meet and fall in love suddenly and unexpectedly. But their marriage cannot take place because they are parted. There are shipwrecks, pirates, slavery, prison, miraculous rescues, recognition scenes, court trials, and sleeping potions. The story ends happily, with the marriage of the two lovers. (Clark & Holquist, 1984, p. 281)

It is the original boy meets girl, loses girl, gets girl story line.

This genre, for Bakhtin, illustrates the essence of *adventure time.* There are only two major events, falling in love and getting married, and the action occurs *between* these points. Adventure time is completely abstract; there is an absence of biological, maturational, or psychological change in the characters. All the events of the story, quoting Bakhtin (1981), "are a pure digression from the normal course of life; they are excluded from the kind of real duration in which additions to normal biography are made" (p. 90). Time is made up of "short, unrelated segments, set off by words emphasising their alienation from developmental time, such as 'suddenly' or 'at just that moment'" (Clark & Holquist, 1984, p. 281). As they move between these two events, the heroes and supporting characters are caught up in a process that is unalterable; their lives follow a certain course over time, based on chance, contingency, and mere happenstance. It is a course that leaves no developmental trace on their identities. In adventure time, the characters do not evolve or grow; they do not reconsider and reconstruct their lives. Instead, they undergo trials and ordeals and, after surviving them, move through the plot to the final event—in essence no different at the end of the novel than the beginning.

Coupled with adventure time is a broad and varied geographical space: a space that is both expansive and generic. Bakhtin (1981) argues that the geographical diversity gives an utterly abstract sense of location, "an interchangeability of space" (p. 100). The shipwreck occurs in an ocean, but which ocean is not important. The prison exists in a foreign country, but which country is unspecified. While the events in time are reversible and could even be reordered, the movement across space is interchangeable as well, thus reducing the specificity and concreteness of the world within which the heroes and events are embedded. Bakhtin (1981) notes that this absence of defining features—geographic, political, or economic—allows the world described to operate with the freedom and flexibility of chance. The details that are described and offered to ground the story are isolated and disconnected, and taken together do not provide an illustration of any cultural or physical world as a whole. For example, customs and animals may be described, but without comparison to what the reader knows. As representations in the text they remain difficult to link with what has been experienced in the reader's world.

In Greek romances, both time and space are abstracted from real contexts and completely nonspecific, giving the reader the feeling that this narrative could happen in any geographical space and at any historical time. Indeed, "adventure-time leaves no trace" (Bakhtin, 1981, p. 110). Time is, in effect, timeless and space, purely physical or material, is universally generic.

Time and Space in Relationships: Identity and Alterity

What happens when we employ a literary concept like the chronotope to human lives outside of print-based or literary texts? Is this a viable form of "interpretation" or "translation" for Bakhtin? For us? There is some evidence to argue that this shift from literary worlds to the world of human experience not only can be made, but also can form the basis of a fruitful analysis (e.g., Bloome & Katz, 1997; Leander, 2002). And perhaps the easiest way to substantiate this move is to note Bakhtin's (1981) words: "Out of the actual chronotopes of our world (which serve as the source of representation) emerge the reflected and *created* chronotopes of the world represented in the work (in the text)" (p. 253, emphasis in original). Indeed, the chronotopes of

texts *are* based on the chronotopes of life; the times and spaces reflected in texts are *founded upon* the experiences of real and imagined
lives. Mapping the chronotope then, from text to life as a lens or
method for understanding experience, ought to hold as well.

Bakhtin links written texts to experiencing "life as text" by expanding the relationship between author and text. He notes that even
people who have not written a literary piece or a novel are
authors—each act of speaking is also an act of authorship. Our ultimate act of authorship is the text that we call our self. This process is
both dialogical and dialectical. We perceive the world not only
through our eyes, but also through our speech (Vygotsky, 1978), ultimately crafting our selves with and through mediational means, such
as the speech genres and social languages we appropriate, and our
relationships and contexts. Central to this mediational construction of
self and other, identity and alterity, is the chronotope: as speakers we
are positioned in both time and space. This positioning is described
through a visual metaphor that locates people and their conversational partners, or interlocutors, in a social space at a particular time
(Clark & Holquist, 1984).

Envision, if you will, a conversation between two people, in terms
of time and space. As I view an event, I view it from a specific place,
with a particular visual perspective, and at a specific moment in time.
By necessity, because my partner cannot be in exactly the same space,
at exactly the same time, his or her perspective must be different.
Bakhtin calls this *noncoincidence*. Our reciprocal noncoincidence provides both of us with a *surplus of seeing*: my partner sees what is behind me and all around us. I, as well, have a surplus of seeing: I see
my partner embedded in the visual surround in front of me (Clark &
Holquist, 1984). It is the combination of, and difference between, these
two perspectives that position us in social space and time.

Bakhtin notes that the construction of the self is a social process, a
reflection of self and other relationships, and as such it is fraught with
both tensions and comforts. For example, we perceive ourselves as
continuously shifting and changing, from moment to moment in time
and through differing contexts and spaces. Our own perception of
achieving selfhood is a timeless, incomplete, and contextually bound
process. Indeed, we are always *becoming*. This sense of becoming is

not felt in the same way—and sometimes not felt at all—by our speaking partners, the others in our lives, and those less obviously connected to us. Others tend to view us from a particular moment in time and from a particular position. Our identity is captured, like a snapshot, and "refracted" back to us through the visual lens or filter of the other. Bakhtin calls this receiving a sense of *completeness* or a fixed identity from the other. This momentary view of a self, refracted through the other, reflects one moment in time and one position in space, rather than a dynamic of becoming. Captured in the view of the other, our history and future is collapsed into a singular, static image embedded in the present moment.

Through this exchange, which Bakhtin conceives of as a "gift," the social construction of identity takes place. Situated within this relationship, the other gives me the gift of my self, however the offering, central to human relationships, is not unproblematic. My experience of the relationship, along with the experience of my self, is shaped by the speech genres and social languages available to me. It is reflected through material bodies and gestures, and also by my ability to convince my interlocutor, or speaking partner, of my position through my performance. That social languages are ordered hierarchically, privileging some over others, is highlighted by Bakhtin through his discussion of "heteroglossia" and the struggle of "centrifugal," differentiating and richly complex, and "centripetal," unifying and unproductive, social discourses. Here, Bakhtin's work benefits from more explicit conceptualisations of power theorised by Bourdieu (1977, 1991), for example, in his development of habitus and disposition. Through disposition, people evaluate and judge the value of the social languages of others and, in doing so, they may recognise, re/produce or resist dominant, or "centripetal," linguistic or symbolic capital. Habitus are a collection of dispositions that are inscribed on and lived through the body. Cultural differences and matters of "taste," and the mediational means we use to represent our selves in terms of social languages and clothes, gestures and posturing, are linked to social class and our relation to forms of capital (for further discussion, see Panofsky, 2003; Portes & Vadeboncoeur, 2003).[4]

The parallels between the social context in works of literature and the social context of the school, the lived experiences of literary characters and the lived experiences of students, provide productive ground for analysis through chronotopes. By examining and tracing the relationship of time and space across institutional and narrative landscapes, I am able to situate the students' construction and negotiation of identity and alterity.

INSTITUTIONAL CHRONOTOPES: LIVING TIME AND SPACE

The research presented in this chapter is part of a larger ethnographic study that examines how young people construct their identity in relation to their school context and the larger sociocultural context outside the school. In the larger study, I explored the way language—speech genres and social languages—was used as a resource to negotiate interpersonal relationships and social identities. I examined, for example, instances of casual conversation and talk about young people, classroom dialogue between teachers and students, and newspaper texts regarding the activities of young people in an alternative program (see Vadeboncoeur & Portes, 2002). I relied on ethnographic methods including observations, field notes, interviews, and text analysis for journals, papers, and poems produced by the students, and newspaper articles about the program written by journalists. The data were organised and analysed using constant comparative analysis (Glaser & Strauss, 1967) and aspects of critical discourse analysis (Chouliaraki & Fairclough, 1999; Fairclough, 1995). The data presented here are a small slice of the larger ethnography organised around chronotopes that surfaced at the institutional level and within identity narratives.

Place and Participants

The Canyon Program[5] is located in a small northwestern university town of approximately 32,000 people. Some ninety-six students were enrolled during the 1999–2000 school year. The students reflected diverse backgrounds and the majority were from working-class families. Fully 21% of the students had become working-class themselves as independent minors. The students had different and varied reasons for being at the school. Several young women were pushed out of the main high school due to pregnancy, or lured out through the promise of childcare offered by the alternative program. Many of the young women and men claimed that they simply did not "fit in" at the main high school. In addition, several young women were homeless. Approximately 27% of the students appeared on the "F list" at the main high school, prior to applying to the Canyon Program. The "F list" was the name given by the guidance counsellors in the main high school to the students who failed a class over a quarter or term.

Each student voice in this chapter refracts the "speaking consciousness" (Wertsch, 1991) of a member of a mixed-grade writing class, a course team-taught by a male and a female teacher. The voice of Janette,[6] a senior student, is highlighted in the third section. The data used here were gathered from field notes, poems, narratives, and formal and informal interviews with students in the writing class.

Physical Chronotopes in Institutional Contexts

While I temporarily separate time and space in order to focus on particular features of institutional structure, it should be noted that within chronotopes, time and space are perceived and experienced as a whole. Evidence for this can be found in the comments of students discussed at the end of this section. Though this may seem an obvious point, many theorists, including Bakhtin (1981) himself, have noted the privileging of time over space: "...it has been temporal relationships by and large that have been studied—and these in isolation from the spatial relationships indissolubly tied up with them" (p. 258). Soja (1989, 1996), Foucault (1975/1995, 1986), and Harvey (2000, 2003) have highlighted the importance of reinserting space in critical social theories. More particularly, Soja (1989) has argued for a historical and geographical materialism. My aim here is to balance time and space, rather than privileging one over the other.

For this analysis of institutional contexts, I begin by identifying and characterising the *official school chronotope* of the mainstream high school, and then juxtaposing it with the *chronotope of the Canyon Program*. The official school chronotope was marked by the abstraction and decontextualisation that surfaced so strongly in the adventure time of the Greek romances described earlier. Time was segmented into forty-six minute periods, each perceived to be discrete and reversible; it made no difference in which order the classes occurred. The subject matter "covered" in each of the periods was narrowly identified through disciplinary frames, such as biology, chemistry, and geometry, with additional course offerings including choir and band. The students moved through space physically, from science lab to rehearsal hall, as if the practice of scientific thought, for example, only surfaced within the specified laboratory space. Interestingly, while science conversation, science homework, science questions, and science thought did not surface anywhere outside the lab, the work that was done in science class was also not perceived by the students to be the work of scientists. Science, and many of the other subjects studied by students in the high school, was not perceived to be relevant to "real life" or necessary for future possible lives.

With respect to time, I note in Table 1 the three most obvious shifts that the Canyon Program offered the students as distinct from the main high school program. For example, the left column shows

Table 1. *Comparing the Canyon Program chronotope across time*

Similar to the Official School Chronotope	Different from the Official School Chronotope
• Same schedule for class periods Class periods are in forty-six minute segments, with four minutes to change rooms.	• Late passes are offered or given frequently so students may finish their work Teachers discuss with each other the students and their projects and inform students when this option is being over used.
• Same attendance policy The students have the same requirement for number of days of attendance per quarter and per year.	• Saturday School This is an optional day for making up hours, classes, or a whole day.
• Same graduation requirements The number of units required is twenty-one total units.	• Alternative completion sequence Students may take English II and III at the same time, for example, in order to catch up with their graduation requirements.

the aspects of the program related to the organization of time that remain similar to the main high school's *official school chronotope*, while the right column highlights the ways in which time is lived flexibly for the students in the alternative program. At the Canyon Program, some aspects of the chronotope were similar to the official school chronotope. For example, students followed the same schedule for class periods, and the same attendance policy and graduation requirements. Time in the *Canyon Program chronotope*, however, allowed for late passes that privileged the pace of the students and the importance of completing projects. The option for Saturday School marked the commitment of the teachers and the students to education and emphasised that learning could occur outside of "normal school hours." Flexibility in course sequencing, while potentially more problematic for younger children, worked with these high school students, in particular when the activities remained fairly similar across the curriculum though the subject matter changed.

In Table 2, the left column shows the aspects of the program related to the organization of space that remain similar to the *official school chronotope* of the main high school, while the right column highlights the ways in which space is dissimilar and more fluid for the students in the alternative program. At the Canyon Program, six teachers had designated rooms that identified spaces for the study of certain curricular areas. There was a traditional style lunchroom, where "hot lunches" could be purchased on plastic trays. In addition, the Canyon Program had a library, with books, magazines, and newspapers, and a part-time librarian. However, with respect to space, the *Canyon Program chronotope* also included the sharing of facilities (with teacher permission), a "coffee shop" atmosphere for lunch in the student centre, and the provision of several areas deemed "community spaces," including both the library and the auditorium. Access to these spaces, and the negotiation of suitable tasks within them, was an ongoing process that occurred inside boundaries identified by the administration and teachers. However, the students in this program were seen as, and saw themselves as, community members: living, working, and using these spaces in concert with their teachers.

These are basic examples of the way in which the Canyon Program allowed for different types of experiences of time and space for the teachers and students at an institutional level. This became possible given a faculty and staff commitment to being responsive to students' needs, coupled with the ability to offer a flexible school environment given smaller class and school size. These two features, a

Table 2. *Comparing the Canyon Program chronotope across space*

Similar to the Official School Chronotope	Different from the Official School Chronotope
• Six teachers have designated rooms, organised by curricular areas Math, science, shop, English, art, and history have specific spaces.	• Room use changes by teacher permission If students want to use a room, to meet or study when the room is not in use, they ask the teacher.
• Lunch may be purchased in the "lunch room" This is the gym with metal tables and benches that fold out of the walls.	• Student centre This open room includes a stove, two microwaves, pop and snack machines, five tables, and numerous chairs.
• The library is a place of scholarship, a quiet place for individual work.	• The library is also a community space for intimate conversation on couches, class meetings, individual work, study hall, tutoring The library is organised by a part-time library aide.

commitment to students and a small school size, became the ground for respectful and lasting relationships between teachers and students, and across students. An example of the kinds of negotiations made possible within an alternative school chronotope, a school-wide meeting called by the students themselves, is elaborated next.

On one Wednesday, a new student left her wallet behind in the room where the writing class was held. By the time she realised she had forgotten it, and gone back to retrieve it (about eight minutes), it was gone from her desk. She returned to her current class and told her teacher and her classmates. After some discussion with the teacher, she and a friend were allowed to leave class and meet with the principal to tell him of the incident. After talking with additional students in the writing class, without resolving the situation, the new student—supported by peers in her writing class, her teachers, and the principal—scheduled a school-wide meeting for Friday afternoon for the last half of fifth period and the first half of sixth period. The student chose the time and the student centre as the appropriate place for the discussion, and wrote an announcement for the principal to read over the intercom noting that if the person who had accidentally picked up her wallet returned it before the meeting, then it would be cancelled.

This example illustrates a shift in time and space in the school schedule in response to a school community problem that was requested by a student and approved by the principal and teachers. The ability to schedule this school-wide meeting, to reorganise time and space during the school day, was of profound importance to this student and her community. The ability for participants in this institutional context to respond to the situation was likely to have partially effected the positive outcome: the wallet was returned intact to the office manager through "the friend of a friend of a friend" shortly after the meeting. The student who took it said she mistook it for her own.

It is important to emphasise that while I was present for this situation, I was not present for the other two student-led school-wide meetings that occurred during the 1999–2000 school year. However, because they were initiated for different purposes, I want to mention them. One was used to plan the school float for the spring parade, and the other was used to organise the students for the coming year—seniors for graduation and the freshpeople, sophomores, and juniors for their optional group activities (e.g., leadership groups). At the Canyon Program, the use of school-wide meetings created the time and space for working through difficult situations, such as a missing wallet, as well as organising upcoming and celebratory events like the parade and graduation.

Discursive Chronotopes: Reflections of the Canyon Program

When talking about their experiences in the Canyon Program, students made reference to both time and space in their comments. In general, comments reflected time and space as both flexible and non-linear in that the students were able to negotiate alternatives to the typical structure of the school day. This included, for example, working on a film project in science class and completing schoolwork on Saturday. In fact what they described was quite different from the official school chronotope created by "factory space" and time "efficiency" studies that still seems to govern what is done today in mainstream high schools. What follows are three examples of students' discursive construction of the alternative chronotope.

In the following quote, the students needed more time than originally planned to design their film project, and as a result they found themselves working in their science lab without having finished what they had hoped to complete during their film class.

> We got caught up in our film project. It took us a long time to make decisions about what we wanted to show. But we were done with our science lab, so we asked Lynn if we could get the cam [video-camcorder] and keep going. She let us. [Jean, eleventh grade, 5/21/00]

Once their work in science was completed, they were allowed to use "science time" and "science space" to continue recording the commentary for their film. After that aspect of the film was completed, they asked to go to the office to see if they could film the office manager, and were allowed to do this until class ended. For these students, the time and space allotted for the study of science was not intractable. The structure of the school day shifted to meet the needs of the students, who articulated a rationale for the shift.

In the second quote, Todd talked about the time he needed to see an assignment as relevant to his school work, and to the year-end play.

> I felt like the first assignments were—like—the same ol', same ol'...So I didn't get started right away. When it seemed like we were...like we would have to really use them...the character stuff [character development for a play]...then I got busy to finish. I went to Saturday School. [Todd, twelfth grade, 5/14/00]

Once Todd understood the connection between the assignment and what he really wanted to pursue—the year-end play that was produced for both the school and the outside community—he worked non-stop on writing a history of and motivations for the actions of two characters in the play. He worked through his study hall and lunch periods for over a week, sped through his classwork to continue this character development during his other classes, and then finished his contribution during Saturday School, an alternative time and space created specifically for this option. Todd was able to spend extended periods of time working on this project, and he remade the spaces he was in as spaces for addressing this project regardless of where he was. Ultimately, what he achieved was a great deal more than what was required.

Finally, Tiffany discussed openly the successes and the difficulties of completing schoolwork while pregnant.

> Some days are good and some days suck. I don't feel good. The baby is due in July and I feel huge...basically, I AM huge. [laughs] Sometimes I fall asleep on the couch in the library, but other times I just work here on this couch. It feels better than a desk. [Tiff, twelfth grade, 4/30/00]

Tiffany's experience of pregnancy during school hours brought home to the students and teachers the central and often forgotten role of the body during learning. In a sense, while pregnant her body became the centre of her spatial experience and others' experiences of her. This lesson was not lost on the teachers, who worked to balance physical comfort, in terms of sitting at tables or on couches and providing food, with social comfort in terms of relationships to promote successful engagement in academic subjects for all the students. As for Tiffany, she was specifically allowed to privilege her body when choosing where she wanted to work and when she needed to sleep. She was never forced to choose between being pregnant and going to school. She was allowed to be both a future mother and a student at the same time.

Overall, students commented about the time they needed to be creative and noted their appreciation of teachers who did not treat them "like machines," expecting them to consistently pump out assignments at predetermined intervals. Indeed, it seemed that at least in the Canyon Program, teacher recognition and willingness to negotiate different ways of living time and space supported student responsibility. Knowing that the teachers were sensitive to this and were willing to make shifts in the structure of the school day, increased students' efforts to meet the original expectations for study and project completion. For example, there were more days than not when Tiffany declined the couch and sat at a table with her peers to work, and times when late passes were offered to students, and they were declined or proved unnecessary, as the student completed the assignment. Sometimes just knowing flexibility was an option seemed to encourage these students to focus and finish.

NARRATIVE CHRONOTOPES: AUTHORING IDENTITY

This section refracts the speaking consciousness of one female student, Janette. Janette was a student in the writing class at the Canyon Program set up to support students as they developed their reading and writing skills. Students were both engaged in a standard curriculum and encouraged to choose additional poets, authors, and song lyricists whose work they read, studied, and analysed. The students were provided with a flexible working environment within which, on a regular basis, they shared their work with each other and their teachers (see Vadeboncoeur, Torres, Swingle, & Anesi, 2000). This representation of Janette's authorial voice, however, is one-sided. Her work is not reflected alongside interviews with her teachers or peers. Instead, I want to highlight the relationship between the flexibility characteristic of the Canyon Program chronotope described earlier and the chronotope that develops over the course of Janette's writing.

Janette was eighteen years old during the 1999–2000 school year and graduated in June 2000. She described herself as having fairly typical school experiences through elementary and middle school, and even through the ninth grade. During her sophomore year, however, her father left and she "dropped for a semester," needing time to sift through and reconstruct her family relationships. When she returned to school she skipped almost every day, feeling disconnected and "out of place," and then ended up applying to the Canyon Program for her junior year. Here, she "worked hard and caught up on" her credits, and as a senior maintained "straight A's."

Populating the Margins: Interanimation as Agency

In terms of identity and alterity, the relationship of self and other, Janette was positioned by those around her, negotiating affordances and constraints with the people in her family system first and foremost. In an early narrative, she described her family as:

> supportive, but...schizophrenic. A very odd mixture of some very odd people. I've known some bizarre and beautiful people in my life, they have influenced me as a student, a person, and as a woman. [N: 12/00]

For Janette, the people in her family were unusual, "odd"; they were perceived as people who stood out from the crowd and had influenced her identities as student, person, and woman. Janette used words not typically associated with families—"schizophrenic" and "bizarre"—to characterise her family. Yet, there was a balance here between "bizarre" and "beautiful": using her words, difference was tempered by beauty and her family was both. Recognising their influence on her identities, Janette willingly took up this juxtaposition between pathology—as located outside the norm—and the aesthetic quality of beauty, a beauty pointing beyond superficial appearances and evocative of an inner beauty. This positioning of the odd and bizarre as beautiful, and in ways desirable, surfaced in another narrative later in the school year:

> Born and raised in [small town], Montana and damn proud of it. A peirced [sic], tattooed freak playing in the mountains. I like being a freak, it's not an insult, it's a freedom like no other. To be a mixture of everything, to see and be seen, to be noticed from three blocks away. [N: 4/00]

Janette positioned herself as "freak," a role that allowed her both freedom and visibility. Her body piercings and tattoos were the ways she had chosen to mark herself, using her body as a canvas of semiotic identifiers. This role offered generativity, it was "a mixture of everything," a position that obtained access to multiple ways of being.

The role of freak shares at least one quality with the rogue, the clown, and the fool—figures analysed in European novels by Bakhtin. Each of these roles, including the freak, share a privilege:

the right to be "other" in this world, the right not to make common cause with any single one of the existing categories that life makes available; none of these categories quite suits them, they see the underside and the falseness of every situation. (Bakhtin, 1981, p. 159)

These roles offer a way of being "outside of" positions, groups, and categories typically extant in a particular context. Perhaps even more important, attaining the role of fool or freak obtains and marks a position of knowing. It is an epistemic stance that bestows the freedom or the licence "to see" more clearly, to see through false appearances to the intention underneath.

While Janette's schooling began typically, and continued that way through the ninth grade, she endured an event that precipitated a turning point in her life as a sophomore: her father left and her parents were divorced. After working through the dissolution of her family as she knew it, and working to reconstruct a new way of being "family" with her mother and brother, Janette returned to school, transformed. At this point in time, returning to the same context did not return her to the same identity, and she was unable to reconnect. She felt displaced and no longer fit into the peer groups that existed in the main high school, noting that she fell "between cliques," or categories in Bakhtin's words, rather than in them. Ultimately, she left the main high school and enrolled herself in the Canyon Program.

Janette's experience may be viewed through "the politics of location," a phrase used by hooks (1990) to describe "the spaces where we begin the process of re-vision...pushing against oppressive boundaries set by race, sex, and class domination...a defiant political gesture" (p. 145). hooks (1990) defines the margins and the population of marginal spaces—historically symbolic of oppression and exploitation—as:

a central location for the production of a counter-hegemonic discourse that is not just found in words but in habits of being and the way one lives...a site one stays in, clings to even, because it nourishes one's capacity to resist. It offers the possibility of radical perspectives from which to see and create, to imagine alternatives, new worlds. (p. 149)

While Janette was positioned on the margins upon her return to the main high school, her interanimation of this marginal space—populating the margin with her own intention, identified perhaps most obviously by her move to the Canyon Program—symbolised the uptake of a new identity: one that was agentic, intentional, and celebratory.

Celebrating Carnival: A Chronotope of Liberation and Danger

Janette's sense of freedom, her embrace of the margins, is reflective of the literary features of the Renaissance carnival, a subject of Rabelais' work identified and analysed by Bakhtin (1984). The *carnivalesque* refers to the carnivalization of everyday life, the twisting and mutating of standard societal themes, and the inversion of societal hierarchies and norms. Janette was better able to "see" or gain a sense of her sociocultural context, by attempting to be outside of it. According to Bakhtin (1984), this process is an example of the heteroglossia of social languages and enriches the dialogue between standard culture and the culture of the carnival, with productive and diversifying results. In a journal entry, a few months before the second narrative recounted above, she wrote:

> Those who stand outside of a "typical" high school experience are blessed and cursed. Being one of these outsiders shaped who I am today. The beauty of being removed from the mainstream is you can act like a sort of diplomat moving between all the cliques. [Journal: Reflections, 2/00]

As an act of resistance, being outside of the mainstream was a method for gaining freedom from domination (Bakhtin, 1984); Janette navigated this line with mastery. She was able to be the "peirced [sic], tattooed freak playing in the mountains"—a complex combination of style and activity—and still achieved success by school standards. Just before graduation she wrote:

> Life has not always been happy and free, but it never is for anyone. That's not important though. What is important is that I write. I love literature and independent film, B-movies are the best, and I dig music. I travel around to concerts whenever I get the chance. Life is what you make, every situation can be customized to benefit you, depending on how you look at it, depending on what you see. [N: 5/00]

The *carnivalesque* in everyday life, the carnival grounds, is important as a marker for a kind of privileged space: the space where challenges to norms occur, the space where the body—the grotesque, the beautiful, the old, the young, the living, the dead—reigns. The carnival is a space where the prohibitions of social life are tossed out and replaced by spectacles. The carnival is also a temporal space, marked by temporary challenges to hegemony, and a fleeting and impermanent celebration of the dialogism between the standard system (centripetal) and alternatives to the norm (centrifugal). Janette's poem, entitled *Girl's Room*, exemplifies the recursivity between the celebration of the margins and challenges to societal norms evident in the chronotope of the carnival.

Girl's Room

Why are there so many girls in the bathroom?
It's not a very hospitable place.
Stalls with toilets.
Toilets filled with TP and tampon wrappers.
I wonder exactly how they get those spots of thick menstrual blood
   on the floor and sometimes the walls.

Maybe they're in there for the sinks?
Sinks filled with paper towels and occasionally vomit.
I often wonder how such supposedly gentle creators create an atmosphere
   of filth.

I've got it, I know why they're in there.
The mirror.
The large mirror smeared with lip gloss or chapstick,
   whatever was available at the time to distort their image.

Out of the inner decay and filth of the girls' room emerge the painted
   beautiful girls.
Out of the vomit and blood come the girls wanting to be women,
   wanting to belong,
   wanting to be loved.
To see the reality of teenage girl, you need not look further than the girls'
room.

The two prominent and interrelated features in *Girl's Room* I want to address here are Janette's celebration of the physical body and her social critique of the emphasis that society places on a certain kind of physical appearance: the image "distorted" by make-up, the beauty created out of "paint." The attention paid to the form and function of female anatomy represents "the whole remarkable complexity and depth of the human body and its life" (Bakhtin, 1981, p. 170). This contrasts with what has become acceptable in society and schools, namely the bifurcation of mind and body, and the privileging of the cognitive over the physical. Janette linguistically explores the girls' room in her poem, recognising each of the tasks attended to in that physical space, without censoring herself or giving up her control of her discursive space: she quite intentionally entitled this poem, *Girl's Room*, to reflect her authorial voice, her representation of the girls' bathroom. While ostensibly focused on the space of the girls' room, this poem forces the reader to consider embodied space and the meaning given to certain kinds of gendered performances. Janette's words "are aimed primarily at destroying the established hierarchy of values, at bringing down the high and raising up the low, at destroying every nook and cranny of the habitual picture of the world" (Bakhtin, 1981, p. 177). She speaks of things that most schools would not celebrate, most teachers would prefer to silence, and most people would rather not discuss. In doing so she exposes the falseness of social custom and the underside of gendered expectation as a moment for imagining something "other"—a different and non-apologetic way of performing "girl" and "woman."

Similar themes surfaced in another poem Janette wrote while in the writing class at the Canyon Program, though more indirectly. The emphasis in *Roadkill in the Sky* is on time and the life lost when it is misspent. For Janette, the necessity of exchanging a cosmetics bag for a friend was a waste of "precious time," an experience akin to a slow death. In that moment, an everyday responsibility became an obstacle, resulting in "words unsaid, dreams unfulfilled, knowledge unattained, verses unwritten." What stood in Janette's way was a friend's desire for something—something that represented to Janette the social control of young women's bodies—a floral cosmetics bag.

Quite unlike the abstraction and decontextualisation inherent in *adventure time*, Janette's experience of the world is deeply connected to her relationships, activities, and contexts. Rather than reflecting a

Roadkill in the Sky

Spring ahead,
one more hour taken
precious time sold
to the lowest bidder.

Auction away life
seconds, minutes, hours, days.
Anyone who wastes your time
murders you slowly.

Words unsaid, dreams unfulfilled,
knowledge unattained, verses unwritten.
All for a floral pattern cosmetics bag
without a price tag.

lack of character development as in Greek romances, the chronotope of Janette's written and oral narrative discourse reveals a young person experiencing a great deal of maturational and psychological change. Her sense of her self—a joint construction based on the *surplus of seeing* of the people around her and her own temporally and spatially positioned perspective—shifts and changes with context and activity, and is continually renegotiated within relationships.

Gee, Allen, and Clinton (2001) note that young people use language to "fashion" themselves into different kinds of people as they move from one context to the next. The chronotopes of Janette's identities surfaced in both her formal and informal writing and were in keeping with the triumphant and *centrifugal* features of the carnival, exemplified by the multivocality in this journal entry:

My conversation with the river changed me and then I realised that we are in a constant state of change. I became many different people during the course of that day. [Journal: Hello, hello, 4/00]

While we construct identities by identifying our selves with others, we also construct alterity and difference from the other. As noted by Bucholtz (1999), youth "to a great extent consciously choose and display their identities through language and other social practices" (p. 210), processes that simultaneously construct "identity with" and "difference from." This relationship, however dualistic it sounds, ought not to be seen so. The dialogics of carnival afford us the possibility of moving beyond binary relationships, toward a position of both/and, a feature that is explicitly challenged from the margins and reflected in Soja's (1996) conceptualisations of "thirdspace." These are places of deconstruction and transformation that refuse, among other things, the binaries so central to western thought, including subject/object, natural/social, man/woman, self/other, and that offer potential for generativity.

During my final interview with Janette, we discussed her plans for university, travelling, and writing. She talked about life being a balance between "what you do with what you get." And she felt she gained freedom to construct both her self and the world from her privileged "position outside the norm." She had a sophisticated sense of when and where to push the boundaries of conservative adult sensibility, and she gained the admiration of her teachers and peers. With respect to life she noted, "It's like I'm acting it out here and now, making choices and doing things with what appears. Sometimes I have to go out looking too, but that's all in a day's work."

I find myself wanting to end on a positive note here, to portray Janette as completely successful in her carnivalization of everyday life. But even though hers is a success story, the carnival is not a benign space for Janette, and the freedom it brings is fleeting and temporary. It is important to recognise both the liberatory power and the danger[7] of carnival, in particular for a young woman. Carnival does create a generative chronotope that affords the celebration of difference, of the body, of what is considered to be "low culture," of the bawdy and bizarre. But Janette returns to being a young woman in an alternative high school program, with all the stigma that this involves, after the celebration. In addition, participation in the carnivalesque includes acts of exposure, articulating what others cannot, leading to increased vulnerability. As the context shifts, as the schoolday passes,

Janette experiences worlds where her challenges to the dominant discourse, which are centred by the carnival chronotope, are moved to the periphery and marginalised again. hooks (1990) writes that the margin is at once "a space of radical openness" and a "profound edge"; "locating oneself there is difficult yet necessary. It is not a 'safe' place. One is always at risk" (p. 149). Janette's arrival at university, something that both she and her mother—and I, for that matter—see as a sign of success, can neither be taken to mean that the road was easy nor that her teachers were able to provide safe trespass for the journey. The freedom Janette experienced in the writing class, and in the Canyon Program, was earned in spite of the dangers at the margins.

CONCLUDING THOUGHTS

When addressing the needs of students who are not experiencing success in mainstream high schools, we frequently depend on counselling and social service interventions aimed at helping *them* find success. While these resources are helpful for many, they reflect a re/turn toward privileging a discourse of reprivatisation (Fraser, 1989), which operates to individualise and locate the difficulties that youth face within themselves or in family and domestic problems. The remedy is often individual or family therapy. Reprivatisation discourses constrain political discourse and conversation regarding the experiences of young people who, for whatever reason, do not seem to "fit in" with mainstream schools. They focus on individual pathologies and neglect social structural critiques. For example, why is it that the comprehensive high school model seems to fail so many young people? Why is it that so many young people are being marked as "at risk of school failure"? How do changing economic markets, information technologies, and consumer tendencies influence today's youth? An analysis of chronotopes in mainstream and alternative school contexts, coupled with the experiences of students, offers empirical results that illustrate the possibilities made available to students in the Canyon Program.

Considering time and space across institutional landscapes—along with the way in which students and teachers are positioned within that landscape—may enable us to better construct alternative environments for students to successfully complete high school requirements. Indeed we rarely, if ever, analyse the structure of the program or more specifically, the chronotope that defines and is defined by the experiences of the participants in the program, whether teachers or students. Willis's (1977) seminal work, examining the lives and struggles of working-class youth in public schools, is almost thirty years old and the stories reflected here are not new. However, using an analysis of chronotopes is a different way to re-visit an old issue. It provides a new lens for understanding or seeing the difficulties of students who are alienated and marginalised, and the possibilities afforded to them in flexible and more fluid contexts.

Official and Alternative School Chronotopes

There is a tendency in the official school chronotope to assume *adventure time* and decontextualised space. This chronotope construction is imposed on youth, positioning them as liminal, as in between, as uncomfortably underdeveloped. They await their release from school, doing time until they are deemed "ready" to be released. In the official school chronotope, young people are positioned between childhood and adulthood, and frequently constructed metaphorically as characters in Greek romances. Events and "adventures" happen to them, but they themselves do not change, nor do their actions in the world alter the force of their fate. High school begins with ninth grade and ends with twelfth grade: the two poles of *adventure time*. Between these two poles there are many events, but the students themselves remain unchanged, merely surviving until graduation when "real life" begins.

I would argue that the *adventure time* and decontextualised space of the official school chronotope is the typical or unmarked experience of high school for many youth today. However, Janette's experiences in the Canyon Program offer a refreshing narrative that more closely reflects the margin as an agentic space, an area of resistance, carrying with it both the celebration of difference and the danger that difference signifies in society today. The *carnivalesque* elaborated in Rabaleis' celebration of the Renaissance carnival is lived by Janette. As poet, Janette revels in the body—writing about women's bodies and her own embodiment. She positions herself outside social convention through her body piercing and tattoos. These actions are more than acts of resistance; they are communicative acts that celebrate her freedom, her choices. She does not want to simply survive until graduation. She blends her identities with alacrity, at once the freak and the environmentalist, at once the beat poet and the A student. But the carnival is not a permanent feature of life. It is a temporary fracture within social convention, a fissure in the chronotopes created by and through the dominant discourse in the larger sociocultural context. Janette navigates this disruption with expertise, and with the support of her teachers and peers in the Canyon Program. She grows in relation to her social contexts during high school, successfully graduates, and begins university. Her life, thus far, is a success story both by her own standards and by the standards of contemporary dominant society.

It could be argued that part of Janette's experience, her border work between the carnivalesque and standard school success, may only have been possible given her participation in an alternative high school program. Certainly the students and teachers in the Canyon Program have much to teach us about the importance of relationships, the value of trust and respect, the necessity of flexible chronotopes and negotiation, and a host of other lessons. The us/them mentality common in the main high school between teachers and students was nonexistent in the Canyon Program. Dissolution of this dichotomy fostered an unconditional embrace of students like Janette, who performed "the freak" and revelled in her position "outside" society. From the point of view of the teachers and students, the Canyon Program was a success on several levels: in terms of the numbers of students graduating each year, standardised test scores, and deep and long-term relationships between adults and young people.

Alternative School as Heterotopia

At the time of this ethnography, in the state of Montana alone, there were over forty alternative high school programs and thirty-one had been created within the last six years. While the possibilities afforded to students in alternative programs are both necessary and valuable, seminal work by Goldenberg (1978), along with current research by Troyna and Rizvi (1997), highlight the way in which institutions like schools act as "containers" for difference, segmenting the population and separating out those with certain characteristics. With the Canyon Program, "containment" (Goldenberg, 1978) became obvious in the newspaper articles written about the program and the way the students were treated by some of the store managers on main street. Indeed, these students were perceived by community members as the "alternative" students, and their reasons for being in the Canyon Program were stereotyped—from drug addiction, to pregnancy, to school failure—without mention of perhaps the most important reason for leaving the main high school: the simple fact that, with 2,000 students, it was just too big to respect and address an array of students' shifting identities, needs, and performances (see Vadeboncoeur & Portes, 2002).

Goldenberg (1978) argues that "containment" is a structure through which all forms of oppression express themselves. He notes:

> All forms of oppression seek first and foremost to contain or limit the range of free movement available to a particular group. The containment may be physical or psychological (oftentimes it is both), but its primary function is to increasingly restrict and narrow the scope of possibilities that can be entertained. (p. 4)

The final product "is the development of programs and practices that serve to quarantine a large percentage of the population" (Goldenberg, 1978, p. 8), as if by separating these youth with "contagious" differences, other youth will be protected from their alterity and deviance, and not "infected" by it.

Participation in alternative programs, therefore, offers students a beneficial environment with sometimes troublesome consequences. Indeed, the *alternative high school program* has become a metonym for difference, marginality, and delinquent youth—a modern "heterotopia of deviation" (Foucault, 1986). The alternative high school is a space that isolates young people and their differences from the larger society. A heterotopia is literally "a place of a different order," an actual place that exists outside of normative space (Leontis, 1995). Similar to Bakhtin's carnival, heterotopias are utopias enacted to represent, challenge, and invert other social and political places. Indeed, the extent to which alternative programs serve the dominant discourse by providing a setting within which to contain diverse students, makes such spaces highly problematic.

There is no question that the students who graduated from the Canyon Program in 2000 were marked by their graduation from the "alternative" school, in both positive and negative ways. The richness of their experience within the program may have offset their positioning within society at large. While participants were perceived by community members and by themselves as different, I would like to believe that this alterity helped them to gain a vantage point outside the system: a position that allowed them to critically perceive and engage with the material effects of social structures. Janette's experiences at the Canyon Program achieved this dynamic. Perhaps by being positioned on the margins and embracing a celebratory and dangerous chronotope, Janette was afforded, in Bakhtin's words, a privileged right to be "other" in this world.

NOTES

1. The first part of this title is a play on "the spaces that difference makes" from a discussion of Thirdspace by Soja (1996) and an article written by Soja and Hooper (1993).
2. I problematise the word "alternative" even as I use it. Research by both Raywid (1990, 1994) and Aron (2003) reviews, compiles, and presents typologies of the word, noting in particular that while it was originally used merely to signify educational programs that are different from mainstream programs, it has come to be used in a derogatory fashion more recently. There are problems as well with other words, such as "flexible" and "inclusive." Holdsworth (2004) argues that as long as alternative programs are considered "alternative" they will have little effect on mainstream programs. And I would add, not unproblematically, that in some sense the existence and the necessity of alternative programs is deeply "mainstream."
3. Portions of the chapter were presented at two conferences: first, the physical structure of time and space, at the 5th International Society for Cultural Research and Activity Theory Congress (2002) in Amsterdam, entitled *Changing the chronotope to privilege alterity: A documentary of an "informal" educational context for young people* and second, the identity narratives, at the Annual meeting of the American Education Research Assocation (2003) in Chicago, entitled *"I'm acting it out here and now": The use of chronotopes in the identity narratives of young people.*
4. Relating written texts and the oral texts we produce in conversation, Smith (1987) uses "relations of ruling" to capture the way power is mediated by texts; texts that represent our lived experience are standardised and constituted as abstractions. As general forms of knowledge, they exemplify relations of ruling.

5. This is a pseudonym.
6. All names used here for students and teachers are pseudonyms.
7. I am grateful to my colleague Elizabeth W. Hirst for several conversations regarding "dangerous space." For further discussion, see Hirst and Renshaw (in press).

REFERENCES

Aron, L. Y. (2003). *Towards a typology of alternative education programs: A compilation of elements from the literature*. Washington, DC: The Urban Institute.

Bakhtin, M. M. (1981). *The dialogic imagination: Four essays* (C. Emerson & M. Holquist, Trans.). Austin: University of Texas Press.

Bakhtin, M. M. (1984). *Rabelais and his world* (A. Iswolsky, Trans.). Bloomington: Indiana University Press.

Bakhtin, M. M. (1986). *Speech genres and other late essays* (V. W. McGee, Trans.). Austin: University of Texas Press.

Bloome, D. (2003). Narrative discourse. In A. C. Graesser, M. A. Gernsbacher, & S. R. Goldman (Eds.), *Handbook of discourse processes* (pp. 287–319). Mahwah, NJ: Lawrence Erlbaum.

Bloome, D. & Katz, L. (1997). Literacy as social practice and classroom chronotopes. *Reading and Writing Quarterly, 13*, 205–225.

Bourdieu, P. (1977). *Outline of a theory of practice*. Cambridge, MA: Harvard University Press.

Bourdieu, P. (1991). Language and symbolic power. Cambridge, MA: Harvard University Press.

Bucholtz, M. (1999). "Why be normal?": Language and identity practices in a community of nerd girls. *Language in Society, 28*(2), 203–222.

Chouliaraki, L. & Fairclough, N. (1999). *Discourse in late modernity: Rethinking critical discourse analysis*. Edinburgh: Edinburgh University Press.

Clark, K. & Holquist, M. (1984). *Mikhail Bakhtin*. Cambridge, MA: Harvard University Press.

Fairclough, N. (1995). *Critical discourse analysis: The critical study of language*. London: Longman.

Foucault, M. (1986). Of other spaces. *Diacritics, 16*, 22–27.

Foucault, M. (1975/1995). *Discipline and punish: The birth of the prison* (2nd ed.). New York: Vintage Books.

Fraser, N. (1989). *Unruly practices: Power, discourse, and gender in contemporary social theory*. Minneapolis: University of Minnesota Press.

Gee, J., Allen, A., & Clinton, K. (2001). Language, class, and identity: Teenagers fashioning themselves through language. *Linguistics and Education, 12*, 174–194.

Glaser, B. G. & Strauss, A. L. (1967). *The discovery of grounded theory*. London: Weidenfeld and Nicolson.

Goldenberg, I. I. (1978). *Oppression and social intervention: Essays on the human condition and the problems of change*. Chicago: Nelson-Hall.

Harvey, D. (2000). *Spaces of hope*. Berkeley: University of California Press.

Harvey, D. (2003). *Spaces of capital: Towards a critical geography*. New York: Routledge.

Hirst, E. W. & Renshaw, P. (in press). Diverse voices, dialogue and intercultural learning in a second language classroom. In P. Renshaw & J. van der Linden (Eds.), *Dialogic perspectives on learning, teaching and instruction*. Amsterdam: Kluwer Academic.

Holdsworth, R. (2004, June). *Good practice in learning alternatives*. Learning Choices EXPO Opening Address, Dusseldorp Skills Forum, Sydney, Australia.

hooks, b. (1990). *Yearning*. Boston: South End Press.

Kant, I. (1848/1999). *Critique of pure reason*. (P. Guyer & A. W. Wood, Ed. & Trans.). New York: Cambridge University Press.

Leander, K. (2002). Locating Latanya: The situated production of identity artifacts in classroom interaction. *Research in the Teaching of English, 37*, 198–250.

Leontis, A. (1995). *Topographies of hellenism: Mapping the homeland*. Ithaca, NY: Cornell University Press.

Ochs, E. & Capps, L. (2001). *Living narrative: Creating lives in everyday storytelling*. Cambridge, MA: Harvard University Press.

Panofsky, C. P. (2003). The relations of learning and student social class: Toward re-"socializing" sociocultural learning theory. In A. Kozulin, B. Gindis, V. S. Ageyev, & S. M. Miller (Eds.), *Vygotsky's educational theory in cultural context* (pp. 411–431). Cambridge, UK: Cambridge University Press.

Portes, P. R. & Vadeboncoeur, J. A. (2003). Mediation in cognitive socialization: The influence of socio-economic status. In A. Kozulin, B. Gindis, V. S. Ageyev, & S. M. Miller (Eds.), *Vygotsky's educational theory in cultural context* (pp. 371–392). Cambridge, UK: Cambridge University Press.

Raywid, M. A. (1990). Alternative education: The definition problem. *Changing Schools, 18*, 4–5:10.

Raywid, M. A. (1994). Alternative schools: The state of the art. *Educational Leadership, 52*(1), 26–31.

Smith, D. E. (1987). *The everyday world as problematic*. Boston: Northeastern University Press.

Soja, E. W. (1989). *Postmodern geographies: The reassertion of space in critical social theory*. London: Verso.

Soja, E. W. (1996). *Thirdspace: Journeys to Los Angeles and other real-and-imagined places*. Oxford: Blackwell.

Soja, E. & Hooper, B. (1993). The spaces that difference makes: Some notes on the geographical margins of the new cultural politics. In M. Keith & S. Pile (Eds.), *Place and the politics of identity* (pp. 183–205). London: Routledge.

Troyna, B. & Rizvi, F. (1997). Racialisation of difference and the cultural politics of teaching. In B. J. Biddle, I. Goodson, & T. L. Good (Eds.), *International handbook of teachers and teaching* (pp. 237–265). Boston: Kluwer.

Vadeboncoeur, J. A. & Portes, P. (2002). Students "at risk": Exploring identity from a sociocultural perspective. In D. M. McInerney & S. Van Etten (Eds.), *Research on sociocultural influences on motivation and learning, Vol. 2* (pp. 89–128). Greenwich, CT: Information Age Publishing.

Vadeboncoeur, J. A., Torres, M. N., Swingle, D., & Anesi, J. D. (2000). Voices of service and learning: Preservice teachers writing with adolescents labeled "at risk." *Academic Exchange Quarterly, 4*(4), 53–62.

Vygotsky, L. S. (1978). *Mind in society: The development of higher psychological processes.* Cambridge, MA: Harvard University Press.

Vygotsky, L. S. (1986). *Thought and language.* Cambridge, MA: The MIT Press.

Wertsch, J. V. (1991). *Voices of the mind: A sociocultural approach to mediated action.* Cambridge, MA: Harvard University Press.

Willis, P. (1977). *Learning to labour: How working class kids get working class jobs.* Farnborough, UK: Saxon House.

CHAPTER SEVEN

"Wishing and Doing": Foreshadowing Life Choices in Writing[1]

Judy V. Diamondstone

> ...I know people like this that have, particularly people that have come from
> a poor environment...As soon as they reach a certain level of education and
> sophistication, they don't want to have anything to do with this poor envi-
> ronment because that was like embarrassing...That is not her at all. She is
> very comfortable in [where] she came from, she still has the same friends
> that she had through all of high school, and this is a great source of pleasure
> for her, and she knows that she is not like them...I think that is another rea-
> son why I think this is a great individual...because you know life is still very
> real to her and she has not become lost in whatever you get lost
> in...[H–Int–12–00][2]

The speaker, whom I will call Tom, is speaking about Jocelyn, whose
story is the subject of this chapter. However, it is not only Jocelyn's
story written in the fifth grade that I am concerned with here. This
chapter is also about the relations that form between the story she told
then and the life she is still composing now. Jocelyn is, at the time of
this writing, in a graduate program in the biological sciences. Tom,
quoted above, became Jocelyn's mentor when she applied and was
accepted to an apprenticeship program at the chemical company in
University Town where Tom worked and near to Center City where
Jocelyn lived. It was through her interests in high school science that
Jocelyn initially established a relationship with Tom, a working scientist with an interest in mentoring high school students. Tom
introduced Jocelyn to the professional practices of laboratory work

and report writing, and later to a new job and eventually a new mentor.

There is a great deal more to the story of this apprenticeship, of course, but that is not the story I tell here. I open with Tom's characterization of Jocelyn to show Jocelyn as a subject in a social world, the subject of someone else's story about her. I do this to construct a basis for my story about her—to suggest, from my perspective as an analyst, a narrative that can link the story I analyze below to the life of the storywriter years later. Specifically, I am interested in the relationship between three protagonists: (1) the protagonist construed by Tom as "a great individual"; (2) the protagonist in Jocelyn's self-narratives in interviews with me; and (3) the protagonist of the fictional story she wrote in first-person in fifth grade. From both Tom and Jocelyn's perspectives, based on interviews with me, Jocelyn moved away from the restrictive conditions of a "poor" urban environment while remaining faithful to the concerns and interests of those who lived there. To represent the trajectory of Jocelyn's life in these terms, shared by both Jocelyn and Tom, is to echo the theme of Jocelyn's fifth grade story, and to presciently suggest how that story foreshadows the trajectory defined by her life choices later on. I begin, then, with an intuition of structural analogies between a child's fiction and the life of the writer later on, and proceed to derive terms for further defining those analogies from a close linguistic reading of the fifth grade story.

I begin with some assumptions about what it means to make meaning, and how our development as persons depends on ways of relating meanings in an evaluative order, as narrative does (Bamberg, 1997; Brockmeier & Carbaugh, 2001; Bruner, 2001; Gergen & Gergen, 1986). To this end, I explore how grammatical choices at one level of creating meaning—the choices of wording in a written narrative—might be relevant to choices at a much higher level, at the level of the writer's composition of her own life story. I do not mean to suggest, of course, that the stories we tell determine our lives in any direct or causal way. Rather, persons participate in their own development through authorial acts. My aim is to shift from a psychological to a semiotic perspective on development (Venn, 1984; Walkerdine, 1984) so as to locate developmental principles in the making of meanings—not to overlook social and historical concerns. Meanings are necessarily social and historical; meanings are not delimited by individual minds. At the same time, a semiotic perspective on development must concern the individual by locating the individual in social and historical terms, as an agent, among others, in her own development. To move away from a notion of psychic potential embedded within the individual, I draw attention to the grammar of authorial acts—to a changing potential dialectically produced by individuals acting within and on the social systems of which they are a part.

DEVELOPMENT: A GRAMMAR OF AUTHORIAL ACTS

While I include *choices of wording* in my definition of grammar, I understand *grammar* broadly to be an ordering principle. Construed this way, grammar is not a recipe for static structures, but a structuring potential. I focus first on relations between *utterance* grammar, the subject-predicate relation, and *narrative* grammar, the ordering of events in time from a particular narrative perspective. Every utterance is formed as a subject-predicate relation, which realizes a speaker-addressee relationship in a specific sociocultural context. Here I am following Halliday (1978) in presupposing that grammatical relations are motivated by and responsive to social organization. Accordingly, grammatical choices are motivated by and responsive to the subjectivities of social actors. In addition, *narrative* is a kind of grammar: an ordering principle and a means for rendering experience coherent.

So I start on the assumption that our "being" as persons depends on some system of meaning. Because we act through signifying systems, shared with others, we are able to produce complex and changing artifacts, both material and symbolic, thereby anchoring our lives as individuals in social and cultural terms. As constituents of a larger social reality, we develop in terms of systems of production and consumption that are more than material—they are systems of value and identification. By naming our world, we collectively produce value in excess of our reproductive needs. The "we" implicated here is essentially semiotic and social.

As subjects in complex, post-modern societies, "we" acquire a sense of individuality across temporally bounded activities and distinct associations of others. Our senses of self are accordingly complicated, discontinuous, and often contradictory. Our experience *as* individuals resists definition, classification, and semiosis. For the authorial subject, it invites a reformulation of social categories, affording new terms for subjectivity, entailing a transformation of the social through its subjects.

It is in this sense of a transformative subject that I speak here of development as a grammatical act, a matter that cannot be restricted to a predetermined trajectory. To speak in this way, I need a theory of the subject as it relates to grammar—a theory of how meaning is made. Following Benveniste (1966/1971), let me first posit the subject as a position in language: the subject of what is said, ordinarily taken for granted, or the subject as *theme*. Next, following Halliday (1994), I propose the subject-predicate *relation* to be the minimal grammar for an exchange of meaning. It is the minimal structure of a complete utterance, addressed to someone real or imagined, and, as such, it invites a response (Bakhtin, 1975/1981). Halliday refers to grammatical resources that are integral to the mood system of English grammar as *interpersonal*. They enable an exchange of meaning, and in doing so, index the speaker's perspective, even when the speaker is not the subject of the utterance.[3] These simultaneous functions—the thematic ordering of information and the ordering of interrelating social actors—are realized in the grammar of utterance as ready-made cultural strategies for discursive performance.

I begin with the subject of utterance in order to consider, in elemental terms, the subjectivity of one who speaks, specifically, one who takes up the "I" position in the grammar of English. The subject of speech and the speaking subject are fused in the position of grammatical first-person. To take up the "I" position is to be already positioned in a system of signification. As a user of this system, a cultural agent may, under situational constraints, extend, qualify, and question what has already been said and done. The speaker is positioned in a social system made possible by language. I am only concerned about positions in language and other systems of signification insofar as persons take them up. I am concerned with meanings, which must be made by those who use the grammar of a system based upon what has already been done. I am concerned specifically with the first-person subject position, the position from which a person becomes a subject in a social world. It is the "I" position from which subjectivity is performed and recognized by others.

Now let us consider the person, the subject of much speech and the speaker in innumerable grammatical acts throughout a lifetime. Many positions from which to speak—multiple subjectivities accumulated historically—are available. When people account for their own experiences, they use their turn at interaction to claim a social identity and frame themselves as a subject in discourse. They act as an authorial self—a self narrator. A self-narrative registers the narrator's sense of being over time: "the person I have been" projected forward to "how I want you to see me." Registered in time and space, a self-narrative can index a possible self for life choices later on. I am concerned here specifically with the authorial "I" performance that is self-narrative.

Self-narrative also subjects the speaker's sense of being-over-time to new formulations in response to speaking situations, recontextualizing the subject "I." Thus the subject of self-narrative unfolds in time, through social interaction. Just as the grammar of utterance folds past into present and implicates a speaker's perspective, so does the grammar of narrative. First-person narrative can thus be a means to stage one's own development. From the perspective of grammatical first-person, narrative is a means to extend and elaborate the subject-predicate relation, and thereby rework one's own subjectivity.

The conditions for the development of persons are not delimited by language use; they depend on the world that language points to. However, that world, of which we are a part, or what we can know of, is largely dependent on language use. Development may be staged linguistically, and it is this staging of what is possible that I am concerned with here: development as a grammatical act. Development is a grammatical act that selectively folds past experience into present circumstances, thereby creating new understandings, new subjects, and new subject relations.

LOCATING JOCELYN

In this chapter, I offer one illustration of a semiotic perspective on development, based on a remarkable story written by a fifth grade student, Jocelyn. Jocelyn was the first in her family to graduate from college and will be one of the very few in her high school cohort to complete graduate school.

Tom, Jocelyn's mentor quoted at the beginning of this chapter, told me that Jocelyn had taken a trip to Puerto Rico to learn more about her Latina heritage. In interviews with me, Jocelyn alluded to herself not specifically as Latina, but as a person of color. When explaining, for instance, that she preferred high school to elementary school, she described how there were more people like her in high school. Her high school, the only public high school in Center City, was predominantly made up of people of color, most of whom, though, were African American. Her elementary school had been predominantly white. In a later interview with me, Jocelyn defined her community as people who were without resources when they were growing up, thus highlighting social class as a primary influence categorizing her experience. I mention these several identifications—ethnicity, race, and social class—to underscore Jocelyn's investment in each of them, and to indicate that they overlap implicitly, if not explicitly, in complicated ways in Jocelyn's self-narratives.

As we would expect, gender also significantly influenced Jocelyn's accounts of who she was and who she wanted to be. These narratives were often pointedly refracted through her relationship with her mother. Jocelyn's social landscape was dominated by her mother in childhood. Her fifth grade story told of her desire for individuation and how she resolved it at the time, a resolution that was reinscribed in her life choices as a young adult. It is Jocelyn's story that first illuminated for me how authorial acts can mediate relations between wishing and doing.

Wishing

Through processes of identification and resistance, we imagine ourselves in imaginary worlds—our selves as we *wish* to be. Because we are subject to multiple identifications and our desires are expectably conflicting, it requires imaginative labor to forge a position from which we wish to speak. Through authorial speech, we can "wrest" language (Bakhtin, 1975/1981) from the social formations that shape our experience and use it to formulate alternatives—*possible* worlds, *possible* selves.

Doing

Possible worlds can be realized only through our participation in actual worlds and in interaction with others. It is in their address to a speaker, and their allusions to and representations of one who has already spoken, that others afford one a place in the world, the position of social subject from which to speak. Actual worlds constrain what is possible for the subject to imagine by providing the resources for imagining.

FIGURING THE WORLD OF DISCOURSE

Jocelyn's relationship to her mother was a highly salient theme, both in the fifth grade narrative (shown below) and in her self-reflections during our interviews, conducted four years after she graduated high school. It is not surprising that mother-daughter relations would be at the heart of a daughter's project of identity. From the perspective of developmental psychology, the caregiver-infant relationship is an integral unit out of which developing children progressively distinguish themselves. I treat the theme of mother-daughter relations as a culturally *figured world* to which Jocelyn's story responds.

The term *figured world* highlights the imaginary dimension of cultural practices and the social institutions that sustain them (Holland, Lachicotte, Skinner, & Cain, 1998). Vygotsky (1978) observed that a child learns through play to detach an object, such as a broom, from its meaning and to assign another meaning, such as "horse," to the broom. The new meaning "pivots" the child into a pretend world. The degree to which children treat the pretend world as real allows objects and their relations, including the social roles of children themselves, to be transformed (Vygotsky, 1978). Holland et al. (1998) extend this insight to the taken-for-granted world of adults, who also treat fabricated worlds as real—specifically the specialized activity systems of cultural institutions.

> A figured world is peopled by the figures, characters, and types who carry out its tasks and who also have styles of interacting within, distinguishable perspectives on, and orientations toward it. (Holland, et al., 1998, p. 51)

In related terms, Gee (1999) defines a big "D" Discourse, for example, the Discourse of lawyers, or the Discourse of biochemists, or even the Discourse of students-of-color-in-the-honors-track-of-their-high-school, as an "identity kit" that affords social roles, values, a universe of meanings and concerns, and ways of talking, thinking, and acting for its participants. The specialized activity systems of a culture, given the degree to which they become taken for granted, sedimented, and socially available practices, are collective fabrications that must be treated as real by would-be participants. Both terms—*figured world* and *Discourse*—implicate a thematic framing that stabilizes the possibilities for meaning, saying, and doing across space and time, a framing that endures beyond the participation of any individual. But while *Discourse* highlights the objective, institutional, and enduring character of culturally recognized practices, the *figured world* highlights the performative dimension of Discourse. While big "D" Discourse emphasizes the *limit* on ways of combining interests, values, and roles available within a particular field, the term "figured world" implicates a particular view of the landscape against which improvisations take place. Big "D" Discourse, as the agent selectively experiences it, is from the agent's perspective. I am, thus, treating a child's discourse about wishing to be free of a mother's constraints as indexically related to the Discourse through which children in European American cultures try out their independence from caregivers. I am presuming that children's conflicting desires about their mother's world are not private but widely shared. They describe a taken-for-granted world of mother-daughter relations, itself arguably an effect of urbanized, modernist cultures.

Mother-Daughter Relations

I first interviewed Jocelyn during the year after she graduated college. She was living with her mother, who worked at a biochemical company in a nearby suburb and in the process of applying to graduate schools. The biographical details most salient in our interviews concern her relationship to her mother. When I asked her to describe her mother, Jocelyn said:

> ...*we're a lot alike, but I'm kind of trained to change that.* I don't know, she's very quiet, well she talks a lot, well I talk a lot too with the people that we are

close to, like friends and family, but in front of strangers she's very quiet
which she's trying to get out of, and I am too. And uh, I don't know, *she's
kind of just very homey and just likes the very traditional and just likes a homey
family life. I like to travel and do things and she's always, she says that I look for
danger.* [J–Sum–nd–2000, italics added]

Jocelyn is the younger of two daughters. When she was three years
old, her mother divorced and moved into her own mother's house.
Jocelyn's mother supported herself by caring for the children of
neighbors and relatives in her home. Later she worked in day care. In
our interview, Jocelyn's mother told me that she *understood* children,
with a special emphasis on "understanding," as if to contrast her own
sympathetic grasp of a child's world with that of other adults who see
less of it. She may have been aware, through childcare licensing programs, of popular advice on preparing children for literacy. If so, it
resonated with lessons from her own struggles as someone who had
entered school without early literacy experiences. She told me that
school had been hard for her, and she did not want it to be hard for
her children. She read to even very young children in day care, and to
her own children until they could read better than she could. She also
told me that she played educational games, did art projects with
them, took them on trips outside the home, and helped them with
homework until it was too hard for her. At that point, they had to
"figure it out for themselves."

Jocelyn's mother was very strict with her daughters. Both she and
Jocelyn stressed this. She prohibited them from dating until they were
sixteen and made sure to meet the parents of each of their friends. The
girls were required to report where they were when they were not at
home and to account for whatever they did. Jocelyn's mother walked
Jocelyn to school until the fourth grade, even though the school was
only a few blocks from home. She would not allow her to attend a
better school that was further and required bussing. She also wanted
Jocelyn to attend a nearby college and cried when Jocelyn decided instead to attend college in another state.

In short, Jocelyn's mother was both loving and strict, a self-
sacrificing mother who channeled all her intelligence, creativity, and
determination into raising two daughters in a city, which, in her own
words, "wasn't very safe back then."

THE MAGIC RING

In 1986/87, when Jocelyn was in third grade, her school district began collecting on an annual basis prompted narrative writing from all students in her cohort as preparation for the eleventh grade High School Proficiency Test, first administered in 1994. The same prompt was assigned in both fifth and seventh grades (Buddemeier & Raivetz, 1987; Raivetz, 1996). Although I do not have the exact words of these prompts, I do have the wording of other prompts, and have reviewed the archive of student texts responding to them. I was able to infer from the many different versions of the text and the wording of other prompts that the directions went something like this: "You decide to explore a room in your house, like the attic or basement where you don't usually go. You find a special box that has your name on it. You open the box. Tell a story about what you find." Students had forty-five minutes to write.

The narrative prompts addressed the students in the second person pronoun "you," inviting them to write a fictional account in the first-person, as if it were really happening to them. The prompts were also written in present tense, inviting students to write as if the events were being narrated as they were happening. First-person narrative is a familiar genre even to young children, but typically stories are told about events that have already happened. Like virtually all the students, Jocelyn responded in first-person, but wrote in simple past.

The following is Jocelyn's fifth grade story. I have parsed the narrative with subheadings in capitals. Words in the text are coded in two ways. First, in **bold italics** to indicate interpersonal grammar, such as **mood**—imperative and interrogative; **modality**—possibility/obligation; and **polarity**—negation. Second, words [in brackets] are other linguistic resources for indexing the subjectivity of the narrator, such as verbal/mental processes, lexis of appraisal, and intensity. Please note, in addition to being bracketed, lexis of appraisal is also underscored and *intensity* is also italicized. Finally, **_polarity_** is also underscored. These codes are further elaborated in the discussion that follows the story.

The Magic Ring

INITIATING EVENT 1. Mental processes

1.	Sitting on the bed with **_nothing_** to do and **_nobody_** to play with
2.	[I thought] about things.

3.	Then [I thought],
4.	**_"Why don't I_** explore the attic?"

INITIATING EVENT 2. Material processes

5.	So I took a flashlight
6.	and headed to the attic.

7.	In the attic there was lots of cobwebs and dust
8.	but that **_didn't_** stop me.

9.	While walking around I found a little box with a note attached to it.
10.	I picked it up
11.	and blew the dust off of it.

12.	It had my name engraved on it.

INITIATING EVENT 3. Verbal processes: dialog

13.	I [read] the note.
14.	It [said],
15.	["Dear Julie,]
16.	In this box there is a [special] ring.
17.	It has three wishes.
18.	**_Just tell_** it what you want
19.	and it will give it to you.
20.	When you've made all 3 wishes
21.	**_get_** a box
22.	and [**_write_** the name] of your youngest cousin.
23.	[**_Write_** a note] like this one
24.	and **_put_** it back in this closet.
25.	From: your ancestors."

INITIATING EVENT 4. Mixed processes

26.	I opened the box.

27.   In it was a [beautiful] ring.
28.   I put it on
29.   and went back downstairs.

30.   [I thought] of what I could wish for.

EVENT SEQUENCE # 1

First wish

31.   Suddenly my mom [called] me
32.   and [said] that it's time for dinner.

33.   We were having liver, spinach and lima beans.

34.   Then [I said],
35.   ["I wish] we *could* eat some McDonald's food!"

36.   Suddenly the food became McDonald's food
37.   and [I remembered] about the ring.

Second wish

38.   After I ate
39.   I went back in my room.

40.   Again [I thought] of things to wish for.

41.   ["I wish] I *could* do [anything I want,"]
42.   [I said].

43.   After that day I did everything
44.   and my mom ***didn't*** care.

45.   I saved the last wish
46.   till I was older.

EVENT SEQUENCE # 2 (years later)

Third wish

47.   Ten years passed
48.   and I was 21.

49.   I [*still*] lived with my mom.

50.   One day I used the last wish.
51.   [I wished] I would meet [*the man of my dreams*].

52.   I met him that same day.

CRISIS

Fourth wish

53.   Then I got a phone call.
54.   My mom had a heart attack
55.   and was in the hospital.

56.   I drove over there with the man I met.

57.   The doctor [said] she was going to die.
58.   I took the ring off my finger
59.   and [said],
60.   ["I wish] my mom __*wouldn't*__ die."

61.   __*Nothing*__ happened.

62.   Then [I remembered] I used all my wishes
63.   so she died.

+ EVALUATION

64.   That week I __*couldn't*__ stop [crying].

65.   I *could have* saved her
66.   but I [*wasted*] my last wish.

RESOLUTION—action

67.   Instead of putting the ring in a box,
68.   I took a hammer
69.   and [smashed] the ring.

RESOLUTION—result

70.   Suddenly I find myself back in the attic.

71.   I went back in time.
72.   My mom was alive
73.   and I was [only] 11 years old.

CODA

74.   I didn't find the ring
75.   but when I became 21 again,
76.   my mom didn't die
77.   and I didn't meet [the man of my dreams],

+ EVALUATION

78.   but I lived [happily] with my mom.

The End.

Interpretation of Narrative Structure

I have parsed Jocelyn's narrative according to progressive stages or functional "moves." My decisions reflect what I perceive to be generic elements of both fairytale, such as Initiating Sequence and Sequent Events, and self-narrative, such as Crisis, Evaluation, and Resolution (Hasan, 1996). The story, organized around an extended wish sequence, draws on the fairytale genre, which is a readily available cultural vehicle for figuring wishes and fears. But the story also progresses to a turning point (Bruner, 2001), due not to fate or accident, but to a change in the protagonist's thinking and feeling. Rather than positing a universal value, as the moral of a fairytale would, the evaluative framing given at the end characterizes the world of the storyteller. Such structural elements typify self-narratives, which individualize the lives of their heroes and antiheroes (Bruner, 2001).

In the Initiating Sequence that sets the stage for what is to follow, I marked shifts in grammatical patterns, specifically, the types of processes encoded in primary verbs, or the kinds of experience reported by the narrative "I." In the Sequent Events, I divided episodes at a major, temporal disjuncture—a ten year gap—which reflects a shift in significance of the episodes.

Interpersonal Resources

I have also highlighted the various linguistic resources that signal the writer's *presence* in the text—those that fall within the range of the *interpersonal metafunction* as defined by authors such as Halliday (1994), Martin (2000), and White (2000, n.d.), as well as Quigley (2000) and Hunston and Thompson (2000). Halliday (1994) contends that language as a system developed in response to contextual pressures to fulfill basic social and cognitive functions within human society, including the primary function of language to negotiate relationships required for the exchange of goods and services. In every interaction between a speaker and addressee, speakers' utterances position participants in relation to others and to the content of the utterance itself. It is predominantly the resources of language that serve an interpersonal metafunction by registering the speaker or writer's stance toward characters and events in the story and toward an audience, both of which index the subjectivity of the speaker or writer. These include constituents of the mood system, such as negation and modality, processes of projection (mental and verbal processes), verbal processes that signal dialog and/or reported speech, and signs of affect, including judgment, appreciation, and the like (White, n.d.). While these categories inform the reading that follows, they are more fully and precisely explicated elsewhere (see Halliday, 1994; Martin, 2000; White, 2000, n.d.).

READING "THE MAGIC RING"

The Subjunctive Subject

Interpersonal resources in the introductory passage of Jocelyn's fifth grade narrative are various. Note the negation (e.g., nobody, nothing) in the beginning of the narrative. Negation implies a resistant reading of reality; it opens a subjunctive space, the *irreal*. To assert the negative is to allow that things could be otherwise. Notice also the projected clauses (the narrator thinking to herself, her ancestors instructing her), which mark a rhetorical space of engagement, both inter-psychologically, with others (ancestors she does not know, aspects of a past she must imagine), and intra-psychologically with herself (as she knows herself at the moment). Although the ancestors speak directly to the narrator in quoted speech and speak in imperatives, their demands are actually offers: they offer wishes and desired futures. The narrator is under no obligation to accept the offer, but she is obligated to respond to it somehow. That obligation opens the space of the narrative. We have at the outset a highly *subjunctive* social space, which makes room for semiogenesis (meaning-making)—the staging of possibilities. This is the authorial environment, which, through grammatical first-person, indexes the subjectivity of the writer and, through the grammar of narrative, figures a world of mother-daughter relations.

Wish Fulfillment

In the subjunctive space construed by the introductory passages, the narrator also acts agentively. She finds a box with a note attached and a magic ring inside; her ancestors speak to her and grant her *three wishes*. Her mother then calls her to the dinner table. Once interpellated into her mother's world, the narrator wishes for the world to be otherwise. She makes three wishes which are granted and *a fourth illegal wish* which is not granted.

By examining the first three wishes in relation to the world as it was initially presented in the story, the following oppositions, tensions between what *is* and what is *wanted*, are set up:

WHAT JOCELYN HAS	WHAT JOCELYN WANTS
#1 *liver, spinach, & lima beans*	*some McDonalds food*
#2 *[by implication, restrictions imposed by mom]*	*I wish I could do anything I want...and my mom didn't care*
#3 *Mom*	*the man of my dreams*

What she *has* is a healthy, home-cooked meal; what she *wants* is McDonalds—a generic, mass-produced meal. What she *has* is strict limits on her free time; what she *wants* is to be able to do whatever she wants without her mother worrying. The third wish occurs ten years after the first two wishes: what she *has* when she grows up is Mom; what she *wants* is the man of her dreams. In sum, she wants to find herself beyond the boundaries of her mother's world. This is the first figuration.

Crisis: Refiguring Mother-Daughter Relations

The third wish occurs in an imagined future, immediately followed by a phone call. Here, the narrator is addressed not by her ancestors but by a stranger, a doctor, who does not report the wonderful news that she can have her wishes fulfilled, but the terrible news that her mother has had a heart attack and is going to die. The narrator then utters a fourth illegal wish for her mother not to die, which is not granted. The third wish, which realizes a final separation from mom, is fraught with ambivalence, which is figured in the fourth, illegal wish, to bring her mother back. The third wish projects a future, one in which the man of her dreams would effectively replace her mother. The third wish, then, precipitates a crisis, because the protagonist is not willing to live entirely free of her mom.

While the first three "legal" wishes defy the taboos imposed by "mom" in lived experience (before wishes are fulfilled), the fourth *illegal* wish seeks to re-consecrate life with mom. In response to the crisis—the narrator's inability to save her mother's life—the narrator smashes the ring, which unravels all the wishes but the last, illegal one: she "goes back in time," as can happen only in a storied space. Life returns to what it was before the first three wishes were granted. This is the final figuration of mother-daughter relations.

The narrator's first three wishes demarcate the terms of the writer's (Jocelyn's) ambivalence. They are the terms through which Jocelyn, the authorial subject, tells her story—a fictional, first-person narrative. The story of mother-daughter relations, which is the figured world that dominates Jocelyn's childhood, is an anchor of healthy identification and the reaching beyond. I suggest that Jocelyn's imagining of individuation from her mother serves as a heuristic for actual individuation within an autobiographical project. The text itself, as a predication on the theme of mother-daughter relations, can be related, I propose, by Jocelyn herself or by an observer like myself, to what Jocelyn in biographical time (distinguished from Jocelyn at the time of writing) says and does. Like the dynamic staging of the text itself, each authorial move sets up the possibilities for another one.

The Turning Point

Let's *reconsider* now what was effected in this "space of authoring" of the fifth grade narrative. The introduction, where negation, projection, and dialogue open a space of possibility, sets up the wish sequence. The wishing and wish *fulfillment* lead to crisis—the mother's death—which is followed by a highly emotional moment, the narrator cries for a whole week. This is the first moment when the narrator inscribes what she *feels*. The subjunctive up until this point was a flat projection, a space of wishing without marked emotional content. Here, the narrator is not wishing, but feeling—a shift in tone within the overall narrative register. It is at this moment that the narrator announces to herself: "I could have saved her but I wasted my last wish."

Although the grammatical processes in this statement are not mental processes, the statement heightens the reflective space of the opening scene—in which the narrator sat thinking to herself, line #2, and prompted herself with internal questions, line #4—because here the narrator *comments upon* her own past actions. She inscribes on her wish for separation her simultaneous love for her mother, and on her sense of self, a sense of responsibility, realized in the modal "could." She turns around on her own figured world of ambivalence and, by smashing the ring, inscribes a resolution: desire for individuation from her mother. This figured world of ambivalence is both fully imagined and then resolved by the fifth grade Jocelyn by returning to the circumference of mother's world.

Here then is the turning point, in which the protagonist's story changes direction because of a shift in the protagonist's cognitive state. Notably this turning points back toward a familiar, already-given world, away from an imaginary alternative. Nevertheless, the effect is to produce, in the naming of wishes and then choosing to unravel them, a distinctive sense of self (fully imagined) in the figured terrain of mother-daughter relations.

Dispositional Grammar

Considered in context of the writer's life-world, the writing of this story in school is but one move on the paths of identification and individuation that the autobiographical Jocelyn has yet to take. As we will see, it is not the structure of returning to mother's world that is reproduced, but a kind of dispositional grammar—a way of relating wishes and choices. In *The Magic Ring*, the protagonist recalculates what she wants and embraces her reality as a transformed subject. The story registers the option of learning about the value of one's world by reaching beyond it—reaching, turning, and changing. The narrative, as such, is a resource for an autobiographical project in which the relations between wishing and doing would be worked out over time.

RELOCATING JOCELYN

Now let's jump ahead from fifth grade to the year after college, by revisiting the quotation cited earlier, where Jocelyn compares herself to her mother.

> *.... we're a lot alike, but I'm kind of trained to change that.* I don't know, she's very quiet, well she talks a lot, well I talk a lot too with the people that we are close to, like friends and family, but in front of strangers she's very quiet which she's trying to get out of, and I am too. And uh, I don't know, *she's kind of just very homey and just likes the very traditional and just likes a homey family life. I like to travel and do things and she's always, she says that I look for danger.* [J–Int–Sum–nd–2000, italics added]

Jocelyn described her mother in reference to herself, stating that they were "a lot alike," enumerating two ways in which they were similar: they both talk a lot "with the people we are close to," but with others they are "quiet." Both Jocelyn and her mother are trying "to get out of" being quiet around strangers and in new situations.

Jocelyn, however, qualified her opening statement that she and her mother were a lot alike by adding, "but I'm kind of trained to change that." Moreover, she concluded her utterance by focusing on a significant difference between them: her mother was "homey" and "traditional"; Jocelyn liked to "travel and do things." Jocelyn reached beyond the circumference of her mother's world. Her mother insightfully said she "reached for danger." In fact, Jocelyn took risks within the calculus of her relations to a familiar world, which she elaborated over many authorial acts. Jocelyn started dating before she was sixteen without telling her mother. She went outside the state to attend college, despite her mother's tears. She took vacations with girlfriends, and when she met a young man in Mexico, she took vacations to be with him too. But Jocelyn was also living with her mother after college, when I interviewed her. When she went away to college, she made sure her mother visited, met her friends, saw her dorm, and felt okay about Jocelyn's living situation—that it was safe. She yoked her mother to her own expanding world.

Trained to Change

Jocelyn said she was "kind of trained" to change the ways in which she was like her mother. Ideally, the institution of public schooling guarantees that students are introduced to worlds beyond those which figure in the activities and artifacts in even the most privileged homes and neighborhoods, and certainly beyond those available to impoverished families in poorer areas. Schools are supposed to introduce students to the advances in knowledge and technology our institutions and economy depend upon. Schools employ teachers that students have never met, often from outside the area, who can thus provide new role models. As we know, schools do not serve this function for all students. But for Jocelyn, they did. When Jocelyn said, "I'm kind of trained to change," she invoked her schooling, and her apprenticeship with Tom as expressions of being different from her mom.

The story of that apprenticeship warrants telling elsewhere. I mention it here again, as in the beginning of this chapter, to frame Jocelyn's expanding autobiographical story beyond the fifth grade, beyond her family, in terms provided by someone who knew her well. As Jocelyn's mentor, Tom appreciated the "huge gap" between excelling in high school science and practicing science as a professional:

> ...figuring out if you want to end up playing the big game of science...what kind of skills you need to start developing.... (It's) not something you can say okay...at the end of this course I will know how to write...I mean you

have to build on this for year after year after year and it just takes such a huge amount of time and how do you get a student to understand what the world of writing is about? (H–Int–12–00)

Interestingly, Tom characterized Jocelyn's journey into the professional practices of a scientist as a journey into a world of writing, as if she had yet to learn to write. Of course, Tom was not referring to the writing of fictional narratives, nor to writing in first-person. He was referring to writing in the big game of science, in which the self is, supposedly, not a subject. The Discourse (Gee, 1999) of science thematizes *things*; it construes a taxonomic universe, in which happenings are turned into states and the specialized objects of scientific practice. Scientists serve not as a subject in a world of wishes, affections, and fears, but as a faithful observer of a supposedly objective universe (Bazerman, 1988; Halliday & Martin, 1993). To become a scientist, Jocelyn had to figure the world accordingly. As a neophyte, she had to learn to represent the obdurate materiality of chemical processes in "objective" time and space, and to know herself in relation to unfamiliar others in more professional rather than autobiographical terms. She would do so in a way that Tom would represent as the performance of "a great individual." And Jocelyn would later, when applying to graduate school, reflect on her high school student-self and wonder at the difference. Yet she also learned, as she eventually had to, that Tom did not know everything and that she had to make her own decisions about her writing and her future (J–Int–1–18–01).

Grammatical First-Person as a Temporal Pivot

How might the figured world of mother-daughter relations, indexed in the fifth grade story Jocelyn wrote, relate to the figured world of scientific practice that Jocelyn was apprenticed into? What could link the circumscribed world of childhood with the expanding (but also contracting) universe of professionalization? Only the grammatical first-person, and the autobiographical subject named here as Jocelyn, who spoke through it. Jocelyn wrote the story as a school assignment. Jocelyn chose to take an internship with Tom. Jocelyn spoke in first-person in interviews with me. She described her relations to Tom, like her relation to her mother, in a way that evoked the protagonist of her fifth grade narrative, even though that story was written in response to an assignment embedded in the school district's language arts practices, i.e., in a figured world that was not figured in the story itself. Yet, because the assignment invited writing in grammatical first-person, it invited reference to the writer's world in the story-world. In the story, Jocelyn wrote about a protagonist whose family life mirrored her own: after being granted liberation from a constraining world, she discovers the cost of liberation and chooses to return to the circumference of that world.

Tracing a similar narrative, the autobiographical Jocelyn made the choice repeatedly, in the years following her writing of the story, to embrace the world she came from, even as she acquired resources that linked her to other distant worlds. In doing so, the autobiographical actor, like the writer of the story, chose the terms by which the subject, indexed by grammatical first-person, would be defined.

Like but Not Like

Let's return once again to the opening quote of this chapter. At the end of the passage, Tom states that Jocelyn:

> ...is very comfortable in [where] she came from, she still has the same friends that she had through all of high school, and this is a great source of pleasure for her, and she knows that she is not like them...I think that is another reason why I think this is a great individual...because you know life is still very real to her and she has not become lost in whatever you get lost in...[H–Int–12–00]

Tom states, "She knows she is not like them." By "them," Tom is referring to Jocelyn's friends in high school. I interpret Tom to mean by "a great individual" someone who does not get lost in all there is to get lost in that Jocelyn was someone whose professional identity would not eclipse her social history. In the Honors Track of the city's only public high school, Jocelyn knew that she was like her friends—a person of color and an Honors student. But in pursuing a graduate degree and a career as a laboratory scientist, Jocelyn moved beyond the circumference of her friends' world.

"Them" might be generalized to refer to all those in her past Jocelyn still identified with when she chose to pursue a career in the sciences. In interviews, I tried to elicit from Jocelyn the dimensions on which she felt solidarity with others from her past. Whenever Jocelyn spoke to me about her future, she made reference to her past—to where she came from:

Judy: Can you...When you talk about you know, where you are going and what is important to you, your values, your community comes up a lot...Can you say more about what that means? Community?

Jocelyn: I guess to me, community would be people who were raised in the same type of situation that I was and with not as many resources or as much guidance to succeed or to go onto college or have a career...And in order to serve them you have to get the resources and get your own guidance, if that makes any sense...Or take advantage of what you know in order to come back and tell them what is out there. [J–Int–Spr–nd–01]

Jocelyn knew herself as different from the dominant culture but like those who were also different on the several dimensions already mentioned in the introduction to this chapter: ethnicity (her Puerto Rican heritage was important to her); "race" (she identified with the population of her high school, which was predominantly students of color); and social class. As a Latina raised by a single working mother, she had grown up in an environment without resources.

In Jocelyn's self-narrative commentary on the term "community" she shared with me, "I" indexes not the protagonist of a fictional narrative responding to her "ancestors," but the protagonist in the speaker's own unfolding life story. That protagonist now claims a *collective* identity, a subjectivity that extends to those whose interests she claims as her own. It is an ideological investment, one that does not subsume her person but one that invokes a sense of responsibility from her emergent, academically and professionally, successful self.

Dislocations, Expansions, and Dispositional Grammar

When addressing herself to me, a university researcher, and reflecting on her own becoming, Jocelyn opens a subjunctive space of rhetorical engagement in which her agency and her feelings of responsibility predominate. As she told me, she feels obligated—she has to—get the resources, the guidance. She has to take advantage of what is available to her, if she is to come *back*, to tell others what is out there. The opposition here is not between what the protagonist has and what she wants, but between what the protagonist *has* and what others like her *ought* to have. Jocelyn identifies with her past, with a younger self, and would yoke what is out *there* to what was *here* for Jocelyn growing up and still *here* for many others. Jocelyn understands her trajectory into "the big game of science" as a means to widen the scope of *here* for others like her, and to bring the resources of a wider world, such as medical cures, to them.

Referring to the "intense contradictions" experienced by (white, feminist) working-class academics, Hey (2003) discusses crossing class boundaries as a kind of "chosen self-alienation" (p. 327). She suggests that sustained identification with a working-class past is a willful "psychic and political defense against the truth" (p. 331), a denial that one has become alienated from a past one can never return to. While Jocelyn's relation to her past seems, from my interviews with her, less alienated, she no doubt has experienced the "intense contradictions" of moving beyond the social class parameters that defined her past and still define the present for many of her high school peers. According to Hey (2003), social class relocation is a "psychic territory" structured as "longing, being, becoming, un/becoming, remaking and unmaking" (p. 329)—reaching, turning, and changing.

Individuation Is Not Only Individualization

A child's individuation from her mother foreshadows the often overlapping, sometimes recurrent identifications and processes of individuation that will motivate her learning and spur development throughout her life. Presumably, the meanings she narratively ascribes to her most intimate relations somehow inform her relations to others and choices of action in the future.

Jocelyn's way of relating wishes and choices in *The Magic Ring* was transformed in the context of her life later on into a means to connect the past to her expanding world. The expansion of her world was *intentionally*, that is, authorially, related to her past, across different fields of interests, different networks of relationships, and different subjectivities.

THE GRAMMATICALIZATION OF HISTORY IN PERSON

To sustain a sense of "self" across such different figured worlds, changing circumstances, and changing subjectivities requires imaginative labor—the story about who one is, and who one wants to be or not to be, must be continually reworked. That story, in each instantiation, makes available a sense of being-over-time that is projected forward—a way of ordering experience for social action. Collective identities—identifications with those who share one's interests and concerns—can span fields of action and join networks of relationship. Collective identities within families, groups, and discourse communities can thus provide for the individuals who invoke them a kind of coherence across discontinuous space and time. The authorial subject is one who works and reworks multiple identities into some kind of coherence. Identities that frame wishes and mediate choices are a kind of "higher level artifact," a means by which people, as authorial subjects, may direct their own behavior (Holland, 2003, p. 6).

As in Holland's (2003) discussion of identities as higher level artifacts, so in her book, *Composing a Life*, Bateson (1989) argues that a life must be deliberately, determinedly improvised, when intergenerational continuities are disrupted, as they often are in postindustrial nations, especially for women. To make a life cohere requires improvisation, an orchestration of narrative (accounting for), dispositional (wishing for), and actional (doing of) elements. When considered in semiotic terms, *development* can be understood as an open-ended improvisation that agentive subjects engage in when they turn around on themselves, recalculate what is important, and who they want to be. In the broad sense in which I use the term, the *grammar* of development can be thought of as principles for improvisatorial composing of an unfolding autobiographical identity whose coherence is always emergent and contingent.

NOTES

1. This chapter extends a presentation for the American Anthropological Association given in 2002 in New Orleans. The writer I discuss is one of a cohort in an urban school district whose written texts from third grade through graduation were collected in an archive that was, some years later, handed over to me by Richard Buddemeier, the Language Arts Supervisor at the time. I was able to locate and

interview some of the graduates about their literacy history and current uses of literacy. The original study was supported by a post-doctoral fellowship from the National Academy of Education, 2001. All identifying names have been replaced by pseudonyms.

2. Interviews are referenced by interviewee (for publication purposes, a single initial); type of data (Int), and date (month–day–year: 00–00–00), or, if the exact date is unknown, the season–no–date–year (e.g., Spr–nd–01).

3. "Interpersonal grammar" includes the requisite finite marking on a verb form, which encodes the temporality of the utterance with respect to the time of speaking. (In "John catches the ball," for example, the "es" ending marks "catch" as the finite verb and indicates that the action occurs as the speaker speaks. It anchors the utterance to speaker time.) The resources of interpersonal grammar also include optional elements (modality and polarity) and, at the level of discourse, the resources of appraisal, as noted in the section in this chapter on *The Magic Ring*.

REFERENCES

Bakhtin, M. M. (1975/1981). Discourse in the novel. In M. Holquist (Ed.), *The dialogic imagination: Four essays by M. M. Bakhtin* (pp. 259–422). Austin: University of Texas Press.

Bamberg, M. (1997). A constructivist approach to narrative development. In M. Bamberg (Ed.), *Narrative development: Six approaches* (pp. 89–132). Mahwah, NJ: Lawrence Erlbaum.

Bateson, M. C. (1989). *Composing a life*. New York: The Atlantic Monthly Press.

Bazerman, C. (1988). *Shaping written knowledge: The genre and activity of the experimental article in science*. Madison: University of Wisconsin Press.

Benveniste, E. (1966/1971). *Problems in general linguistics*. Coral Gables, FL: University of Miami Press.

Brockmeier, J. & Carbaugh, D. (Eds.). (2001). *Narrative and identity: Studies in autobiography, self, and culture*. Philadelphia: John Benjamins.

Bruner, J. (2001). Self-making and world-making. In J. Brockmeier & D. Carbaugh (Eds.), *Narrative and identity: Studies in autobiography, self, and culture* (pp. 25–38). Amsterdam: John Benjamins.

Buddemeier, R. & Raivetz, M. (1987). '95 or bust: Studying writing in an urban district as the class of '95 heads toward a high risk, statewide graduation test. Unpublished paper, Trenton Public Schools.

Gee, J. P. (1999). *An introduction to discourse analysis: Theory and method*. New York: Routledge.

Gergen, K. & Gergen, M. (1986). Narrative form and the construction of psychological science. In T. Sarbin (Ed.), *Narrative psychology: The storied nature of human conduct* (pp. 22–44). New York: Praeger.

Halliday, M. A. K. (1978). *Language as social semiotic: The social interpretation of language and meaning*. London: Edward Arnold.

Halliday, M. A. K. (1994). *An introduction to functional grammar*. London: Edward Arnold.

Halliday, M. A. K. & Martin, J. R. (1993). *Writing science: Literacy and discursive power*. Pittsburgh, PA: University of Pittsburgh Press.

Hasan, R. (1996). The nursery tale as a genre. In C. Cloran, D. Butt, & G. Williams (Eds.), *Ways of saying, ways of meaning: Selected papers of Ruqaiya Hasan* (pp. 51–72). London: Cassell.

Hey, V. (2003). Joining the club? Academia and working-class femininities. *Gender and Education, 15*(3), 319–335.

Holland, D. (2003). *People in activity: A cultural-historical approach to identity, agency, and social change*. Unpublished manuscript, University of North Carolina, Chapel Hill.

Holland, D., Lachicotte, W., Jr., Skinner, D., & Cain, C. (1998). *Identity and agency in cultural worlds*. Cambridge, MA: Harvard University Press.

Hunston, S. & Thompson, G. (Eds.). (2000). *Evaluation in text: Authorial stance and the construction of discourse*. New York: Oxford University Press.

Martin, J. R. (2000). Beyond exchange: APPRAISAL systems in English. In S. Hunston & G. Thompson (Eds.), *Evaluation in text: Authorial stance and the construction of discourse* (pp. 142–175). Oxford: Oxford University Press.

Quigley, J. (2000). *The grammar of autobiography: A developmental account*. Mahwah, NJ: Lawrence Erlbaum.

Raivetz, M. (1996, April). *High stakes testing in an urban school district: Survivors of the class of 1995 from grade eight to graduation*. Paper presented at the Annual Meeting of the American Education Research Association, New York.

Venn, C. (1984). The subject of psychology. In J. Henriques, W. Hollway, C. Urwin, C. Venn, & V. Walkerdine (Eds.), *Changing the subject: Psychology, social regulation and subjectivity* (pp. 119–152). London: Methuen.

Vygotsky, L. S. (1978). *Mind in society: The development of higher psychological processes* (M. Cole, V. John-Steiner, S. Scribner, & E. Souberman, Eds.). Cambridge, MA: Harvard University Press.

Walkerdine, V. (1984). Developmental psychology and the child-centred pedagogy: The insertion of Piaget into early education. In J. Henriques, W. Hollway, C. Urwin, C. Venn, & V. Walkerdine (Eds.), *Changing the subject: Psychology, social regulation and subjectivity* (pp. 153–202). London: Methuen.

White, P. R. R. (n.d.). An Introductory Course in Appraisal Analysis. Available: www.grammatics.com/appraisal/.

White, P. R. R. (2000). Dialogue and inter-subjectivity: Reinterpreting the semantics of modality and hedging. In M. Coulthard, J. Cotterill, & F. Rock (Eds.), *Working with dialog* (pp. 67–80). Tübingen: Verlag.

CHAPTER EIGHT

Who Gets to Play? Kids, Bodies, and Schooled Subjectivities

Lisa Hunter

Young people in their middle years of schooling are commonly referred to as *adolescents, early adolescents,* or *young adolescents*. The categorisation of young people as *adolescent* occurred at the turn of the last
century and coincided with the introduction of compulsory mass
schooling (McCulloch, 1991). The widely used term, first coined predominantly by educational and developmental psychologists to study
young people, has resulted in a limiting of the discourses available to
young people. Understanding adolescence as a cultural construction
provides the theoretical space to question totalising and objectified
characteristics, and to explore more generative ideas about young
people (Lesko, 2001). Departure from dominant developmental bio-
psychological conceptualisations of adolescents affords space to consider the subjectivities of young people as shifting, multidimensional,
diverse, negotiated, and embodied.

   While some researchers have attempted to address the categorisation of young people, and have worked to reconceptualise ways of
thinking about young people (e.g., Wyn & White, 1997), there seems
to be little evidence of this work being taken up in the practices of
schools and teachers. This chapter provides an illustration of the *doxa*
(Bourdieu, 1998), or common sense taken-for-granted beliefs, about
young people that are evident in the practices of schools, teachers,
and students (e.g., Burns, 2002). As an attempt to break from this

doxa, I refer to young people or students, to index the heterogeneity and diversity of students in middle years of schooling contexts. Essentialising categories work in several ways to locate, name, and often oppress the subject. For example, categories symbolically mark the body by naming chronological stages (e.g., adolescent, senior, elderly) and physical changes (e.g., toddler, pubescent, menopausal). These categories, used by different groups of people to talk about other groups of people, are self-reifying and further legitimate, define, and impose homogeneity on the individuals they address. Indeed, the application of a category by one person to another may be in conflict with how the latter person identifies her or himself. Categories are also temporally and spatially situated in particular contexts, given interactions and understandings within that context. Common to this understanding of categorisation is the body, the corporeality of inscription. Yet the playing out of embodied subjectivity is under-theorised in general. Categories like gender, class, and race work to reduce possible subject positions available to the body, while also inscribing performances on the body. With respect to young people, embodied subjectivity is also under-theorised in relation to schooling and society. The Cartesian hierarchy of mind as separate and superior to the body continues as a doxa within schooling (Hunter, 2002b). A more appropriate way to situate young people in society would be to conceptualise them through the social processes that shape the embodied subjectivities of individuals and differing collective groups, including the relationship between the two.

In this chapter, I focus on the social space (Bourdieu, 1990a) of a physical education (PE) class within the wider spaces of schooling and society. First, I describe a conceptual framework for the research included here. Second, I discuss the research context and introduce four students from the PE class to help illustrate several themes from the data. In the third section, I explore the themes of the good student, hetero/sexism, and controlling the body in the construction of the students' embodied subjectivities and their positioning within the class. Using Bourdieu's (1986) forms of capital, I explore essentialising categories, as embodied, to theorise the social space of the class, student positioning, and the social construction of subjectivities within it. In the closing discussion, I argue for the importance of critiquing and challenging the discursive spaces and, in particular, the discursive production of the body. I suggest a shift to practices that recognise learning as inherently embodied, and challenge traditional rules of "who gets to play the game."

THEORETICAL FRAMEWORK: THE FIELD
AND PLAYERS IN THE GAME

A growing number of researchers have explored the significance of the corporeality of students within the discourse of schooling (Gore, 1998; Kirk, 1998a; Reid, 1998). Much of this research focuses on the discipline or control of students' bodies. Findings from this work strongly suggest that the surveillance and control of students' bodies has been a dominant discourse in schooling, manifested through formal schooling practices such as lining up, raising one's hand to speak, asking permission to urinate, and even informal playground practices, such as boys playing out physical violence within a frame of acceptance not available to girls. These practices become perhaps more obvious, although no less insidious, within aspects of the curriculum that apply directly to the body. Physical education is one formal space in the school curriculum where the body becomes a focus of, and for, observation. The cultures of PE have been analysed by a small number of researchers who suggest that the history of PE has been discursively driven by controlling, disciplining, gendering, and shaping an objectified body (Kirk & Tinning, 1994; Vertinsky, 1992; Wright, 1998). These discourses become apparent in the ways sport, health, and gender, for example, are understood.

A more dynamic understanding of teaching and learning as contextualised, contested, and embodied necessitates a theoretical framework that illuminates multiple, interrelated dimensions. I draw heavily upon the work of Bourdieu to explore the ways in which discourses associated with the body, both within the classroom context and through the field of PE, create discursive spaces for constituting the embodied subjectivities of those acting within the social space. In an interview, Bourdieu refers to *field* as:

> a network, or a configuration, of objective relations between positions objectively defined, in their existence and in the determinations they impose upon their occupants, agents of institutions, by their present and potential

situation (situs) in the structure of the distribution of species of power (or capital) whose possession commands access to the specific profits that are at stake in the field, as well as by their objective relation to other positions (domination, subordination, homology, etc.). (Bourdieu & Wacquant, 1992, p. 97)

The field of PE, then, is made up of a structured system of social relations between the educational authority, PE teacher educators, PE curriculum writers, health specialists, and sport professionals who have influence over curriculum and practices, individual school administrators, PE teachers, and PE students. Any analysis of discourses and the individual devoid of a social context is flawed and limited because it denies the relational positioning of the individual within social fields. The body, highlighted by Bourdieu's concept of habitus, is paramount in reading, categorising, and positioning an individual within a field.

Interconnected to the concept of field is *habitus*, the corporeal dispositions that interact with social relations. Habitus works similarly to subjectivity, but emphasises embodiment and the role of the body in constituting habitus, as well as being constituted by habitus (Bourdieu & Wacquant, 1992). This dialectic becomes important in understanding the intertwining of material and symbolic practices in the construction of the subject, such as linguistic conceptions of the construction of corporeality. Bourdieu's emphasis on social structures is balanced by his conceptualisation of agency. However, acting as an agent may be mediated by influences that are beyond conscious realisation. Therefore, agents may actually reproduce the very structures that limit them. These become important points to discuss when arguing for peoples' ability to reflect and be reflexive, to act as agents. Agency can be contextualised in the positioning of young people as not-adults—as students within the discourses of particular subject areas such as PE. It is through the tension between being subjected to meaning inherent in the discourses of PE and becoming embodied agentic subjects that PE may constitute and construct the various habitus of young people. At the same time, young people also have the potential to constitute and construct the PE field. This dual process, being constituted and constituting, is central to understanding habitus as being constantly negotiated—constructed/ing, reconstructed/ing and maintained/ing.

While Bourdieu's concept of habitus has been critiqued for under-theorising internal diversity (McNay, 2000), this concept is still useful in that it attends to the intersection of symbolic and material dimensions of power on the body. As a compatible concept, *embodied subjectivity/subjectivities* provides a conceptual tool that is a generative structure rather than a determining principle—an orientation that suggests potentialities (Grosz, 1994; Wright, 1996). A person can be conceptualised as a multifaceted intersection of various subject signifiers or markers including, but not limited to, gender, class, race, sexuality, and corporeality. Within categories such as adolescent or boy or Aboriginal there are more differences than similarities. Local and contextual factors are important, and are variable across contexts for any one individual (Brooks, 1997). Because of this variability, the post-structuralist notion of subjectivities is more helpful than that of identity to encapsulate multiple, unpredictable, contradictory, and complex contextual inter-relationships of selves that make up a person in any one timespace (Lovell, 2000). It allows for conceptualisations of difference within and between individuals—as both internal and external diversity (Hird, 1998).

Along with habitus, bodies, and subjectivities, we must also attend to *practice* (Bourdieu, 1998). Culture is embodied and reproduced through participation in social practices in day-to-day activities produced by the interaction of fields and habitus, through social structures and agents. Through practice, social structures become embedded in the habitus, mediated by discourses within social fields. As with the considered concept of agency, actions occur through processes that may be beyond conscious control or awareness of the individual. "Habitus reveals itself...only in reference to a definite situation. It is only in the relation to certain structures that habitus produces given discourses or practices" (Bourdieu & Wacquant, 1992, p. 135). Practice is therefore "the product of a habitus that is itself the product of the embodiment of the immanent regularities and tendencies of the world" (p. 138). This is illustrated when people unknowingly reproduce oppressive practices that exist in the society in which they were born.

In this chapter, the analysis of practice is conducted within the social space of the PE class. This space is held together through the concept of *capital*. Capital acknowledges the value of something for members of a particular field and, in turn, the distribution of that value yields two principles of differentiation: economic capital and cultural capital (Bourdieu, 1998). The more people have in common in a given social space, the closer they are. They are distributed according to the volume of the different kinds of capital they possess, and according to the relative weight of the different forms of capital (Bourdieu, 1998). The forces active in the field define specific capitals, in relation to a field, and confer power over the field (Bourdieu, in Wacquant, 1989). Bourdieu's conceptualisation of capital therefore goes beyond that of an economic form, to include social, symbolic, and cultural capital, differentiating between the source and nature of the operating power.

While economic capital still refers to wealth, the other forms of capital ultimately translate into economic capital, provided there is a means for exchange. A network of lasting relations, a belongingness or connectedness with others in the field defines social capital. Cultural capital marks the product of education, the academic market, as connected to individuals in the form of accent and disposition, and learning as connected to objects such as books, qualifications, and possessions. These are in turn connected differentially to institutions, such as a secondary school education in a state school as opposed to a private school or university. Symbolic capital draws from any of the above-mentioned capitals and is given value by a particular groups' perception of what is legitimate and/or valued (Bourdieu, 1998). For example some young people may be perceived as good students and therefore afforded more symbolic capital than those not perceived as such. The accumulation of symbolic and material forms of capital determines one's location in social space, and that in turn determines the kinds of possibilities for accumulating different forms of capital and the abilities to redefine or legitimate the forms of those capitals.

Physical capital, defined by Bourdieu (1986), is a form of cultural capital, although Shilling (1993) argues that "the corporeal is too important to be seen merely as a subdivision of another form of capital" (p. 58). Shilling develops the concept more broadly through his contribution to the sociology of the body, arguing that physical capital encompasses the symbolic value of the exterior surface of the body in the form of shape, physique, and appearance. The physical body is the external manifestation of the habitus, as well as constituting the habitus warranting inclusion in understanding the definitions and practices where the body is central. This is particularly pertinent to schooling and PE.

To complement this theoretical framework, several other concepts require mention. *Illusio* acts as an investment that one has in maintaining the game—the social space and its outcomes. One does not necessarily play the game consciously but "one is born into the game, with the game; and the relation of investment, illusio, investment, is made more total and unconditional by the fact that it is unaware of what it is" (Bourdieu, 1990b, p. 67). Those who have a feel for the game are complicit in reproducing the doxa through illusio so as to maintain their positioning, the allocation of capital, and the legitimation of the forms of capital to be allocated. *Symbolic violence*, then, is "the violence which is exercised upon a social agent with his or her complicity" (Bourdieu & Wacquant, 1992, p. 167). Symbolic violence may occur through misrecognition when the violence is not even recognised by the individual, or "the fact of recognizing a violence which is wielded precisely inasmuch as one does not perceive it as such" (p. 168). A distinction between people must be made so that some may accrue capital and be positioned in a way to maintain the game. As such, those not able to access capital must give consensual validation to those who can. As this chapter demonstrates, the field of PE attends to the body formally, as an object of gaze, performance, measurement, and categorisation. Such attention often means that the symbolic violence constructed through unofficial discourses that maintain and reproduce mind/body dualism and essential categories is neither perceived nor problematised.

THE GAME IN PRACTICE: WHO IS ON THE TEAM, SIDELINED, A "NO SHOW," OR BANNED?

Twenty-four students participated in an eighteen month study that formed the data source for this chapter. The students, from one year seven class during their final year of primary school, then moved to nine year eight classes in their first year of secondary school or middle school. A classroom generalist teacher and PE specialist teacher worked with the students in year seven, and five specialist Health and Physical Education (HPE) teachers were primarily involved with the classes in year eight. The primary school was situated within a working-class/lower middle-class suburb of an Australian metropolitan city. Although several students transferred to middle class schools in other suburbs, most moved to the corresponding government co-educational high school in the same suburb.

I used a multi-method approach for data generation in an attempt to include as many students' perspectives as possible over the eighteen months of fieldwork. The methods included interviews, field observations, questionnaires, journals, videoing, and photography. The data were analysed using the tools of both qualitative and quantitative methods, critical discourse analysis, descriptive statistics, and Qmethodology. The study drew from a number of theoretical perspectives including critical theory and pedagogy, post-structural feminism, cultural studies, and youth studies. Through the use of these perspectives, I analysed the relational positioning of four students within their physical education class.

MEET SOME PLAYERS IN THE SQUAD: EMILY, NITRO, SALLY, AND ASHLEY[1]

To introduce four young people from the class, I draw upon two forms of representation from the data sources mentioned above. The first data source, as noted from the quotes below, is students' narratives developed from student quotes during interviews.

Based on interview data, Emily was able to access social capital because of her confidence and ability to read many social situations to her advantage. Her family life had been difficult with parents divorcing, but she had learned ways to benefit from it. Her economic capital was low. Her mother supported two children on a low-income wage, but Emily worked on obtaining cultural and symbolic capital through her friends. Her large size worked against her obtaining physical capital, as many within her social group preferred a more common idealised female appearance. Yet Emily was competent at many physical activities and sometimes used her body aggressively.

Being rather outspoken, Emily challenged many of the routines of school, often in ways deemed inappropriate by teachers.

Emily:

> I do tap dancing, karate, jazz, um cricket, netball and softball. I live with my mum and sister and my dad is whatever they are, I don't think they're married. They split up when I was in grade 4. It's good coz you get two of everything. I'm concerned about getting really, really fat. I've counted up in the past two years, had to go up and see the principal 43 times (laughing). I go ice-skating with Mandy when they've got their discount night and I ride my bike around on the street.

Unlike Emily, Nitro had a lot of economic capital from his physician father. As a result, Nitro could access many goods and services that Emily could not. It did not seem that Nitro's ethnicity had been used to marginalise him. His strong body was endowed with skill and speed, and he spoke with confidence, manipulating his social environment to remain popular with students and teachers. He was able to achieve well at school without too much effort and enjoyed the social aspects while recognising the importance of doing well.

Nitro:

> I play sport and do school work at school, I like PE and all that, I like the teachers. It's a good school I guess and they have good sports and I'm into playing games, I play with my friends a lot. I like having fun which I get to do at school sometimes. I get in trouble sometimes. I came here from Bangladesh when I was nine. I've been living here for four years so far. [School there] used to have PE but they don't have swimming pools and all that. In PE I feel good all the time except for when I get in trouble maybe. I was gonna join a go-kart club but I couldn't, it's too expensive. I ride bikes sometimes.

Like Nitro, Sally had a very supportive family where English was their second language. Their economic capital was low and Sally had little access to cultural capital. Like Emily she worked hard to position herself as a friend to all and therefore one who was able to comment on the legitimation of symbolic goods and her ability to obtain them. Unlike Nitro, however, Sally was not deemed "good looking" by her classmates but neither was she described as "fat" like Emily.

Sally:

> I like getting fit, hanging with my friends, watching TV, eating, um reading, just like having fun (laughs). I go to the pools, go shopping, go to the movies and go [skate] blading and play hit and run, when you knock on people's houses, on their door then run away. We don't do that anymore, it's too boring. I go blading every day with my sister. My parents smoke and I'm concerned they're gonna, well, pass away any minute. I hate the war in Bosnia, that's where my parents come from.

Like Sally, Ashley was also physically competent and motivated. Ashley, like Nitro, was also one of the older students in the class, and he had high levels of fitness and motor skill. He described his life as happy and his family as supportive. Unlike Emily, however, Ashley was a serious and highly motivated student, successful socially and academically at school, achieving high marks in all subjects and holding the title of school captain. Generally speaking, Ashley was able to access capital through being in a position to engage effectively with dominant discourses.

Ashley:

> I enjoy doing athletics, sport, playing video games, reading, my family, my sporting ability, probably being able to play video games and have free choice of stuff is important. I like numbers but English is boring—no challenge. I play for the club, soccer.

As these representations illustrate, there is a considerable degree of diversity and complexity within the class even when giving attention to only four members. In addition, there are differences within essentialised categories (e.g., female) and in the ordering of signifiers for individuals, for example, whether one identifies initially as female or working-class. This diversity and complexity is further complicated by changes in context, time, space, and a fluidity of subjectivities not necessarily captured in such limited representations. Attempting to construct more complete representations highlights the difficulty and slipperiness of capturing subjectivities.

The Field: Physical Education or *PE-as-Sport*

Many students regarded PE to be synonymous with sport: "[PE is] running and swimming and playing like soccer or something" [Student, I1. 78][2]. The nature of the field of PE, how it impacts the embodied subjectivities of young people and how it is experienced as a social space, acts as a structure. Within this structure, particular discourses such as sport, health, fitness, age, body, gender, sexuality, social class, and ethnicity interact through agents to shape the field, circulating between the macro and micro levels (Hunter, 2002a). For example, as the student noted above, discourses associated with PE have strong roots within sport, and vice versa, to the point where they are understood to be synonymous. Programs such as *Aussie Sport* (Bluett, Bluett, & Australian Sports Commission, 1986) and *Health Promoting Schools* (National Health Promoting Schools Association, 1997), supported by government and practiced in schools, are underpinned by dominant discourses of sport and health. So too does sport, health, and fitness dominate the official discursive practices of PE (Tinning, Kirk, Evans, & Glover, 1994). PE-as-sport has constructed a narrow conceptualisation of movement as technical and utilitarian, emphasising regimented and controlled sport-based movements at the expense of expressive physical activities such as creative dance. Worse, the replication of oppressive practices, such as those found in competition, are misrecognised as normal. In a more subtle and elusive way, the unofficial discourses associated with sport, including gender/ing, sex/ing, and body/ing, also operate to constitute the field of PE.

Many students spoke of PE by naming it as sport: "Yeah, coz like if you like didn't do sport or anything you like wouldn't be fit and healthy" [Emily, I1. 145]. Emily's words also illustrate the assumption of the positive relationship between PE participation and health, an illusion with respect to her lived experiences but one no less upheld by the field of PE. The doxa that equates sport, health, and fitness is based upon presuppositions that work as unofficial discourses. These include healthism, or blaming the individual for their perceived un-wellness, rather than considering social situations, individualism, competition, and the positivist scientism that governs sports sciences in particular. The subject positions that are rewarded and legitimated in PE are the competent display of skill performance, appearance of health and ideal body type (not being "fat"), and knowledge about the objectified biomedical body—all indicators of competitive fitness as a good student. Those students able to take these positions accrue capital and therefore have an investment in reproducing the game, unaware of their complicity in maintaining these legitimated subject positions. Misrecognising that sport is good for one's health, and therefore worthy of participation, justifies PE in the curriculum, under a restricted conflation of sport with PE. As such, even those students who cannot take up legitimated subject positions, those labelled unfit or fat for example, but continue to participate are also complicit in re-producing the social space, albeit as targets of symbolic violence.

PLAYERS TAKE UP THEIR POSITIONS ON THE FIELD: THREE THEMES

The construction of positions in the field of PE is partially realised through the teacher's role. The teacher is central, but not exclusive, in the legitimation and assigning of capital valued in the field. Many of the students referred to the teacher's centrality in the form of know-ledge and codes of behaviour: "He might show you the stroke or he might demonstrate it and he'd just tell us what to do" [Ashley, I1, 408]. "The teacher says you've done it very well that's when you know you've done it correctly" [Nitro, I1, 322]. A form of symbolic violence common in schooling kept many of the students "in their place" as they mis/recognised their role as unquestioning of auth-ority. Others created pockets of resistance which in turn labelled them as "bad" students by both the teacher and "good" students. Although various forms of capital were being legitimated and afforded within the PE class, here I focus on physical capital to illustrate how students' positioning may be conceptualised.

The value positions toward PE taken up by the teacher and students in the class are represented in Figure 1. Those in Group A, including the teacher and students such as Ashley and Sally, valued working hard through skill acquisition, good grades, and social skills such as cooperation and tolerance. These were perceived to be the more serious students or those who wanted to please the teacher. The

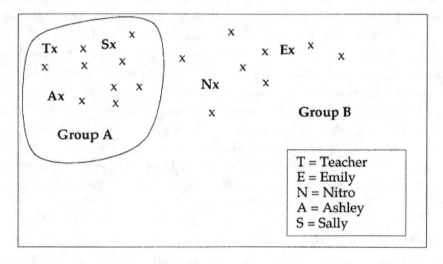

Figure 1. *Representational value positions toward physical education*[3]

students in group B, including Nitro and Emily, identified strongly with different values, including a chance to talk with friends, have fun, and get good grades without too much effort or having to think about others. The students in this group were marginalised and labelled as resistant, disruptive, or not keen workers by the teachers and other students.

> Mr. Spears: Mmm, in relation to other year 7's we've had [here] the last few years they were quite a difficult class to take...I find them particularly in phys ed unmotivated, not overly keen, um been a difficult class since they've been in grade 1...Nitro I think is uncooperative unless he's doing

something he really likes and if he doesn't really like it he spits the dummy,[4] and the girls like Emily, constantly, doesn't matter what you say, it always have to end up with laughs, it annoys me. [I1, 7–22]

Those who did not value PE for the same reasons the teacher did had less access to capital and less influence on the construction of the field.

Importantly, resisting had different origins and took different forms. This diversity tended to dilute any agency to change the field. Had they operated together, these students might have been able to confront their marginalisation. Students positioned closely to the teacher in values—those perceived to be serious students and pleasers—had bought in to the game and were therefore on the team and part of maintaining the game. Through the doxa and symbolic violence of sport/health/fitness, and through their bodies, they had accumulated the necessary capital to be recognised as good students. Those marginalised were either "sidelined" (e.g., given parental permission to sit out of PE), "no shows" (e.g., excused from PE), or "banned" (e.g., removed from PE by the teacher). These students had their ability to recreate the field reduced, thereby increasing the maintenance of dominant discourses and the practices of PE teachers and their better students. A closer look at three overlapping themes that emerged from the data follows.

The "Good" Student

The discursive space of the good student in the PE class highlights how symbolic capital operated to endorse particular subjectivities and not others. Specific ways of looking and behaving increased one's capital and legitimation as a good student, such as being a male within the context of PE-as-sport. The discursive space of the good student in PE was shaped by the characteristics found in the discourse of sport: competence, competition, comparison, display, skill, and fitness. To accrue physical capital in PE, a student must be able to recognise the discourses of, and operate successfully within, sport. Not to engage with this discourse is to be labelled as "not good," a mantra reinforced publicly every time students participate, or avoid participation. The good student was "Someone…that's [sic] really good at sport coz he wins almost every event" [Emily, I3, 341–342]. Similar to

Clarke's (1992) concept of the competent student, the good student is powerful in being defined as successful through the embodiment of a particular construction of the field. Students who are able to effectively work within the discursive spaces available to them become more closely aligned to the discourses operating through the teacher, particularly when this includes discourses from the school field, emphasising behaviour and effort. This classification or category is explained by Bourdieu (1998):

> Habitus are generative principles of distinct and distinctive practices (what [one] eats, how she eats)…But habitus are also classificatory schemes, principles of classification, principles of vision and division, different tastes. They make distinctions between what is good and what is bad. (p. 8)

Good students embodied subjectivities that were displayed as good at sport, compliant in behaviour, and demonstrative in effort. They had physical capital in the form of skill, fitness, and/or corporeal appearance, legitimated through teacher approval, support, and attention. Through teachers' continual reinforcement of physical capital for those with the right attitude, students learned what a good student was. The discourses of sport and school positioned the good students closer to the teacher. The discourses and physical proximities worked together to maintain and reproduce the dominant aspects of the field.

This was evident, for example, in the teacher's praise of those who finished pool laps quickly and returned to their blocks to wait for the next instruction, as opposed to those who struggled to complete or resisted the activity and were either ignored or reprimanded. Through this pedagogical relationship, those already positioned with power held together the legitimated practices of PE-as-sport. Through this process, students also learned who was not good or bad. Ashley, a good student explained, "There's some people who are [sic] bad at PE but they don't listen much and that's why they're bad at it…Here, here [pointing] there's the badder [sic] ones having a good old chat" [I1. 559, 721]. Students like Ashley maintained this position while others, like Nitro, slipped between good and bad depending on their engagement with various discursive spaces. Nitro was afforded leniency in expectations of effort because others took it for granted that he was a good PE student given his physical capital, his corporeality, and ability to perform skilfully and with speed:

> Most of them are [good]...That'd be me, Ashley, Nelson...Bernie, Emily...Sally, umm Toni. Toni gets into trouble sometimes, Tammy, I think that's all...I'm pretty good at it, I think I'm pretty good I can beat some of my friends when I'm competing with them, that's if I do...And the teacher tells you you're good at it. [I1, 424–37]

Some students, who recognised they were not good PE students, rejected the version of PE expected by the teacher. When given the choice, students took the opportunity to leave PE altogether, focusing instead on their club sports activities, recreation, or more sedentary practices. Some students used their own positions of power or agency to redirect the path of the class activities to suit their own purposes. For example, Emily told a supply teacher that they were to do netball rather than soccer, and Nitro wrestled with another student at the shallow end of the pool instead of continuing with laps. A significant number of students also resisted participation in the dominant field. Strategies included wearing a knee guard in case the teacher announced that running would be part of the activity or leaving the required sun hat behind to be disqualified from participation, an option taken by some when they wanted to avoid what they considered to be the boring stuff.

As with entry into many social fields, a novice's entry shows naiveté to the potentialities of the field. Within PE, the students were not aware of learning and movement possibilities outside those narrowly defined through sport. They were defining themselves as good or bad in terms of this specific field, which in turn opened or closed spaces for engagement. Bourdieu (1990b) explains this perpetuation as follows:

> The greater is his ignorance of all that is tacitly granted through his investment in the field and his interest in its very existence and perpetuation and in everything that is played for in it, and his unawareness of the unthought presuppositions that the game produces and endlessly reproduces, thereby reproducing the conditions of its own perpetuation. (p. 67)

The field of PE reproduces the conditions of its own perpetuation through teacher and student subjectivities, the strong links to sport, and the associated practices and discourses. Marginalisation in, and dissatisfaction with, PE—along with its devaluation by many of the disengaged students—came from practices within the field. Although the good students, like Ashley and Sally, were well positioned to seek continuance when the choice became available, others, like Emily and Nitro, declined the opportunity.

Hetero/Sexism

After age, gender[5] was perhaps the most dominant categorical space in which students were discursively constituted at school. Teacher/student language and practices referenced individuals as either boys or girls. This discourse, construed as natural, gendered many of the practices within the social space. Students articulated the significance of their bodies in gendered practices of sexuality and sexual orientation in less visible ways. Gendered discourses worked through language, corporeality, physical proximity, and relationships to establish a dominant order of heterosexual masculinity over heterosexual femininity (Wright, 1996), with other ways of embodying sexuality silenced.

The PE teacher, like many other teachers, constantly referred to students as boys and girls and always in a particular order, "OK, let's make a start. Boys and girls walk up to the other end behind a block" [Fg1: 52]. The gendered language became constituted in the students' subjectivities, and they then reconstituted the dominant discourse through their practices. Gender separation in some activities also reified heteronormative dualism by reinstantiating as natural the assumed biological differences attributed to boys and girls. When testing for fitness, for instance, the teacher separated the students according to their test results and gender, saying, "girls over here and boys over there. Line up with the highest scores to lowest scores. Stand in order" [Fb3: 8, 15–20]. This was common practice, regardless of whether teachers were measuring sprint speed, height, anaerobic power, or coordination. Performance was constantly on display as physical capital, and it was always differentiated and ordered by gender.

As in primary school, separation according to gender also continued as normal practice in secondary school, played out spatially when students waited for teachers gendered directions at the beginning of class and in different activities. Gender separation surfaced in the teacher's instructions:

> Today we're going to measure. Ok boys, you have to pick the 600 [gram javelin]. You can pick any of these and … [he shows them the green javelin]. The orange is the heaviest—you can usually tell by the thickness. The girls have to have the smaller ones. [Fb3: 6, 29–33]

Unpacking the doxa of ordering gender through sport and the taken-for-granted assumptions about gender also point to the level of symbolic violence through this hegemonic ordering.

Gender was also played out through students' spatial relationships, such as sitting as two gendered groups at the beginning of class. When the students viewed this practice (via video playback during their interview), few could articulate the reason for gender separation: "Oh, because, I don't know, we just sit like that" [Sally, I1, 881–882]. After further questioning, Sally attempted an explanation also used by other students, "Because we don't like boys, they're horrible, I don't know, we just sit like that [there's a reason]…I don't know, I think so but I don't know it [laughs]" [I1. 915–918]. Through her words, Sally references gender as a natural and dichotomised difference, based upon only two opposing ways of being heteronormative—masculine and feminine. Those students who attempted to explain the practice could not go beyond the misrecognitions associated with the gender discourses, continuing to use totalising and polarising explanations such as "like the boys are just mucking around and the girls are usually trying" [Sally, I1, 681].

Through corporeal practices, PE provided a space where structures of sexuality were reinscribed and reconstituted as gendered practices based on complementarity and heteronormativity. The sexual gaze of the opposite sex was noted by some: "Andrew's an idiot…Coz he's so small, he's so annoying…He just sits there and looks at me. Like yuk, piss off" [Emily, I2. 142–146]. Being under the evaluative gaze (Bartky, 1988) of boys was reported as a reason for girls wishing to avoid PE. Postures that covered the body, such as standing with their arms across their torso or across their waist and chest with hand across their face were common among the girls during the swimming lessons, "It's close to swimming and I get nervous coz I hate going in togs[6] with all these boys around. Yaaaah. I hate swimming with all these boys around coz they look at you like that, especially if you've got a big body. Like me" [Sally, I1, 1002]. In turn, however, some girls used their physicality to gain capital. The legitimised appearance was a hyperfeminine ectomorph—not "fat," with developing breasts and a fine-featured face clear of blemishes. Two students, referred to as attractive by students of both genders, often moved around the pool in minimal swimming garb to remain close to several of the boys and to avoid engagement with the physical activity. Some boys had noted the girls' appearance as physically attractive while describing other girls as fat or smelly, indicating a dislike in interacting with them. The tension for some girls was between being physically active and not appearing feminine, or trying to display a feminised sporty appearance while avoiding being labelled butch or lemon.[7]

Within the dominant discourse of sport, hypermasculinity was valued by many of boys who wanted to appear more muscular. Those who were small, not athletic, and not yet showing physical signs of puberty were not able to obtain physical capital through appearance or performance. In Nitro's case, his practices seemed to be a display of heterosexuality as well as same-sex social dominance. During swimming classes, he gained the attention of other students by a clowning display of his well-developed biceps and abdominals. While doing athletics in PE, specifically the shot put, he continued this display, as noted in my field notes:

As soon as the teacher left, Nitro again performed the incorrect technique that looked like a caber toss. On retrieving the shot he held it up under his shirtsleeve imitating a body builder showing off his biceps. He then relocated the shot to his pectorals to display to his two friends either large pectorals, or, given the way he was holding the shot and an imaginary one in his other hand, his large breasts...He commented that the school tracksuit was *gay* and returned to the circle for another *toss*. This time, he picked up a second shot dangling both between his knees like a pair of swollen testicles, laughing as he showed his friends. [Fb4: 9, 38–49]

Particular discourses of body, gender, and sexuality made possible the access to physical capital through performed heteronormativity within the field of PE-as-sport. Simultaneously, this reified capital served to reproduce each of these dominant discourses.

The visibility of physical characteristics and the hormonal changes occurring for some of the students provided a biological reading of the body (Bourdieu, 1990a, 1990b) through the discourses of gender and sexuality. However, many of these perceived displays (e.g., hair cut, clothes worn, ways of walking, ways of talking) had been socially constructed from the gendered positions, understood as biological. All students were obviously male or female despite a visible lack of primary or secondary sex characteristics[8] among many of the students. Routines around public clothes changing and the wearing of togs made some physical characteristics more visible. For several of the girls, exposure of the body—as an object of others' gaze—led to an awareness that others were looking at them and covering practices. Swimming sharpened the merger between bodily and gender discourses.

Like sex and gender, sexuality is also ascribed to bodies. Sexuality was often displayed through heteronormative speech acts, such as calling someone or something gay, indications of illegitimacy, abnormality, or unacceptability. Because of a choice of clothing, a lack of physical prowess, or a lack of friends, some students were referred to as gay and constructed as other, thus linking this discourse with more generalised performances rather than specific comments upon sexual behaviour or appearance. One teacher was labelled gay by students dissatisfied with class activities, while several also justified the label by virtue of the teacher's dress and mannerisms.

In the only other reference to sexualities outside heteronormativity, Emily identified pregnancy and lesbianism as negative states of being attributed to herself and her friend—states neither wanted to be associated with:

> I like Anthony [laughs]…he's the only partially good-looking one (laughs). Tim's an idiot coz in Drama, um, we did this thing, it was like make up and Mia told me that she was a lesbian and I told her I was pregnant and then he went and spread it that I'm a piece of shit. [Emily, I2. 136–138]

When Tim continued the construction of Emily as pregnant, even after the drama class was over, he employed a technique to reduce her capital and positioning within the class. The dominant state of being heterosexual and a virgin had more legitimacy than other ways of being. The dominant discourses had been reproduced rather than challenged.

In practices outside the class, like lunch-time free play, it was interesting to note resistance to the dominant discourses of heteronormative masculinity and femininity, but also the ways in which dominant practices reinscribing, and reinscribed by, gender were reasserted with a reference back to PE. As one student noted:

> Since girls never bring a ball, we play with the boys…football and soccer as well…girls are on one team and the boys are on the other. Sometimes if the girls are doing really badly one good person on the boys team will come over and help us and it's mainly just like PE when we do it. [I1. 203–211]

In statements like this made outside of PE, but referencing PE activities, the dominance of boys over girls in sport is again reified. This student, like many others, took for granted that if the girls were not succeeding against the boys, it was because they were girls. Having a boy on the team was expected to rectify the problem. Through practices in PE, under the guise of equity or equal teams, the dominant discourse of a hierarchical gender dualism was reinforced and embedded in the student subjectivities. The belief that males were better and could therefore help females became reinforced in practice.

These few examples of gender and sexuality operating in the field of PE demonstrate how heteronormativity is reproduced and how the field closes spaces for alternatives to dualistic, normative, and gendered heterosexual orientations. Connell (1998) notes:

> Issues of gender are, at one level, issues about how personal lives are arranged and conducted. It is through critical reflection on personal experience, often, that people come to realize the significance of what has been taken-for-granted—such as the [hegemonic] masculinity of sport, and the use of sport to make and confirm masculinities. (p. iii)

Connell describes the critical reflection that is absent from the PE field as manifested in all of the PE sites. The field of PE reproduces dominant forms of gender and sexuality discourses beyond the boundaries of student and teacher consciousness, constituted through both discourse and corporeality.

Controlling the Body

Emily's words highlight the production of the controlled body in PE (Broekhoff, 1972): "[I'm concerned] if I get like really, really, really, really, really fat coz I'm already fat. I'll probably get anorexic or something" [Emily, I1, 39–40]. A particular bodily appearance, or "the look" (Featherstone, 1982), is legitimated through PE, resulting in those close to the ideal accruing capital and those further from the ideal being marginalised. Prior examples have demonstrated that the body is central in the constitution of one's subjectivity, particularly when engaging with the field of PE and in schooling more broadly. The mind/body dualism promoted in schools, in conjunction with emphases in PE on objectification and performance, appearance and gaze, operated to construct particular discursive spaces in which students' subjectivities were differently legitimated and alienated.

Students come to know the body through the physical sciences and objectify the body through gaze, measurement, and comparison (Pronger, 1995). Bodily discourses also operate sensually and emotionally (Lyon, 1997), yet there is a gap in this research and little space within the field of PE to know the body in these ways. Dominant discourses operate to present the student's body as an object to be controlled (Kirk, 1998b). At the same time, students become disembodied in other classes too, such as mathematics and English, where a disembodied mind and cognitive processes become the focus (Davis, 1997). Ultimately, the separation of body from mind is legitimated through the often disparate association of each with particular school subjects, rather than understanding the student as embodied with subjectivities manifested through movement and corporeality. An epistemology based upon Cartesian dualism is reproduced within education, placing the mind as dominant and separate to the body. This is illustrated in many students' comments, like Nitro's differentiation between PE and mathematics:

> Maths? It's more tougher [sic]...Like in swimming it's like you have to do something but in maths you have to concentrate and you have to write

things and all that. So it's more really tough than doing PE. In PE it's just relaxed, you can talk whenever you want. If you're talking in this maths you just get a detention straight away. [Nitro, I1, 816–818]

Nitro differentiates between doing in PE, that is using the body, and concentrating in mathematics, that is using the mind. This separation values particular knowledges, or ways of knowing (cognitive, "theory") over ways of doing (activity, "practice"), reinforcing the mind/body hierarchy.

As described in the previous section, physical capital and social positions were influenced by comparisons of performance, such as placement in races, comparisons of throwing distances, and one's physical dimensions, including height, weight, and arm span. As Sally noted: "You have to weigh yourself…it's just horrible. Look at how skinny and tall I am" [I1, 335 & 910]. The students' bodies acted as a reference point from which they constituted their subjectivities, constrained, however, by a deterministic relationship between field and subjectivity and the accrual of physical capital.

Consequently, some students were very conscious of the look, and how closely their reality came to an ideal shaped by discourses of sport, health, and fitness. Nitro knew the capital to be gained through a muscular physique: "I think [PE's] for your health and um for your fitness, to get you fit…It helps me get more fit, helps me get ah…huge I guess, very big" [I1. 104–110]. By "big," Nitro was referring to his athletic physique and muscle definition. But whereas Nitro's physique was rewarded with physical capital in the form of positive comments from others, other students' capital (e.g., Emily's) was diminished, especially through the increased opportunities of gaze provided by PE: "But I hate [PE] because you have to wear the togs because it makes me look fat and everyone teases me because I'm fat" [I1. 759].

The body was a thing to be looked after and worked on in PE in order to access physical capital: "Because, like you learn how to look after your body and [pause] stuff, and swimming, like you can learn how to rescue people and you could run fast and get a career in sports and stuff" [Sally, I1, 302]. This shape or look of the somatic surface of the body carried with it physical capital. Bourdieu (1990b, 1999), however, also conceptualises the body as a visual manifestation of the habitus. The students used this visuality in a number of ways. Through misrecognition, the performance-competence discourse was played out against those with particular body types. If one displayed competence, as Emily did in swimming, their "fatness" was sometimes overlooked by others, although they themselves made reference to being fat. However, in the case of others, visual markers of a body that were not legitimate within the discourses of either PE or youth culture were associated with incompetence. The body discourse available through PE gave these students the tools to misrecognise the relationship between appearance and competence, thereby rationalising their lack of engagement with the activities.

TIME OUT: MOVING BEYOND CATEGORISATION

The discourses associated with the body through PE constitute embodied subjectivities and therefore necessitate explicit critique both within the field and by the students. Bourdieu (1990b) suggests that this critique cannot be reduced to the familiar concept of "body image," which he explains as being "a subjective representation largely based on the representation of one's own body produced and returned by others" (p. 72). Rather, the body is understood through "classificatory schemes," such as gender, race, and class. These categories pose oppositional values, such as male or female, and are "one of the fundamental principles of the perception that agents have of their body and also of their whole relation to the body" (p. 72). In effect, while some students learn what they *can* do and who they are, many learn what they *can't* do, and who they are not.

Though numerous possibilities for students' subjectivities are conceivable, they are not part of students' formal conversations in understanding how physical capital may be afforded to some and not to others. Instead, these bodily inscriptions are played out implicitly through discourses associated with gender and sport. When these discourses are inculcated, certain students *naturally* acquire physical capital while others do not.

Physical Education as a Learning Area

Learning to be is an important if not pre-eminent purpose of schooling and is predicated on ways of understanding and enacting one's subjectivities. More importantly, discursive spaces created from conceptualisations of young people as adolescents, and therefore still becoming, are problematic. PE is potentially a powerful catalyst for learning through, and as a result of, the somatic surface of the body as manifested in movement and contextualised in social relationships (e.g., Hellison, 1995; Martinek, 1997). Whether this potential is used in socially just and empowering ways is the issue. Given its history and co-optive association with sport, PE has demonstrated the powerful use of these discourses in enculturating bodies and constraining subjectivities, understood and reproduced in particular ways. I argue that these ways marginalise many young people in PE, physical activity, and health, and ultimately reduce positive spaces for different subjectivities to exist. It could be argued that PE does more harm than good: its practices demonstrate failed health intervention at best and construct a damaging learning space at worst (Evans, Davies, & Wright, 2004).

Through the assimilation of legitimised practices, such as those encouraged in sport, some people have been able to access cultural and social capital through their physical capital. However, others have been resoundingly reminded of what they lack, closing spaces for opportunities involving movement, spaces for understanding one's subjectivities, and spaces for difference. By redefining what a good student in PE could be like or could look like, both within and outside sport discourses, more spaces for more students to successfully position themselves (and be positioned by others) as good, as valued, students can be created.

PE as a field can potentially model what being an embodied learner could be like. The first step might be for teachers and students to distinguish between the doxa currently governing PE, and other possibilities for PE. Two learning experiences then need to be worked through with students. The first is the learning associated with one's subjectivities, one's embodiment as a participant in the field of PE. Students need to know how they are constituted within the field of PE and how they participate as agents in the reproduction or re-creation of those fields. The second is the learning associated with one's positioning within society generally as based upon categories, such as age, gender, sexuality, ethnicity, and bodily appearance. These categories afford some people social, physical, cultural, and symbolic capital and not others.

Learning as Embodied

Embodied learning needs to be a part of PE if the field is to break from its oppressive reproduction of essentialised bodies through narrow categories. The disruption of mind/body dualism, objectification and performance, appearance and gaze, offers opportunities for students to understand and explore the ways they have been positioned by competing discourses. Learning particular ways of becoming an adult body—ways of moving, controlling, and regulating the body—seems to be part of the project of schooling that is upheld through the doxa of adolescence. Through PE and schooling, ways of knowing the body need to be challenged as constructed and essentialising. By understanding the construction of knowledge that frames the field, students might recognise the discourses operating around them as well as the need to critically challenge these discourses. Moreover, an awareness of the complicit participation of teachers and students in reproducing discourses and circles of influence needs to be raised. Only when these become explicit can students begin to effectively move beyond the superficial and constraining ways of relating to themselves through the field. By becoming aware of these superficial relations, both students and teachers—and people generally—may come to understand learning as embodied and may then be able to critique their own social construction and positioning within the social processes imposed in institutions such as schooling.

Knowledge as cognitive, learning as an individual process, adolescence as a biologically driven stage, and intelligence as reflected in knowledges from particular fields are all discourses we need to critique to understand the role of school in the creation of particular types of citizens. Such a critique is required if we are to understand the parts young people, individually and collectively, may play in schools and society more broadly. A new knowledge must reflect an epistemological and ontological shift about the role of learners, teachers, PE and schooling more generally. Such shifts might include an understanding of subjectivities as embodied, opening the way for a respect for differences, and a disruption of oppressive practices already deeply imbedded in PE, schooling and the positioning of young people within our society. As Bourdieu (1990b) proposes, the body operates "below the level of consciousness...it does not represent what it performs, it does not memorise the past, it enacts the past, bringing it back to life" (p. 73). This suggests that the body, as the visible manifestation of embodied subjectivities, also needs to become explicit, operating at the level of consciousness if we are to move beyond the reproduction of past oppressions. In this way we may be able to shift toward more inclusive forms of schooling and a more just and generative society.

Acknowledgments

Thanks to Doune Macdonald and Richard Tinning for their guidance with the research on which this chapter is based, Delia Hart for her comments on drafts of this paper, and particularly those individuals who participated in the research. Thanks also to Lisa Patel Stevens and Jennifer A. Vadeboncoeur for their suggestions and patience in teasing out and communicating the important issues.

NOTES

1. All identifying names have been replaced by pseudonyms.
2. Indicates data source for speaker or field notes.
3. A Qsort test was employed (ordered 40 value orientations towards physical education). Figure 1 shows value orientations of the teachers and students to physical education. By focussing on Function 1 (Eigenvalue of 73.2%) it is possible to recognise two groups of people within the class (Group A and B). Function 1 separated the class on their values towards physical education as a chance to talk with friends, have fun, and get good grades without too much effort or having to think about, or take into account, others. A further separation using Function 2 was valid between cluster 2 and 3 within Group A (although with a much lower Eigenvalue of 26.8%). This discriminated between those who highly valued being with friends, agreeableness towards the teacher, and not having to work too hard and those who were very motivated towards working hard through skill acquisition, for good skill outcomes and therefore grades.
4. "Spit the dummy" is a colloquialism for having a temper tantrum.
5. Gender is used to denote the socially constructed, dichotomised categories of masculinity and femininity into which young people are placed. Although these categories are assumed to be based upon the biology of sex, there is argument to suggest that sex, in turn, is also a socially constructed category within the doxa of

biological determinism. For a discussion of this position, see Butler (1993) and Petersen (1998).

6. Togs are bathing costumes or swimwear.
7. A lemon is the disparaging term used to refer to a lesbian.
8. Primary sex characteristics are the actual reproductive systems, such as ovaries and testes, whereas secondary characteristics are bodily characteristics of adult males and females produced from hormones. These would include pubic hair, change of voice, breast development, and sexual desires.

REFERENCES

Bartky, S. (1988). Foucault, femininity and the modernization of patriarchal power. In I. Diamond & L. Quinby (Eds.), *Feminism and Foucault: Reflections on resistance* (pp. 61–86). Boston: Northeastern University Press.

Bluett, B., Bluett, L., & Australian Sports Commission. (1986). *Aussie sports activities manual.* Canberra: Australian Schools Sports Council.

Bourdieu, P. (1986). The forms of capital. In J. G. Richardson (Ed.), *Handbook of theory and research for the sociology of education* (pp. 241–258). New York: Greenwood Press.

Bourdieu, P. (1990a). *In other words: Essays towards a reflexive sociology.* Stanford, CA: Stanford University Press.

Bourdieu, P. (1990b). *The logic of practice.* Cambridge: Polity Press.

Bourdieu, P. (1998). *Practical reason: On the theory of action.* Cambridge: Polity Press.

Bourdieu, P. (1999). Language and symbolic power. In A. Jaworski & N. Coupland (Eds.), *The discourse reader* (pp. 502–513). London: Routledge.

Bourdieu, P. & Wacquant, L. (1992). *An invitation to reflexive sociology.* Cambridge: Polity Press.

Broekhoff, J. (1972). Physical education and the reification of the human body. *Gymnasium, 9,* 4–11.

Brooks, A. (1997). *Postfeminisms: Feminism, cultural theory, and cultural forms.* New York: Routledge.

Burns, J. (2002, July). *Addressing needs of young adolescent learners: An integrative perspective on development and practice.* Paper presented at the International Middle Schooling Conference, Adelaide, Australia.

Butler, J. (1993). *Bodies that matter: On the discursive limits of "sex."* London: Routledge.

Clarke, G. (1992). Learning the language: Discourse analysis in physical education. In A. Sparkes (Ed.), *Research in physical education and sport: Exploring alternative visions* (pp. 146–166). London: Falmer Press.

Connell, R. W. (1998). Forward: Where the boys are. In C. Hickey, L. Fitzclarence, & R. Matthews (Eds.). *Where the boys are: Masculinity, sport and education* (pp. i–vi).

Davis, K. (1997). *Embodied practices: Feminist perspectives on the body.* London: Sage.

Evans, J., Davies, B., & Wright, J. (Eds.). (2004). *Body knowledge and control: Studies in the sociology of physical education and health.* London: Routledge.

Featherstone, J. (1982). The body in consumer culture. *Theory, Culture and Society, 1*(2), 18–33.

Gore, J. (1998). Disciplining bodies: On the continuity of power relations in pedagogy. In T. Popkewitz & M. Brennan (Eds.). *Foucault's challenge: Discourse, knowledge, and power in education* (pp. 231–251). New York: Teachers College Press.

Grosz, E. (1994). *Volatile bodies: Toward a corporeal feminism.* St. Leonards, Australia: Allen & Unwin.

Hellison, D. R. (1995). *Teaching responsibility through physical activity.* Champaign, IL: Human Kinetics.

Hird, M. (1998). Theorising student identity as fragmented: Some implications for feminist critical pedagogy. *British Journal of Sociology of Education, 19*(4), 517–527.

Hunter, L. (2002a, July). *Teachers as gatekeepers to physical and social capital.* Paper presented at the Australian Council for Health, Physical Education, and Recreation National Conference, Adelaide, Australia.

Hunter, L. (2002b). *Young people, physical education, and transition: Understanding practices in the middle years of schooling.* Unpublished doctoral dissertation, The University of Queensland, Brisbane, Australia.

Kirk, D. (1998a). *Schooling bodies: School practice and public discourse, 1880–1950.* London: Leicester University Press.

Kirk, D. (1998b). Education reform, physical culture and the crisis of legitimation in physical education. *Discourse: Studies in the Cultural Politics of Education, 19*(1), 101–112.

Kirk, D. & Tinning, R. (1994). Embodied self-identity, healthy lifestyles and school physical education. *Sociology of Health and Illness, 16*(5), 600–625.

Lesko, N. (2001). *Act your act!: A cultural construction of adolescence.* New York: Routledge.

Lovell, T. (2000). Thinking feminism with and against Bourdieu. *Feminist Theory, 1*(1), 11–32.

Lyon, M. (1997). The material body, social processes and emotion: "Techniques of the body revisited. *Body and Society, 3*(1), 83–101.

Martinek, T. (1997). Serving underserved youth through physical activity. *Quest, 49,* 3–7.

McCulloch, G. (1991). Educational history and the politics of human learning. In J. R. Morss & T. Linzey (Eds.), *Growing up: The politics of human learning* (pp. 171–187). Auckland: Longman Paul.

McNay, L. (2000). *Gender and agency: Reconfiguring the subject in feminist and social theory.* Cambridge: Polity Press.

National Health Promoting Schools Association. (1997). *National Health Promoting School Initiative: Final Report.* Brisbane, Australia: Author.

Petersen, A. R. (1998). *Unmasking the masculine: Men and identity in a sceptical age.* London: Routledge.

Pronger, B. (1995). Rendering the body: The implicit lessons of gross anatomy. *Quest,* 47, 427–446.

Reid, J. A. (1998). New times, new ways: Methodological problems researching the Nintendo generation. *Australian Educational Researcher,* 25(3), 37–60.

Shilling, C. (1993). The body, class and social inequalities. In J. Evans (Ed.), *Equality, education, and physical education* (pp. 55–73). London: Falmer Press.

Tinning, R., Kirk, D., Evans, J., & Glover, S. (1994). School physical education: A crisis of meaning. *Changing Education: A Journal for Teachers and Administrators,* 1(2), 13–15.

Vertinsky, P. (1992). Reclaiming space, revisioning the body: The quest for gender-sensitive physical education. *Quest,* 44, 373–396.

Wacquant, L. (1989). Towards a reflexive sociology: A workshop with Pierre Bourdieu. *Sociological Theory,* 7(1), 26–63.

Wright, J. (1996). The construction of complementarity in physical education. *Gender and Education,* 8(1), 61–79.

Wright, J. (1998). Reconstructing gender in sport and physical education. In C. Hickey, L. Fitzclarence, & R. Matthews (Eds.), *Where the boys are: Masculinity, sport and education* (pp. 13–26). Geelong, Australia: Deakin University.

Wyn, J. & White, R. (1997). *Rethinking youth.* St. Leonards, Australia: Allen & Unwin.

CHAPTER NINE

Doing Popular Culture: Troubling Discourses about Youth

Elizabeth Birr Moje & Caspar van Helden

"Young women lose their senses."

This line appeared recently in boldfaced print in the entertainment section of a local newspaper. The reporter was describing reactions to the performance of a "young Latin superstar" (Amaya, 2003). One might ask why young women were a focus of the report. One might even wonder what constitutes *young* in such an account. More probably, however, very few people asked those, or any, questions when they read those words. Most readers would be likely either not to question the sentence or to chuckle and nod their heads as they read the report, perhaps visualizing a mass of screaming *girls* swarming at the feet of a male performer.

In this chapter, we notice and trouble that line and the assumptions that go with it. We ask the question, "What does it mean to be young?" What do popular discourses—everyday talk, images, and signs—communicate to people about what an adolescent is? Further, what is it about *adolescence* that leads people to believe it is a special time period in human development, a time of searching, confusion, vulnerability, and crisis? What is it about adolescence that leads people to fear that certain influences will prey on the alleged confusion, vulnerability, and crisis of youth?

Consider, for example, the following excerpt of a response from "The American Decency Association" to the sales catalog published by the popular youth clothier, Abercrombie & Fitch (A&F) (www.abercombie.com) where images of scarcely clad male and female youths are used to advertise their brand.

WHY A&F'S CATALOG DRAWS OUR GRAVE CONCERN

(1) Because A&F relentlessly shows no regard for the *innocence of our children*...[emphasis added]

(3) Though the vast majority of American corporations avoid using pornography to target our youth for sales and the lining of their pockets, A&F shamelessly and aggressively uses eroticism to bring youth to its doors and to their cash registers...

(6) I have four children. Through their growing up years, I have desired and prayed that each of my children would save themselves for marriage. I'm not finished with parenting and all of my children haven't finished growing up. Any corporate entity, TV program, magazine, video game, movie, catalog that attempts to undermine the sexual purity of any of my children... (www.americandecency.org)

One might argue that this text is the product of a small, radical, religious group unique in its position against A&F's marketing campaign. However, other groups also protested A&F's targeting of youth. For example, Desantis (2002), published an article entitled "Unbelievable: We control who you think you are," in *XY* (see Figure 1). Desantis, who was nineteen years old at the time, describes how gay youth such as himself were being controlled by A&F's self-proclaimed *"coordinated lifestyle reinforcement"* campaign [emphasis added].

We do not necessarily disagree with the argument that corporate entities use various forms of mass media and popular cultural texts to sell not only goods but also *desires and identities*, via brands, to people. What we are concerned with, however, is the assumption that young people, people between the ages of ten and twenty-five years (Arnett, 2002), are somehow more vulnerable, more open to such exploitation through branding and other media outlets than are adults (e.g., Buckingham, 2003). The assumption implicit in such discourse—that

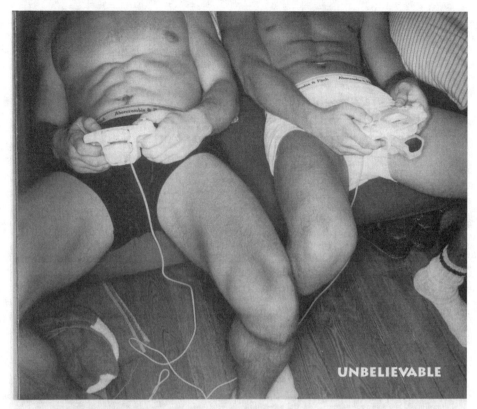

we control who you think you are

Figure 1. *Photo and text from Desantis (2002) in XY*

young people will move from "innocence" to some sort of deviance as a result of their engagement with artifacts of popular culture—reveals what adults[1] believe about both young people and popular culture.

Such discourse suggests adults believe youth of a certain age to be highly vulnerable to certain influences as they search to *find themselves*, to *become* something or someone. The idea that popular cultural texts, if left unchecked and unmonitored in the hands of youth, will turn innocent children into confused, lazy, or even deviant adolescents reveals the assumption that popular cultural texts prey upon young people, and that young people are not capable, perhaps as a result of diminished rationality (Lesko, 2001), of reasoning through the influences of those texts. That the same concern is not directed toward adults using popular cultural texts suggests that young people are assumed to be in a special category, a transitory period during which they are especially susceptible to the wiles of those who might lead them astray. Adulthood, in this view, is apparently a state of mind and body in which a person has achieved a stable identity and no longer experiences significant confusion or uncertainty.

For our part in this book on deconstructing common constructions of "the adolescent," we examine some of these assumptions about youth, with a particular focus on how some youth use popular culture. We focus on adolescents/youth because adolescence is a highly "marked" and over-determined category. A number of assumptions about people in the adolescent age group are made simply by virtue of *age*, regardless of the person's ethnicity, race, social class, sexual orientation, gender, or religious affiliation. Of course, assumptions are made about all sorts of social groups, including racial, ethnic, gender, sexual orientation, social class, and religious groups. But adolescence is a unique grouping because it is assumed to be a transitory grouping, a stage or time period that people assume one enters and eventually leaves. It is also commonly assumed that adolescence is a time of searching, of establishing one's identity, of *becoming* (e.g., Lesko, 2001; Moje, 2002).

We give special attention to popular culture because it is so often linked in both popular and research literatures with dangerous influences on "the adolescent." Popular culture is all too often reduced to the crazy stuff that kids listen to, watch, and wear. On the flip side, young people and youth culture often get represented by images of all youth as immersed in and overwhelmed by popular cultural texts, caring about nothing and nobody else, and living their lives in a swirl of brands, logos, music, television, film, and Internet web pages. Although many youth both enjoy and produce popular cultural texts, they cannot be reduced to those texts. Young people make *youth cultures* from a complex intersection of home, school, community, peer, and popular cultures. Youth cultures can be thought of as practices and meaning systems enacted by, and unique to, particular groups of youth as they use popular cultural texts, among many other cultural texts and models, to interact with each other and with parents, teachers, older siblings, and other elders.

Distinguishing youth cultures from the more broadly disseminated popular cultural texts that people enjoy is also important to challenging essentialized conceptions of youth cultures. When youth cultures are positioned, for example, merely as fourteen year olds watching MTV (Music Television), wearing a certain brand of clothing, or engaging in Instant Messaging, there is no sense of how particular groups of young people, of particular ages and subjectivities, in particular geographic spaces, at particular points in time, using particular aspects of particular forms of popular culture, are making sense of it.

There is also little empirical sense of how people of any age make use of popular culture texts to move in and out of different cultural arrangements. Several of the participants in the first author's research project, for example, listen to what is popularly labeled "gangster rap," but also avidly enjoy cumbia, merengue, mariachi, and salsa. They listen to, discuss, read, and write about different musical genres in different groups, but they do not necessarily confine the genres to those groups. While attending one young woman's *quinceañera* practice, or fifteenth birthday celebration, for example, Elizabeth observed the youth moving in and out of different popular musical texts, practicing for traditional dances as they listened to Mexican folk and pop songs, and weaving in hip hop moves and singing the lyrics as they danced. They interacted with the adults who were present and with each other around these texts.

Thus, the notion of something stable called youth culture should be a contested notion, as should the notion that youths are only interested in popular culture. People of all ages make cultural meanings and systems, and they all use popular culture, among other cultural models, to do so. They carry those cultural forms and models into other cultural groups of which they are members. So-called youth do not make culture by themselves; they make youth cultures while living in relation with so-called adults, and adults participate in the making of youth cultures and popular culture. Indeed, adults often control the making of popular culture, even as they critique it. Thus, how young people use popular culture should be studied in local and particular ways, and researchers should examine how youth are powerful and strategic in their uses of popular culture.

At the same time, studying youth culture in local and particular ways can reveal the dangers inherent in youth using popular culture, albeit different kinds of dangers than those feared by adults who believe that young people are somehow more susceptible to the vagaries of popular culture than are adults. There is a real danger of a large group of young people falling for simple consumerism offered via popular cultural texts. But there is also another group of young people engaging in a cynical rejection of the world as they become more aware of what these texts mean for their lives. A careful examination of the relationship between youth cultures, adult cultures, and popular cultures can point to ways educators might learn from youth about how and why they use various cultural texts, allowing educators to support young people as they learn new cultures, knowledges, literacies, and ways of knowing.

JUST WHAT IS POPULAR CULTURE?

We have used the phrases *popular culture* and *popular cultural texts* a number of times in the preceding passages, but these are phrases with few clear definitions. In their introduction to a *Harvard Educational Review* issue on popular culture, the editors refer to figures from film, music, and sports as they introduce the topic of popular culture (Gaztambide-Fernández & Gruner, 2003). Notably, they refer first to the movies made from the widely popular Harry Potter book series, implicating the novels as forms of popular culture only at the end of their essay, thereby suggesting that the "popular" in popular culture relies most heavily on electronic forms of dissemination such as television, film, radio, or Internet, although books and magazines remain important venues for popular culture.

The *spread* of popular culture, however, has a great deal to do with the technologies that carry pop culture texts. Cell phones, pagers, Palm Pilots, laptops, board-computers, e-check in, e-mail, chat, messenger, blogs, and video games are just some of the high-tech hardware and software that surround people, not to mention the mechanisms of film, television, and radio. Other technological means of communicating are also widely available, including the branding of various items, from clothing to equipment. People of all ages, for example, sport clothing labels that carry with them, whether the wearer likes it or not, identities of "punk," "grunge," "prep," "rapper," or "retro." The identities attached to such styles are not accidental; the word *brand* has multiple meanings, from varieties of a product to labels that, metaphorically and literally, *brand* and identify wearers and users.

Since World War II, the entertainment industry, now intimately connected with every other industry, has significantly enhanced its all-encompassing presence and influence in the lives of young people and adults alike (Horkheimer & Adorno, 1972). There is hardly an hour, or even a minute, that the average person is not confronted with some kind of commercial media, brand identity, or logo, whether on television, radio, Internet websites, billboards, or print magazine. These texts and brands, of course, are sold to people, who use and consume them even as they adapt them to serve their own purposes. Popular culture, then, seems to be intricately connected with many aspects of most people's identities, social lives, socio-political situation and views, economical situation, and the massive political and commercial machinery that operates around all people.

Why has popular culture in all its current manifestations become so popular? It could be said that legal, medical, and educational discourses of adolescence have all had their moments, but that popular culture discourses are dominant at this time. Furthermore, the cultural models provided through various forms of popular culture seem to frame Discourses (Gee, 1996)—ways of knowing, doing, believing, reading, and writing—which are more used, connected to, and liked by youth. Or it may be that we notice the popular cultural texts and accompanying discourses that youth use because of the unwavering gaze we direct at young people. Whatever the explanation, popular culture appears to be an explicit and significant aspect of the cultures that young people make for themselves every day (e.g., Dolby, 2003).

At least three dominant critiques of popular culture are prevalent in educational, sociological, anthropological, and psychological research literatures, and reflected in mainstream society. Often these critiques are aimed particularly at young people's uses of popular cultural texts. For example, despite and perhaps due to its dominance, many people consider popular culture to be "low" culture, trashy, non-artistic, and representative of the baseness of contemporary society (e.g., Bennett, 1994; Hirsch, Kett, & Trefil, 1987). Popular culture aimed at or taken up by youth, in particular, is often accused of being deviant in orientation, exposing young people to drugs or "immoral" behaviors, or encouraging them to be unproductive, or "slackers." The common lament that television programming, for example, has led to shorter attention spans among children and youth is routinely taken up in research studies. Cottle (2001), for example, argues that television and other popular cultural forms have led to a culture of "distraction" in which young people cannot sustain focused attention, suggesting weakened cognitive processing abilities. Such views of popular culture imply that popular culture is worth less than *high* culture, and that it can even threaten high culture or the development of higher-level thinking.

A second critique of the popular is that it represents an explicitly manipulative tool of domination (Horkheimer & Adorno, 1972) or a highly seductive, hegemonic arm of capitalism (Grossberg, 1995). Popular culture, it is argued, encourages users to consume material goods by selling not just the goods themselves, but also desires and needs. As a result, consumers require material goods designed to sate their desires or to build relationships with others who have similar desires. Consumers of popular culture, especially youth, then, are seen at best as co-opted by the popular cultural texts they consume and, at worst, as duped into thinking that the texts are expressions of their own interests and desires. The notion of consumption is particularly important in this critique, suggesting that users of popular cultural texts and brands digest texts without question, awareness, or critique of what they are taking in. In this view, popular culture is neither low nor high culture, neither traditional nor innovative. It is less about culture and more about economics because the artifacts of the popular are mired in neo-capitalist webs of production and consumption that use the consumers of popular culture to sell desires and goods.

Finally, an alternative to both of these critiques is what might be seen as an agentic or romantic critique of popular culture. From this perspective, popular cultural forms are seen as new, inventive, and more advanced forms than the so-called classic forms of culture. People's uses of popular culture are said to represent innovative ways of thinking that far surpass the rigid, bounded modes of representation of days gone by. Two views dominate within this perspective. For some scholars, youths' uses of popular culture should be examined for the pleasure (or *plaisir*, a la Barthes, 1975) that the young people derive from the texts (Alvermann, Hagood, & Williams, 2001; Buckingham, 1991). According to this view, youth can be seen as aware of, but unconcerned with, the ways in which popular cultural texts might be subtle forms of domination and reproduction of social, economic, and political systems that serve some and disenfranchise others. Their pleasure in the texts mitigates against the problematic nature of the texts. A second perspective argues that the popular is an explicitly agentic and even resistant space in which people's innovations will reinvent culture in ways that diminish strict social reproduction and the dominance of traditional forms and ways of thinking (Dolby, 2003; McCarthy, 1998). According to this view, people—especially young people—make culture anew with the texts of the popular as their material. Indeed, their use of brands and various mass media turn the texts back on themselves, diminishing, or at least challenging, the power of the texts to shape their lives.

In each case, we would argue, the critiques are over-determined serving to frame popular culture and youth culture as either good or bad. But popular culture—no less than the youth cultures so often subsumed to it in popular discourse—cannot be reduced to categories of good *or* bad, self-expression *or* other-exploitation, deviance *or* innovation, resistance *or* domination. Popular culture is simultaneously a product of people's imaginations, curiosities, and expressions and an institution with goals of shaping desires and needs, selling products, and manipulating imaginations and expressions. Popular culture is made as people live in the everyday world, and it is made by *both* people living out their lives *and* industries trying to sell people goods. It is the complex, double—indeed, multiple—life of popular culture that makes it hard to study, to use, and to control. It is the multiple life of popular culture that often makes it difficult for educators to decide whether popular culture is something that youth use productively or that uses youth for its own gains. Our data show that youth both use and are used by popular culture, and that work-ing this tension, rather than simply avoiding it by avoiding popular culture, is the job of educators.

JUST HOW DO YOUNG PEOPLE USE POPULAR CULTURE?

Ethnographic research shows that young people especially are heavy users of all forms of popular culture, or *youth lifestyle media*, a phrase which the second author has coined, through all available traditional and new media technologies (e.g., Alvermann, Moon, & Hagood, 1999; Buckingham, 1991; Cottle, 2001; Dolby, 2003; Holloway & Val-entine, 2003; Kress, 2003; Lewis & Fabos, 1999; Mahiri, 2003; Moje et al., 2004; Nespor, 1997). Youth, as shown in much ethnographic youth research, can be sophisticated and critical in their use and re-use of popular culture material, whether electronic or print-based. Popular cultural texts can inform their desires (van Helden, 2002), shape iden-tities (Holloway & Valentine, 2003; Moje & Ciechanowski, 2002), en-hance or change the nature of literacy skills (Gee, 2003; Lankshear & Knobel, 2002; Lee, 1993; Mahiri, 1994, 1998), improve certain kinds of test scores (Gee, 2003), and stimulate creativity (Alvermann, et al., 1999; Gee, 2003; Holloway & Valentine, 2003). Such texts can also do the opposite, or at least leave them indifferent or uncritical, just as they do to many adults (van Helden, 2002). In what follows, we pre-sent some of these possibilities via data drawn from Caspar's work with young men "reading" Abercrombie & Fitch (A&F) catalogs and websites, and from Elizabeth's work with young Latinas as they talk about, read, listen to, and watch music and film.

Doing Popular Culture: Abercrombie Boys

Caspar's examination of youth using popular culture is presented as narratives drawn from interviews with three different young men. The participants in Caspar's research, Jason, Tim, and David,[2] were all twenty to twenty-two years old at the time of his study. Jason and Tim agreed on having some of the characteristics commonly associ-ated with adolescence or as "behaving as an adolescent," while David embraced "being one" and seemed to equal his adolescent status to a constant state of "post-modern bliss," as he put it. He added that there is "really no other way to be anymore, no matter what your age is." In short, given their biological age, the Abercrombie & Fitch target group guideline, and their own claims to adolescence, we were satisfied that these participants would be suitable for this analysis.

Jason was twenty-two years old at the time of the interview, which took place in 2002. He was a business major at an East Coast private university in a major metropolitan area. His parents are Argentinean and American, but he has lived in the United States since the age of six, except for one year in Argentina during his late teens. He identifies himself as gay, and at the time of the research wore A&F clothing almost exclusively. He had worked at an A&F store as a "brand representative." Jason also looked like a model typically found within the A&F advertisements, with a very strong, fit physical appearance, white complexion, and energetic and playful, but serious and masculine behavior in engaging with others. That is, his body language was self-confident and his responses to the interview questions came in a strong, low voice without intonation or fluctuation, suggesting a confident and assertive manner. In other words, he seemed to know what he wanted to say and seemed confident that his comments would be accepted and understood.

David, twenty years old at the time of the interviews, was a student at a large state university in the Midwest United States. He studied comparative literature; was very much interested in different types of music, art, and drama; and often creatively engaged in producing poetry, screen plays, paintings, and photography. He has an Israeli and American background and had done all his schooling in the United States. Specifically, he described himself as "Moroccan, Egyptian, Israeli, with a dash of German and a sometimes nauseatingly overwhelming American coating." He identified himself mostly as gay, suggesting that he didn't "know if he wants to buy into the stereotype all the way." David dressed in a slightly *alternative* style mixed with some university logo-wear.

Tim lived down the hall from David in the same apartment building on campus. Tim was a twenty year old European American philosophy major at the same Midwestern state university. He was a rather short, skinny young person who wore baggy, oversized "streetwear." Tim identified as heterosexual and spent a lot of time with

David socially. He was born in the Midwest and did not have a great deal of travel or living experience outside that area.

Caspar interviewed Jason in a structural manner about his opinions of the A&F brand and his experiences working for them at an East Coast store. David and Tim engaged in a more informal conversation in David's apartment, and later at a restaurant, while they reflected on some of the things Caspar suggested, and offered topics and opinions of their own as well. During this second conversation, Caspar asked them about A&F in a more integrated manner as part of a larger conversation of popular culture and identity, while leaving the table free for anything they might want to offer. Because Caspar's goal was to examine whether and how the A&F brand was taken up as a popular cultural text by these youth, his analysis focuses primarily on the young men's interpretation of A&F. Tim, however, did not view A&F as integral to his identity, and so Caspar allowed the focus of the interview to expand to the popular cultural texts with which Tim did engage. Consequently, Tim's case allows for an interesting comparison of the ways the young men used and were used by different popular cultural texts. We present each case, or narrative, in succession, beginning with Jason.

Jason

Caspar met Jason while attending a linguistics conference where Jason served as an assistant to the conference organizers. When Caspar asked Jason, after several days of observing him, why he always wore A&F, Jason explained that it was because he had worked there in the past and they gave him discounts on clothing purchases. As a student, he added, he was too poor to buy new clothes. He immediately added that he did not wear A&F because he particularly liked them, their clothes, or their image, adding that it was actually "pretty anti-gay."

Jason acknowledged the appeal of A&F's advertising campaigns insofar as the models used were "hot." He explained that he did not really know anything about A&F other than they sold "boring men's clothes which my father used to buy," and only realized their merchandise and image had changed when he went for a job interview at the suggestion of a friend. He was surprised nobody wanted to know much about his background; the recruiters were only interested in whether or not he was "trainable" and whether he "had the look." He received a "brand representative" contract. Jason noted, A&F staff are not "sales people," an expression which seemed to leave a bad taste in his mouth. He soon moved up to be assistant manager and started hiring and firing people himself. To do so, he said, he used the "look-book," which consisted of guidelines on what job applicants were supposed to look like in order to fit A&F's brand image. It also described the colors that staff could wear during working hours: clothing colors matched skin tones. Jason said that he became appalled by the obvious anti-gay and anti-black attitudes of the district managers:

> The district manager made it pretty clear to me that I needed to hire hot, A&F-look boys and girls. Black people were obviously not welcome, not even as customers, really. He eventually forced me to fire a boy for swishing too much while he walked around the store. It just really pissed me off, and eventually I quit. I know I still wear their shit, but that's just financial. I can't believe people buy into all those bimbos and yeah, the boys are hot, but are they brainless or something?

In his talk, Jason made sure to distance himself from what he claimed are A&F's racist and sexist policies, while he defended his own A&F outfits. He did acknowledge that the models are sexy and that he liked them, but also associated the models and, seemingly, the consumers with being "brainless."

A&F as a brand has a prominent place in popular, mass-produced, consumer gay youth culture, although not necessarily in local versions of gay youth cultures, because of its attractive models, who wear little in the way of clothing, and because of the homoerotic nature of much of its photography. These erotic notions are, in the advertising, connected with youth or young people. With its repeated photographs and videos of all-male interactions—A&F presents fewer all-female photographs—and its emphasis on body, beauty, and virility (van Helden, 2002), the photography of A&F, and thus, the brand itself, may present to some gay cultures a version of an "ideal gay world" in which everyone is young, beautiful, and gay. This is also why, according to Jason, some men outside the target age group wear A&F clothing:

> Well, when you see guys in their forties wear A&F T-shirts in a bar then you know you've gotta stay away from them...they're after young boys. Total chicken hawks who pretend to look young and cool by putting on Abercombie. I think it's pathetic those guys who go after boys twenty years younger and I usually stay away. Especially when they wear A&F, that's like a warning signal.

Jason accepted the A&F brand for two reasons: the models are attractive and the business model is admirable for its success. As a young gay man and a business major, for Jason, those claims seem perfectly understandable, and in line with his sexual and professional identities. Simultaneously though, he rejected corporate policies for being racist and sexist, while showing that he had little respect for the "brainless" people who so easily buy into the A&F concept. On yet another level, Jason seemed fine with college age boys wearing A&F while accusing significantly older men of trying to look younger and pursuing young gay boys. He constructed a conditional view that the brand targeted a certain age group and that trying to belong in that group when no longer within the target range was not acceptable.

Jason's story shows how young people can make complex meanings out of a particular expression of popular, commercial culture. Some premises of a brand can be accepted, while others of the same brand are rejected, and so Jason developed a system that apparently was a comfortable way for him to think about A&F. Comfortable, here, does not mean simple.

David

Caspar has known David longer than the others, and so David was, at the time of the interviews, perhaps more aware of Caspar's interests in popular culture, youth culture, and identity. In fact, during previous conversations, David had accused Caspar of being a "pop culture slut." David generally tried to be witty, ironic, and smart and always tried to find some unusual or "twisted" connection to any interview topic. He had the following to say about the A&F brand:

> Oh yum, those boys are beyond fuckable and totally porny. Just a touch slick and modern, for my taste, but that wouldn't stop me. What I don't get is the whole gender mix that's going on there, I mean, why design screen savers

with boys and tits? Either the boys don't like it or the girls don't. Anyway, I wouldn't seriously wear any of their stuff, unless one of those jocks would rip it off me [laughs].

David did have an A&F T-shirt, which he wore "ironically" and not "seriously," he said, especially when he wanted to feel "slutty." When asked about other popular culture items or websites that he uses, he mentioned an expressly gay website first. It is a portal that offers information on travel, movies, shopping, and other lifestyle topics, but is mainly used by registered participants as a chat site:

> ...gay.com [a website], I use the most. Where else I am going to meet guys in this town? It totally is part of and feeds my identity, because not only do I talk to them and get to express myself, which is all cool in a virtual sort of way, but eventually you can hook up and connect with actual flesh and blood. A lot of socializing I do there, and the shift from an anonymous virtual life to the moment where you have coffee with someone, or sex, is fabulous. You create every moment exactly to your current metaphysics.

It seems that David was far more interested in such a website than in a commercial site or a brand such as Abercrombie. These latter seemed too "fixed" to him, or too "modern," as he put it, which he meant as opposite to post-modern. By contrast, gay.com offered him space to perform and express different moods, values, desires, and even bodies: one can manipulate one's online profile any way one wants. With each new contact, or chat, it is possible to build a relationship from scratch, and this contact can eventually lead to a game of pinball, a cup of coffee at Starbucks, or a hook-up, a one-time sexual encounter.

David seemed to love inventing himself and every situation continuously, and somehow seemed to feel very powerful and excited about doing that. The static beauty of A&F models who could not communicate was boring to him. However, he used A&F branded clothing to send messages to others, in class or in a bar, to tell them something about who he was. In doing so, he said that he made sure not to come across as a "typical" Abercrombie jock, although he did not elaborate how he portrayed an image contrary to what he saw as the typical Abercrombie image. What is important in David's talk about A&F is the sense of agency he seemed to convey as he made use of and took some pleasure from the erotic and sexualized image that A&F carries in the gay community. His comments indicate that he was aware of what he was doing and that he engaged in some level of critique of A&F as a brand, even as he used the brand as a way of building and maintaining relationships within his own youth culture and with others he encountered in a variety of contexts in which A&F could be read in particular ways.

Tim

To the question of what his favorite popular culture artifact or website was, Tim immediately responded, "my bong." That statement came with a smirk on his face, as Tim intended his labeling of the bong as an artifact of popular culture to be ironic, a joking response. But whether or not he recognized it, Tim's behaviors in a number of settings suggest that his bong really did serve as both an artifact and symbol of his taking up of popular culture. Tim showed Caspar his room, where he was just painting a bong-stand, a wooden device he constructed himself to keep the glass bong from falling over, in a design he had previously worked out on paper. David and Tim often smoked pot together in Tim's room, which was a small dark one-bedroom studio crammed with books, laundry, a bed, a desk, and a computer.

> Really, it [smoking pot] has to go together with the Simpsons. I can do them separately, but it's not the same. The Simpsons website would also be my favorite one. I use it daily. I don't quite identify with any of the characters, but it's the whole dynamic that I find nurturing. I have this really cool book too that explains how every great western philosophy is represented in episodes of the Simpsons (...) Otherwise I don't really understand pop music, or pop culture. It's such trash and just, no good, you know. I mean, Britney? Is that what you're talking about?

Tim's remarks suggest two important points about how Tim took up popular cultural texts. First, Tim considered "pop culture" to be something tasteless and for the masses, while he saw *The Simpsons* as an exception to his overall impression of what counted as pop culture. During the conversation, it became clear that he saw popular culture as unintelligent, unchallenging, sort of pre-chewed bubble-gum for those with "small brains." His main activities during most days were, according to his own words, watching *The Simpsons*, smoking pot, and reading philosophy (in that order). He had developed a way to link these activities so that he could stay home and watch episodes on his computer screen—he did not have a TV so he downloaded them from the Net—while commenting to David and exchanging the bong. Thus, the bong served as both a tool for the making of his particular youth culture—what he did while hanging out with David and other friends—and as an artifact that connected his particular youth culture to a wider, mass media produced, popular cultural artifact. Watching *The Simpsons* with his college peer transformed the popular cultural text of *The Simpsons* into an intellectual activity particular to him and his friends.

The Internet was another source of popular cultural texts for Tim. Tim did not drink, or have a girlfriend, but he did work some nights in a local restaurant. Outside of class, however, he spent much of his time in his room. Being online "24/7," he surfed the Internet, e-mailed, and chatted often with family members and some friends, "who are a bit tired" of his "obsession" with *The Simpsons*. When offered an article on gay interpretations of *The Simpsons*, he said that would be "totally cool." On the topic of Abercombie & Fitch, he really could not say much, as he was unfamiliar with the brand and the imagery. However, when he looked at parts of the catalog as part of the interview, he responded, "yeah, right, steroid city," and switched the topic. Tim's dismissal of the A&F brand and its merchandise serves to underscore his general distaste for what he labeled popular culture. As he took up popular cultural texts in the privacy of his own room, with his small circle of friends, Tim transformed these texts in his own mind to be intellectually and socially stimulating texts, texts that allowed him to maintain certain kinds of relationships and a certain level of social isolation.

From these few segments of in-depth interviews, it becomes clear how very differently three older youth can talk about, use, and evaluate their ideas and behaviors in relation to popular culture. There is not a simple acceptance or rejection of popular culture. In the case of A&F, Jason and David both appreciate some aspects of the brand, and both use the brand insofar as they wear Abercombie clothes and find the models in the advertisements desirable. At the same time, however, they reject A&F's corporate policies and what they see as empty messages of sculpted torsos and "challenged intelligence." Tim seems to reject most strongly, or demonstrate disinterest in, A&F's brand and image by dismissing the whole thing as fake—a "steroid city." He was also the only participant who identified himself as heterosexual. The other two who acknowledged the attractiveness of the models, steroids or not, identified as gay and did have athletic, muscular appearances very much like the models in the A&F catalog (while Tim did not). Tim, however, also did not comment on, or seem to be interested in, any of the females portrayed on the catalog.

Their use of the A&F brand is sophisticated, as both Jason and David wear A&F clothing in a problematized or complex way. Jason claims to do it because it is all he can afford, but also acknowledges its sex-appeal and its role in the categorization of men of different ages and their interests. He did socialize with men of different age groups and his interview comments suggest that he was aware of what the word "Abercrombie" on his chest might signal to them. David also wore the brand name, but claimed to do it "ironically," to show that his sex appeal is connected with wit, intelligence, and sauciness. In his words, "It says I'm not a dumb jock but I do like to screw." He seemed to think other features of his personality, appearance, and behavior somehow compensate for, or complicate, the "dumb jock" image that A&F carries for him.

It is worth noting that many of Jason and David's comments were connected to sexual identity and behavior. Only Tim stayed away from such remarks, and did not make any sexual comments or jokes under any circumstances during the conversations. The other two connected their discussion of A&F to other popular culture activities or media, such as bars and websites, both of which were again connected to sexual activities. It is clear that the brand had particular meaning for them in terms of sexual identification, and that they carried that meaning with them, via another medium or space such as a bar or a chat room, and communicated it to others. They were aware of the popular meaning A&F carried, and they were aware that they were "playing" with different meanings in their heads, and in their communications and behaviors.

The most important claim that we can make from these interviews is that these three young people took up popular culture very differently. They also consumed, interpreted, and re/used these phenomena in complex and creative ways. Finally, they were acutely aware that this was exactly what they were doing. These interviews hardly constitute a statistical sampling, but they do demonstrate that researchers and popular presses alike must be cautious in oversimplifying the meaning that is made by young people out of popular cultural texts. Adults need to be careful about assuming how youth are influenced by such texts and how they use these texts in their daily lives. This realization must affect how we theorize identity, adolescence, and youth culture, as young people themselves seem to be quite clear about the fact that popular culture has an impact on them. Whether this impact is good or bad remains an open question and depends very much on the youth themselves and the opportunities they have for examining these texts in explicit and critical ways.

Doing Popular Culture: Latino[3] Lovers

Elizabeth has been engaged in an ongoing community ethnography focused on youth culture, identity, and literacy in one urban community for five years. The community, embedded in the city of Detroit, Michigan, is inhabited predominantly by Latino/as. In the larger project, Elizabeth and a multidisciplinary, multi-ethnic team of researchers have interviewed and observed forty-one young people (both male and female) in community, home, and school settings. For this chapter, Elizabeth uses data from four young women with whom she and her team have worked closely over a four-year period. Their self-identified pseudonyms in the study are Pilar, Alexandra, Yolanda, and Jovana. The young women all live in low-income or working-class homes. Although this data is from only four young women, their complex uses of popular culture are, in many ways, representative of the complexity we observed in the larger sample of youth. The young men in the larger study differ from the young women in important ways, but we chose to focus on the young women to provide a contrast to Caspar's male participants.

Background on the Young Women

These young women identify variably as Mexican, Chicana, Tejana, Mexicana, and Mexican American, depending on when and where they were born, and when and where they are asked about their identities. Yolanda was born in Mexico and identifies herself as Mexican. Pilar, Alexandra, and Jovana were born in the United States to parents born in Mexico. Pilar and Alexandra represent themselves most frequently as Chicanas or Tejanas (residents of Texas who are of Mexican ancestry), citing their origins in Texas whenever they name themselves as Chicanas. They also labeled themselves as Mexican, Latina, or Hispanic in various written texts and on a language and identity survey. Jovana chose many of the same identifiers on the written survey, but in her talk with peers and members of the research team, she identified herself as "Mexican and American, too." Thus, the sample is representative in terms of generational status and hybrid identity enactments of a range of Latinas who identify as being of Mexican ancestry in this urban area. What unites all of the Latinas in Elizabeth's research project is (1) their strong ethnic identity enactments (all describe themselves in terms of some aspect of Mexican-ness when asked simply to describe themselves to another person); (2) their explicit attention to a wide variety of popular cultural texts; and (3) their unique usage of popular cultural texts.

Artifacts of popular culture filled their lives, and yet their lives cannot be reduced to popular culture, and certainly not to any one type or one stream of popular cultural texts. These young women were immersed in the popular, but they were also immersed in many other cultural texts, models, and practices, including school, Catholic, home, Mexican/Chicano/Latino, Detroit, Latina (i.e., gendered), and urban cultures, just to name a few. These other cultures are, of course, *popular*, in the sense that *people* make and practice these cultures, but they are not the *popular* in the sense of being broadly—no less globally—marketed and disseminated. What is critical, however, is how these cultures intersected with mainstream popular culture as the young women produced cultural practices unique to their particular physical and social space, to their groups of peers, and to their families and community. In short, these young women used a variety of cultural texts in different ways, at different times, to different ends, thus producing something that one might generically label *youth culture*, but more specifically as *Detroit Latina/Mexicana/Chicana urban popular family youth* culture. They were not simply taking up the mainstream, but nor were they ignoring it.

Doing Popular Culture: Being Latino Lovers

Imagine a seventh grade classroom filled with young people at the end of the period. The teacher has just given the students the last five minutes of the period as "free time." Some chat with one another; some pull out homework due next period; some get up and move around the room. Others—in this case, two young women—read a magazine together. They sit side by side, flipping through the pages, glancing at images, pointing out features and dress of the people pictured, occasionally reading some text. Elizabeth approaches the two girls and asks what they are doing. "We're reading this music magazine. See, this is the Backstreet Boys, we love them, they're so fine [pronounced "foin," a pronunciation taken from an urban colloquialism and used as a marker of group membership]. This is AJ, he's Hispanic." Elizabeth's curiosity is piqued: Why the Backstreet Boys? Why AJ? Why mention that he's Hispanic? She probes the girls with each of these questions, and they respond simply: "They're fine...He's hot...We only like Hispanic boys."

This scene represents Elizabeth's first sustained interaction with two of the young women and is remarkably representative of the different interactions we had with the young women in this study. Many interactions revolved around some sort of text, usually a magazine, a CD, a song playing on the radio, or a local newspaper. A surface look at these interactions might lead one to concur with dominant discourses about adolescents, particularly young women: "young women lose their senses" and live out their lives in relation to hyper-real images of masculinity, femininity, and romantic relationships available in popular culture.

But that reading of the girls' uses of popular culture would be checked upon closer examination of their typical practices. For example, when we stopped to pick up a local newspaper while walking around the community, Pilar, Alexandra, and Yolanda turned to the entertainment section, searching for information on the performances of bands or groups they cared about. On one outing, Alexandra and Pilar both picked up newspapers and quickly turned to the "center-fold" advertisement of an up-coming performance of the all-male group, *Intocable*, at a local dance and music club later that month. They checked out ticket prices and times, but they also talked about saving the centerfold to display in their rooms. Some of the girls present noted the prohibitive price of the concert, stating that they would not be able to attend; others said that they would find a way in, perhaps via one young women's sister who had "connections." Still others noted that the concert started too late and their parents or other family members would not let them stay out.

Even such a brief glimpse at the young women's talk around one popular cultural event can reveal some of the complexity in their take-up of pop culture. The young women, for example, were not talking about a mainstream, mass media musical group, but about following a locally popular Mexican group which sings romantic ballads and pop numbers. Second, the girls did not merely fantasize about the men in the music group; they made social and economic plans around the group's performance, discussing ways to acquire tickets or entrance (without paying), how to make use of social and familial relationships, and whether their schedules and family norms would allow them to attend the concert. The group's performance—represented in the centerfold photograph in a local newspaper—served as a site for social and economic negotiation within a larger network of social, cultural, economic, and even political relations.

Popular cultural tools can also serve as identity tools, part of a larger identity toolkit (Gee, 1996) the young women build through a variety of cultural practices and interactions. When window-shopping in a suburban shopping mall or on their neighborhood streets, for example, the young women spent a great deal of time examining music CDs of their favorite artists. The focus in these texts was, with a few exceptions, on music artists and, almost always, on male artists. However, the artists they were drawn to were different in different spaces, with the mainstream mall space offering more mainstream artists, such as rappers Tupac and Eminem, and Juvenile or boy bands, such as the Backstreet Boys or 'N Sync. In addition, some cross-over

Latino groups, such as the Kumbia Kings, received attention in mainstream stores and in local community stores.

On at least one occasion, when one young woman in the group expressed an interest in mainstream female artists, such as Britney Spears or Christina Aguilera, she was careful not to display her interest in obvious or vocal ways to the others in the group. Her interest was similar to that of another young woman who professed a love for "white" television shows, from which they could learn to "talk like a white girl," dress white, and adopt "white" hair and make-up styles. Indeed, when asked where she got information about how to "talk like a white girl," one young woman claimed, "TV. I learn everything from there" (Moje & Ciechanowski, 2002). It is worth noting that other young women watched the same shows (e.g., *Boy Meets World*), but did not talk about learning how to act like white girls from the show. Instead, they talked about the show portraying "real life" and "just being funny." Thus, their uses of the cultural texts, and the identity tools they provided, differed in significant ways. In all cases, the texts provided the girls with tools they could use to make identity and group membership claims, but the kinds of claims they wanted to make differed in important ways.

For example, although all the girls made gendered claims, Pilar and Alexandra identified more explicitly as "Latino Lovers"—even choosing that phrase as an e-mail address. These young women were stunned to find that the email address they really wanted, something to the effect of "ChicanoLoversKumbiaKings,"[4] was already taken, a point that underscores the power of the popular for both reflecting and shaping identities. These young women named themselves Latino Lovers because, as they announced time and time again, "I love Mexican boys," also adding that they liked "Dominicans, Puerto Ricans, and Cubans." Every interview conducted with Pilar and Alexandra included a discussion of the young men in their lives, both friendships and romantic relationships. They also talked at length about what they labeled the "macho" Mexican male, who "had to be right," who had to be "in charge." Although they talked in critical ways of what they called "part of Mexican culture," they seemed accepting of such gendered relationship practices, and seemed intent on building romantic relationships with young Latinos.

Their Latino Lover identities were tied to popular Latin music texts about love, sex, and relationships. The texts—which varied from sexually explicit raps to love ballads—also were tools for imagining, learning about, or maintaining female-male relationships, reminiscent of the uses of romance novels among housewives detailed by Janice Radway (1984). They imagined, for example, fathers for their future children, referring to certain music artists with phrases such as, "he's my sixth baby daddy," meaning that the artist was one of six men whom they deemed good enough to be a father to their children, if they were to have them. Music texts also were useful for promoting and maintaining actual, present relationships, as well as for living out relational identities. When Elizabeth asked Pilar what song most represented her identity, Pilar responded, *De Uno y De Todos Los Modus [One and All the Ways...*I can possibly love you] "because my boyfriend dedicated it to me and because I have always liked it." Although Pilar self-identified throughout the study as "Chicana" and "loud," claiming repeatedly that "I like to be heard," her representative song focused on love and relationships, underscoring her use of popular cultural texts as ways to maintain certain kinds of relationships.

Alexandra, by contrast, chose the word "bitch" to identify herself, and chose *Move Bitch* by Ludacris—a song performed by an African American male artist and addressed to the many women who have tried to hook up with him for his money and status. Alexandra explained: "I have a very bad temper and I most likely end up calling everybody a bitch." In Alexandra's case, her choice seemed to reflect her sense of self in male/female relationships, her self-positioning as someone who gets in men's faces. Just as Butler argues about the "radical resignification" of the word "queer" (quoted in Olson & Worsham, 2000, p. 759) in queer theory, Alexandra here may be radically resignifying Ludacris's positioning of women as bitches by taking up the title for herself to diminish the sting of the word applied to her and the rest of her gender. In such a move, Alexandra talks back to Ludacris, engaging in what those in marginalized positions have done throughout time when they take up racial or sexual slurs (e.g., nigga, queer): apply them proudly to themselves thereby diffusing and transforming the power of the slur to slur, to hurt, or to marginalize.

In both cases, these young women were representative of a group of girls who talked explicitly and often about male-female relationships, and who used the songs to "hook up" with men or to define themselves as separate from men who listened to the same music. This last point is particularly important: the songs were useful not only for imagining relationships, but also for promoting, developing, and maintaining relationships. Popular cultural texts were tied to actual romantic relationships, to the structure of gendered relationships in their ethnic cultural practice, and to how they identified as young women in their everyday worlds.

Other young women, such as Yolanda and Jovana, were more interested in using popular cultural texts to learn, it seems, about different ways of being a woman. They were concerned with how to talk, dress, or present themselves in certain ways, such as learning how to "talk like a white girl," thinking through life relationships (e.g., with parents, siblings, or young men), or checking out Britney's (and other female performers') latest hair and dress styles. Both Jovana and Yolanda used the texts to learn about other ways of being outside their cultural and geographic space, thus allowing them to navigate different cultural groups, from "white girl" groups to other Latina groups, from school groups to family groups, from male groups to female groups. However, both Yolanda and Jovana enjoyed the same romantic ballads of Mexican male artists as did the previous group. What it seems Yolanda and Jovana did not share with Pilar and Alexandra was an interest in rap and hip hop music, or music that their male peers would be likely to listen to. Pilar and Alexandra, by contrast, did not share Yolanda and Jovana's interest in "white girl" texts and more mainstream *pop* music.

Thus, what linked the two groups of young women was a focus on gendered identities and romantic relationships. What distinguished them were different ways of being in relationships and different goals for the outcome of those relationships. In no case were the young women simply following along with their peers, and in no case were the young women ignorant of the implications of their engagement with the popular cultural forms. Each of them recognized how these texts were emblematic of particular identities, and they emphasized different texts in different spaces and relationships as a way of marking their identities, for example, backgrounding an interest in Britney, foregrounding their enjoyment of certain movies, and so on, depending on the group they were with at the time.

More interesting, these differences seem to generate different sorts of *girl cultures*, with groups of young women referring to each other as "those girls who think they're all that," or as "babyish," or as "acting all naïve, like a little girl." The girls who listened to, watched, or read about older male artists, particularly rappers, could position themselves as "more mature" and could use the "less innocent" texts, as they described them, to identify with the male youth to whom they were attracted to in their neighborhoods. The other girls could position themselves as "respectful" and "responsible" girls who were thoughtful and more careful of relationships. They could also position themselves as standing apart from their urban community, as signaled by the desire some girls expressed to "get out of this community," which they considered dirty and dangerous.

That a consistent pattern of talk about love, relationships, babies, and marriage appears among all the young women—including young women in the larger sample—illuminates an important source of difference in cultural constructions of the adolescent. Elizabeth, a middle-aged white academic, has noted, with some tension, the lack of talk about post-secondary educational and career goals among all of the young women she and other research team members have interviewed. Observing how the young woman take up popular cultural texts which foreground male-female relationships, Elizabeth has worried that these texts, read and listened to *at such a young age* foreclose possibilities for agency and potentially cast the girls into positions of subjugation. But Elizabeth's reading of these texts, and of the young women's practices generally, are framed by her own class, race, age, and particular way of expressing gender. These young women see themselves as emotionally, physically, and socially mature enough to handle the responsibilities of romantic relationships and parenthood. They do not see themselves as children on the brink of adulthood. Indeed, their many domestic responsibilities at home, such as childcare, cleaning, cooking, and overseeing the completion of homework by younger siblings, are similar to the responsibilities Elizabeth currently has in her own domestic life—responsibilities she did not have as a younger person. Her out-of-school time was scrupulously protected for school homework and extracurricular activities. The assumption, then, that these young women, in virtue of their age, are in need of protection, guidance, and oversight; the assumption that their time must be carefully structured for them; the assumption that their school responsibilities should be foregrounded above all else, can be understood as a white, middle-class construction of adolescence as a time of innocence, development, and becoming some particular sort of future person. When examined from the particular Latina perspective represented by these young women, adolescence seems to be a very different thing, if, indeed, a thing at all. Consequently, their choices and uses of popular cultural texts must be read from the particular social, cultural, and economic perspectives that they bring to bear on the texts.

Indeed, the desire for emotional, physical, and relational maturity as represented in the girls' choices of popular cultural texts appeared to be imbricated in the gendered, religious, ethnic, and cultural models, most visible in the traditional *quinceañera* that most of these young women celebrated. The *quinceañera* marks a specific transition from girl to woman for Latinas who practice it. It is only after they turn fifteen that young Latinas are allowed to wear cosmetics, dance, and date young men. And as often as they read teen music magazines, watched television, and listened to various music artists, these young women also read fashion magazines, searched for *quinceañera* dresses, consulted with mothers, aunts, uncles, and godparents about *quinceañera* plans, and made lists of possible *chambelans* (their male escort in the church mass and the party that follows) and *dubas*, or male attendants, for their *damas*, or female attendants. Their preparations for the *quinceañera* demonstrate the power of a variety of cultural models to draw their attention, as *quinceañeras* are rarely represented in mainstream popular cultural texts. To do the *quinceañera*, one had to *do* traditional Mexican culture.

Thus, the talk about and focus on maturity, innocence, love, and romance via mainstream and Latino/a popular cultural texts is not a vestige of the cultural models offered by popular cultural texts alone. Rather, the young women's focus on love, relationships, and maturity bears the trace of multiple cultural models. The desire to be *mature* for these particular young women was drawn from and integrated with models of what it means to be an adolescent, Roman Catholic, Mexican young woman in this urban landscape. The cultural models of maturity, innocence, love, and romance offered to these young women are, of course, not unique to Latinas or Catholics. That is, the cultural models that position young women as innocent objects to be made mature through romantic relationships with men are offered in wide variety of religious and ethnic cultures. What is important here is the recognition that the popular cultural texts the young women identify with do not exist in a vacuum; indeed, these popular cultural texts might not have worked their magic with these young women unless the girls were not already living inside cultural models that positioned them as waiting on the edge of innocence for men to develop them into mature beings. In short, one must question the role of popular culture in "robbing children of their innocence," and examine the role that dominant social and cultural discourses about adolescence, gender, sexuality, and relationships might have in how young people decide which popular cultural texts are most interesting and useful to them.

Doing Popular Culture: Playing at Borders

The group-centered analyses that we have presented are important in illustrating some differences in how young people of the same gender, ethnic background, and social class take up popular culture. However, group analyses fail to emphasize the ways in which all the young women in the study engaged with a wide variety of texts, connecting to certain texts when necessary for membership in one group or another. Group analyses also fail to demonstrate fully how these young women also merged mainstream popular cultural texts with less widely distributed Latino/a popular texts. In this section, we use a narrative constructed from data rendered by Pilar to illustrate the unique ways that these young women took up a host of cultural texts. On one occasion, Pilar, for example, read the contents of her CD case to Elizabeth, emphasizing the contrasts in her musical choices:

P: We're gonna play our CDs, you can hear them. We'll be like, "This is Mexican. This is rap." They're like totally different. I got Juvenile: *I Got Da Fire*. Right next to that I've got Intocable. They're right next to each other.

E: That's cool. That shows all your different identities.

P: Um-hmm...O'Town sings a slow song, *All or Nothing*. Right next to it I've got Pegaso.

In another segment of the interview presented above, Pilar went on at length about popular cultural texts and her ethnic cultural identities, blurring the boundaries between popular culture (in the form of music that anyone could obtain on a CD, tape, or website) and ethnic culture, which Pilar claimed as an important aspect of her identity:

> Penni let me borrow her Kumbia Kings CD, the first one, 'cause I've got only the second one...Have you heard the Intocable CD? I'll put this one on and if it sounds familiar then you'll know if it's *Es Para Ti*...[she is setting up the Intocable CD]...Alexandra is from Texas. I was born in Texas. We're Chicanas, we're Tejanas. In my sketch book, I've got something that says Chicana, then Pilar, then Angel...Oh, here's a song [she says the name, *Azucita*, but Elizabeth doesn't understand what the Spanish means, so Pilar explains]...You know, like sugar...azucar [she spells this for Elizabeth]. It's a really famous song, you might have heard it. "Azucita" she sings to me. "Ay, I love that song." The Kumbia Kings, they have some English songs. It has two songs, but their new CD, it has like five songs.

Pilar's movement from talk about the Kumbia Kings and Intocable to her talk about her friend, Alexandra, who has reminded her of being Tejana/Chicana, is not merely the jumbled ramblings of a hyperkinetic or confused adolescent blissfully hopping from one topic to the next. The links between these texts and Pilar's ethnic cultural identity become clear from studying both the texts, and how Pilar talks about herself and her identity across time. Her talk about Mexican music groups overlaps with her multiple self-labelings ("we're Chicanas, we're Tejanas"), just as her ethnic and gendered identity is represented in the palimpsest of labels she gives herself ("Chicana," "Pilar," "Angel"). When Pilar named herself in the midst of her talk about Mexican music, she sandwiched her named identity between her foregrounded Chicana identity and her gendered identity. Gender was signaled explicitly with the "a" on Chicana, and more implicitly with "Angel," a polyvalent youth cultural term layered with mixed messages about innocence and sexuality for young women. Chicana, in addition to marking gender, signals a hybrid ethnicity of Mexican and American. In this move, Pilar signified her sense of self as more than one individual, as a hybrid of Chicana, woman, youth, and person. In this move, Pilar also signified for the informed reader the importance of gender in her subjectivity. The term Chicana indexes both ethnicity and gender, suggesting that there might be no further need or desire for Pilar to ground her identity in the gendered, "Angel." But the use of "Angel" underscores her identity as a particular kind of Chicana, a sexualized young woman who takes up a North American popular identity while maintaining a resistant, conflicted, borderlands identity. Pilar's choices of musical texts further this sense of self as hybrid.

The music of the Kumbia Kings, for example, is critical to her representation of her polyvalent self as both a Chicana person named Pilar and a woman named Angel, as the Kumbia Kings are themselves representative of borders, hybridity, and polyvalence.[5] The Kumbia Kings' latest album containing both Spanish and English songs (which Pilar specifically marked in her talk), is emblematic of both the group's and Pilar's hybrid identity. As a Chicana who lived in a predominantly African American neighborhood, and attended a predominantly African American school in Detroit, a two-way bilingual immersion school, a predominantly Latino/a high school, and finally a predominantly African American high school, Pilar's ethnic identifications had gone through a variety of transitions. As she remarked in one interview, "At my old school, I didn't talk much Spanish. I didn't talk about being Hispanic. I would never deny my culture, but I didn't talk about it much either. It's different at [middle school name]. I speak Spanish all the time." Just as she shifted her everyday practices in accordance with the dominant populations at her schools, she shifted her choices of popular cultural texts, taking up the Backstreet Boys and focusing on their "Hispanic" members early in her predominantly Latino/a middle school career, then shifting to Kumbia

Kings, Intocable, and other Mexican or Latino artists as she met Alexandra, who identified explicitly as Tejana/Chicana. At the same time, Pilar added rap and hip hop music texts to her retinue, weaving together mainstream popular texts valued in her neighborhood, as well as texts valued in her predominantly African American neighborhood, school, and in the larger Detroit environment.

Just as the young men Caspar represented used and rejected, critiqued and consumed Abercrombie & Fitch, these young women used, critiqued, *and* consumed popular music, movie, and television texts in complex ways. The young women used popular, ethnic, spatial, religious, and school culture to make something unique, a particular youth culture that drew from popular cultural texts, but also drew from interactions with parents, siblings, teachers, and community members. The culture that these youth made and lived each day was situated in particular geographic and physical spaces (Moje, in press), and shifted and changed with each interaction they had. Yes, they voraciously consumed popular cultural texts, but they consumed a wide variety of texts, and they took them up in ways that allowed them to represent particular facets of their identities. They were neither deeply critical nor blissfully acritical of these texts. As educators and parents, we might all continue to wonder about the effect of these texts on these young women, but we cannot look only to the texts, nor can we assume that these girls are more vulnerable than we are, simply because of their youth. They take up the texts because, whether we like to acknowledge it or not, the texts do not deeply disrupt other cultural models in their experience. In this case, the models revolve around what it means to be a young woman, and they are offered by society, religion, and schooling. Rather than focus attention on the youth or pop culture texts, we might do well to look to the interrelationship of popular culture with other more invisible and, perhaps, deeply rooted texts, discourses, and identities offered via other cultural models.

CONCLUSION

We can no longer assume that youth live at the whim of popular culture more than any other age group. We can no longer assume that all young people take up popular cultural texts in identical ways. And we can no longer reduce them to the texts of popular culture. At the same time we can avoid romanticizing their uses of popular culture by highlighting the complexity and contradictions evident in their talk about and use of popular cultural texts. Although it is clear that youth are not the lazy, deviant, hormonally challenged youth they are often depicted to be in the press and some popular media, it is also clear that they are, at times, conflicted about their uses of popular culture, as clearly indicated in data from both of our groups of young people. In particular, Caspar's data indicate that even highly educated, older (on the adolescent age spectrum) youth who are accustomed to "doing critique" are not always as critical of popular culture as they might claim in their talk. For a whole host of reasons, they take up—and often use to particular ends—the texts and the artifacts of popular culture that they say they despise. Such findings lead us to consider a number of questions we believe are critical for deconstructing notions of adolescence and for enhancing the education of young people in a media-saturated world.

First, what does it really mean for young people to analyze critically the role of popular culture in their lives? Do they understand the ways that makers of mass-produced popular culture may be co-opting their interests and desires in order to sell them things and belief systems, which in turn shape their desires and interests? Must one shun a practice or text to fully critique it? What about enjoyment and pleasure? Should educators assume that enjoyment and critique are mutually exclusive? More research is needed to provide insight into how these media succeed in getting people *emotionally* involved, how these artifacts shape the system of meaning of feelings and emotions young people employ or experience, how one engages in critique of a text one enjoys or even loves, and how an active critique of popular culture would influence systems of emotion and feeling.

Second, why is the world so concerned about *youth* and popular culture, even as its major corporations co-opt popular cultural trends for the explicit purpose of selling to youth? Are youth as naive as some researchers, teachers, and parents seem to believe? It seems clear that educators and educational researchers alike assume a lack of sophistication, a developmental vulnerability in *the young person* that makes youth particularly susceptible to the negative power of popular culture. But it is worth asking whether youth need to learn to be critical any more than do adults.

These questions aside, if popular culture is as closely connected to people's identities, belief systems, values, and behaviors as we suspect it is, and if different groups of young people are actively involved in constructing cultures from the many different cultural models available to them, then it is time to take what youth do with popular culture seriously. It is time to give it a more prominent place in research on adolescence and education. It can be argued that popular culture has become the dominant post-ideological force. Its post-modern, polyvalent appearance guarantees its stealth-like quality of being impossible to grasp, comprehend, or attack, while its inner machinery is modernly capitalist, exploitative, and linear. It can also be argued that popular cultures' polyvalent and hybrid appearance is exactly what gives it the power to serve as a tool of agency, expression, and resistance in the hands of those typically marginalized (Knobel & Lankshear, 2001; McCarthy, 1998). From both perspectives, it is important to understand that popular culture frames dominant discourses of our time and that these discourses are important tools in people's identity, learning, and self-expression kits.

If popular culture discourses open up opportunities to teach better, learn better, and understand better (Alvermann, et al., 1999; Dolby, 2003; Dyson, 2003), then educators cannot ignore them. Those who work with or study popular and youth cultures can be sure of three things at least: popular culture is everywhere, it usually has commercial interests, and it pays special attention to young people as a market (Grossman, 2003). Although youth are no more vulnerable to the *immorality* or *commercialism* of popular culture than are children or adults, they are certainly targets of organized "lifestyle reinforcements" and "the quest to be cool" (Grossman, 2003) enacted via popular cultural networks (Dolby, 2003). Systems of education serve as useful sites for such careful attention to popular culture, not because young people are especially vulnerable to the whims of popular culture, but because the school is a space where all cultural models should be closely examined, expanded, and/or challenged.

Before we jump on the popular cultural and education bandwagon, however, it seems important to ask whether we have evidence that some people—other than researchers—are not happy with the current assumptions about how adolescent people use popular culture and about dominant views of popular culture's place, or lack thereof, in the classroom. Although both the popular press and the research literature decry the dangers of popular culture's influence on adolescents, only certain texts are brought under the microscope. Whose interests are served by studying youths' uses of popular culture and by attempts to effect change in those uses? Whose interests are served by maintaining the *status quo*, and simply worrying about the lost innocence of imagined youth? Would those interests be served if young people learned to critique the economic and political reach of popular cultural texts?

If we deconstruct the notion of *adolescence* more fully and demonstrate that young people already engage in critique or that, in many ways, they *build* popular culture, then systems of marketing and advertising will have to be reinvented. If educators teach youth to engage critically with popular culture and to use it to their advantage, then that may change or upset the original balance or "popular commercial ecosystem" in place now. These ecosystems are an integral element of the larger economic and political system that we live in, and do not generally appreciate challenges to its wealth or power. In other words, current discourses of adolescence may be central in some way to the "neo-capitalist" organization and interests of our society. Are we prepared to encounter the consequences of critiquing one of the pillars of the system, and ready to address what happens in a post-adolescent world?

NOTES

1. Age categorizations that distinguish adolescents from children and adults generally range from ten to twenty years. We add another layer of distinction: Adults, for the purposes of this chapter, can be considered those people who talk about *adolescents* as if they no longer belong in that category.
2. All identifying names have been replaced by pseudonyms.
3. We emphasize the use of the "o" or the "a" at the end of Latino/a, which is used to signal gender. When we are referring to males of Latin descent, we will use Latino; for females, Latina. When referring to both genders or generically, we use the term, Latino/a. These distinctions are important in this section, i.e., this header refers to young women who have deemed themselves those who love Latinos.

4. We are purposely vague here, although the exact phrase is noted in our field notes. Although it is unlikely that readers could track down the owners of the exact e-mail address the girls wanted and ultimately chose, we prefer to maintain as much anonymity for these youth as possible.
5. The Kumbia Kings, a musical group, was started by the brother of Selena, a Mexican female artist murdered just as her career was in ascendancy on both sides of the Mexican/US border.

REFERENCES

Alvermann, D. E., Hagood, M. C., & Williams, K. B. (2001). Image, language, and sound: Making meaning with popular culture texts. *Reading Online, 4*(11). Available: http://www.readingonline.org/.

Alvermann, D. E., Moon, J., & Hagood, M. C. (1999). *Popular culture in the classroom: Teaching and researching critical media literacy.* Newark, DE: International Reading Association/National Reading Conference.

Amaya, A. O. (2003, July 3). A musical "journey" with El Central. *El Central,* p. 10.

Arnett, J. J. (Ed.). (2002). *Adolescence and emerging adulthood* (1st ed.). Upper Saddle River, NJ: Prentice Hall.

Barthes, R. (1975). *The pleasure of the text* (R. Miller, Trans.). New York: Hill and Wang.

Bennett, W. (1994). *The book of virtues.* New York: Simon and Schuster.

Buckingham, D. (1991). Teaching about the media. In D. Lusted (Ed.), *The media studies book* (pp. 12–35). New York: Routledge.

Buckingham, D. (2003). Media education and the end of the critical consumer. *Harvard Educational Review, 73*(3), 309–327.

Cottle, T. J. (2001). *Mind fields: Adolescent consciousness in a culture of distraction.* New York: Peter Lang.

Desantis, J. (2002). Unbelievable: We control who you think you are. *XY, 30,* 49–50.

Dolby, N. (2003). Popular culture and democratic practice. *Harvard Educational Review, 73*(3), 258–284.

Dyson, A. H. (2003). "Welcome to the jam": Popular culture, school literacy, and the making of childhoods. *Harvard Educational Review, 73*(3), 328–361.

Gaztambide-Fernández, R. A. & Gruner, A. (2003). Introduction. *Harvard Educational Review, 73*(3), 253–257.

Gee, J. P. (1996). *Social linguistics and literacies: Ideology in discourses* (2nd ed.). London: Falmer.

Gee, J. P. (2003). What video games have to teach us about learning and literacy. New York: Palgrave Macmillan.

Grossberg, L. (1995). Cultural studies: What's in a name? (One more time). *Taboo: The Journal of Culture and Education, 1,* 1–37.

Grossman, L. (2003, September 8). The quest for cool. *Time, 162,* 48–54.

Hirsch, E. D., Kett, J. F., & Trefil, J. S. (1987). *Cultural literacy: What every American needs to know.* Boston: Houghton Mifflin.

Holloway, S. L. & Valentine, G. (2003). *Cyberkids: Children in the information age.* London: Routledge Falmer.

Horkheimer, M. & Adorno, T. W. (1972). *Dialectics of enlightenment* (J. Cumming, Trans.). New York: Herder and Herder.

Knobel, M. & Lankshear, C. (2001). Cut, paste, and publish: The production and consumption of zines. In D. E. Alvermann (Ed.), *Youth's multiliteracies in a digital world* (pp. 164–185). New York: Peter Lang.

Kress, G. (2003). *Literacy in the new media age (literacies).* New York: Routledge.

Lankshear, C. & Knobel, M. (2002). Do we have your attention? New literacies, digital technologies, and the education of adolescents. In D. E. Alvermann (Ed.), *Youth's multiliteracies in a digital world* (pp. 19–39). New York: Peter Lang.

Lee, C. D. (1993). *Signifying as a scaffold for literary interpretation: The pedagogical implications of an African American discourse genre* (NCTE Research Report, No. 26). Urbana, IL: National Council of Teachers of English.

Lesko, N. (2001). *Act your age! A cultural construction of adolescence.* New York: Routledge Falmer.

Lewis, C. & Fabos, B. (1999, December). *Chatting on-line: Uses of instant message communication among adolescent girls.* Paper presented at the National Reading Conference, Orlando, FL.

Mahiri, J. (1994). Reading rites and sports: Motivation for adaptive literacy of young African American males. In B. J. Moss (Ed.), *Literacy across communities* (pp. 121–146). Cresskill, NJ: Hampton Press.

Mahiri, J. (1998). *Shooting for excellence: African American and youth culture in new century schools.* Urbana, IL: National Council of Teachers of English.

Mahiri, J. (Ed.). (2003). *What they don't learn in school: Literacy in the lives of urban youth.* New York: Peter Lang.

McCarthy, C. (1998). *The uses of culture: Education and the limits of ethnic affiliation.* New York: Routledge.

Moje, E. B. (2002). But where are the youth: Integrating youth culture into literacy theory. *Educational Theory, 52,* 97–120.

Moje, E. B. (in press). Powerful spaces: Tracing the out-of-school literacy spaces of Latino/a youth. In K. Leander & M. Sheehy (Eds.), *Space matters: Assertions of space in literacy practice and research.* New York: Peter Lang.

Moje, E. B. & Ciechanowski, K. M. (2002, April). *Literacy, language, and life in the millennial world: A study of Latino/a youth literacy in one urban community.* Paper presented at the American Educational Research Association, New Orleans, LA.

Moje, E. B., Ciechanowski, K. M., Kramer, K. E., Ellis, L. M., Carrillo, R., & Collazo, T. (2004). Working toward third space in content area literacy: An examination of everyday funds of knowledge and Discourse. *Reading Research Quarterly, 39*(1), 38–70.

Nespor, J. (1997). *Tangled up in school: Politics, space, bodies, and signs in the educational process.* Mahwah, NJ: Lawrence Erlbaum Associates.

Olson, G. A. & Worsham, L. (2000). Changing the subject: Judith Butler's politics of radical resignification. *JAC: A Journal of Composition Theory*, 20(4), 727–765.

Radway, J. (1984). *Reading the romance: Women, patriarchy and popular literature*. Chapel Hill: University of North Carolina Press.

van Helden, C. J. L. (2002). *Critical discourse studies of youth lifestyle media: Sexuality and polyvalent meaning*. Unpublished master's thesis, University of Amsterdam, The Netherlands. Available: http://www.umich.edu/~cvanhel/projectp/.

CHAPTER TEN

Talking Together for Change: Examining Positioning Between Teachers and Queer Youth

Mollie V. Blackburn

When I taught ninth grade, I taught, predictably, *To Kill a Mockingbird*, and as a white middle-class woman, I loved it. I knew that many of my students, most of whom were black and working-class, did not. I did not know why. I did not consider what it meant for me to impose this book on my students—this book in which kind white middle-class people are celebrated for saving black working-class people from mean white poor people. Had I listened to my students about why they disliked the book, I could have learned from them what they knew about race and class. Instead I tried feverishly to get them to listen to and learn from me what I knew about symbolism, for example. I insisted on being the one who teaches and, in the process, sacrificed educative opportunities for both my students and myself.

I wonder what it would have meant for me to position myself and my students more tentatively, more tenuously, such that the roles of those who teach and those who learn were open to all of us in any given interaction. I wonder what difference positioning makes in interactions between teachers and young people particularly when it comes to teaching and learning about difference.

The purpose of this chapter is to explore these wonderings. In it, I discuss understandings of adolescent identities, and I consider what identities, language, and positioning have to do with one another. I then describe the study with particular respect to action-implicative discourse analysis, and talk about the ways in which critical race theory and queer theory guided my analysis. Next, I examine the ways in which differences defined by age, race, and sexuality influence interactions between teachers and queer youth. Finally, I argue that in order to better teach and learn across differences, we need to name and discuss these differences as a method for working toward social change.

ADOLESCENT IDENTITIES

Lesko (2001) identifies "four 'confident characterizations' of adolescents: they 'come of age' into adulthood; they are controlled by raging hormones; they are peer-oriented; and they are represented by age" (p. 2). These characterizations work to regulate and contain youth in that they position adults as superior to young people. Adolescents are immature, not fully developed, and perhaps worst of all "beyond social intervention" (p. 3). In addition, narrow and derogatory characterizations of youth limit the roles that educators play in relation to youth, in particular when teachers' perceptions of young people are constrained by society's dominant emphasis requiring the surveillance and control of what is perceived to be an entire stage of development marked by being out of control. In order to free educators from these limits, "[w]e must move between and against the confident characterizations of youth, which involves including teenagers as *active participants* (not tokens) in educational and other public policy deliberations" (Lesko, 2001, p. 199). In this study, I closely examine interactions between a young person and two teachers where the young person is an active participant who exercises adult-like responsibilities in an educational deliberation. I work from the premise that adolescence is a cultural construction rather than solely a biological or psychological construction. And perhaps most important, my emphasis is on coming to understand the contextualization of these interactions, for example, the ways in which each participant is positioned in the dialogue by her partners in conversation.

Accordingly, I draw from a theory of identity that also highlights the cultural. Situating identity within culture, Holland, Lachicotte, Skinner, and Cain (1998) "reject a dichotomy between the sociological and the psychological" and "attemp[t] to articulate the relation of person and society in a way that makes light of neither social life nor the world of the psyche" (p. 270). Instead they focus on what they call "cultural worlds." Foundational to their approach is the Vygotskian emphasis on the social construction of knowledge and identity and the Bakhtinian notion of the dialogic. In other words, they work from the premise that identities are formed in social evolutionary contexts, and therefore, in some ways, identities are shaped by these contexts. However, individuals also contribute to the work of identity formation: they have agency. Individuals interact in and with their contexts to conduct their identity work.

IDENTITIES, LANGUAGE, AND POSITIONING

In this chapter, I explore the relationship between identities and language. More specifically, I explore the ways in which the identities and language of teachers and youth position them relative to each other, and what difference this positioning makes in their interactions and efforts to make schools better places, particularly for queer youth. Based on the assumption that "language users' identities are not essential to their natures but are produced through contingent social interactions" (Bucholtz, 1999, p. 20), I discuss the ways in which identities of teachers and youth are produced through their social interactions in a university classroom at which the youth were guest speakers. In these interactions, teachers and youth respond to the ideologies of what it means to be queer students in typically heterosexist and homophobic schools and what it means to be the teachers of these students in such schools. As Bucholtz (1999) notes, such responses "sometimes challenge and sometimes reproduce dominant beliefs" (p. 20). It is through these responses and with participants' social resources that they produce new identities (Bucholtz, 1999). In this study, these new identities, both chosen and imposed, disrupt the teacher-student binary and, in this way, offer hope in making schools better places for queer youth.

Liang (1999), in her study of the ways in which lesbians and gay men use language both to reveal and conceal their sexual identities, describes the relationship between language and identities as a "process of negotiation between individuals, intentions, and social and cultural forces [that] illustrates the intimate connection between language and identity" (p. 307). Integral to this negotiation is the notion of positioning. Positioning is the work of "speakers in particular settings who assume they can know one another and act on their taken-for-granted relations of power and status, like the relations between students and teachers in classrooms" (Enciso, 2001, p. 166). According to Enciso, when "we interact with one another we often assume certain social positions or expected ways of talking and acting that enable us to locate who we are in relation to one another" (p. 166). Further, she claims one positioning usually implies another related positioning, though often opposing, as in the case of teacher and student. In this case, I focus on the related and sometimes opposing positioning of individuals as teachers and/or students. I look at the ways other identity markers, particularly age, race, and sexuality, influence this positioning. While Enciso considers what difference positioning makes for readers and reading education, I consider what difference positioning makes for teachers of queer students in schools that are often heterosexist and homophobic places.

CONTEXT, PARTICIPANTS, AND RESEARCHER

The interactions I examine took place in a course for pre-service teachers of secondary English in an urban private university in the northeastern region of the United States. The course was taught by a team of five women: a faculty member in the graduate school of education, two local teachers/part-time doctoral students, and two full-time doctoral students, of whom I was one. There were thirty-five pre-service teachers in the class. The class met requirements for several different programs in this graduate school of education. In this particular class meeting, we had three guest speakers who had attended and graduated from the school district in which the university was located where the two currently practicing teachers taught and where some of the students would be placed for their field experiences. These speakers came from *The Attic*, a local youth-run center for lesbian, gay, bisexual, transgender, and questioning (LGBTQ) youth where I had first volunteered and by this time worked. The speakers and I, as an adult facilitator, worked together on *The Attic*'s Speakers' Bureau. The Speakers' Bureau was a group of youth who were hired and trained to conduct outreaches to educate youth and youth service providers about issues pertinent to LGBTQ youth. Coming to this class was one such outreach. As a qualitative researcher, I audiotaped this outreach and transcribed the audiotape.

This analysis focuses on two of thirteen interactions represented by the transcript. Both interactions were initiated by team teachers, both local school teachers. One of the teachers was Donna, a middle-aged white woman.[1] I never heard her state her sexual identity, but she was a divorced mother of a biracial son in his early twenties. The other teacher was Sally, a middle-aged black woman who was partnered with a black man. I understood both of them as initiating the discussion with the youth in an effort to learn how to be better teachers to all of their students, including LGBTQ students.

Kira, the youth speaker who first addressed Donna and Sally's questions, was, at the time, twenty years old. While she may not have been considered to be an adolescent by traditional conceptualizations of adolescence, she was considered by *The Attic* to be a youth—defined as twelve to twenty-three years of age. Kira, a biracial woman, identified sometimes as lesbian, other times as gay, and still other times as a dyke. She was born and raised in the United States. Both of her biological parents died of AIDS-related complications, so she was raised primarily by a black foster mother. Kira had graduated from high school and planned to go to college, but she was not in school at the time of this outreach. The other two speakers were Dara and Kevin, both of whom had graduated from high school and were attending a community college. Dara identified, at the time, as a twenty-three year old African American lesbian, and Kevin identified as an eighteen year old white gay man. All three of these youth had spent the majority of their lives as students, and even though Kira was not a student at the time of this discussion, she had recently been a student and was soon to become a student again. As such, these young people, simply because they were young people, were too often being influenced and authored by others rather than doing their own authoring.

I was thirty years old at the time, and I had been out as a lesbian for just over two years. I had never been out as a student or teacher in a K-12 public school.

ACTION-IMPLICATIVE DISCOURSE ANALYSIS

The method of this study draws heavily from Tracy's (1995) action-implicative discourse analysis. The primary metatheoretical frames that characterize action-implicative discourse analysis in general, and this study in particular, are interpretive and critical in nature. The central questions that guide the analysis are intended to identify participants' beliefs and related tensions in order to solve problems among participants. For example, here, I examine the ways in which people invested in schools interact with one another around issues pertinent to LGBTQ youth. More specifically, I ask questions about the ways these teachers and speakers position themselves and each other through their interactions in order to better understand the difference this makes to the teaching and learning they do together.

Transcription for the purpose of action-implicative discourse analysis requires less detail than that for other types of discourse analysis. Action-implicative discourse analysis attends to "problematic episodes that often last considerably longer (twenty to sixty minutes)" and focuses on "examining strategies at a conceptual level" (Tracy, 1995, p. 202) that can be captured in less detailed transcripts. Related to this, a researcher using this kind of analysis will "extract conversational moves from a longer utterance (and its response) if doing so seems to make an analytic claim clearer" (Tracy, 1995, p. 203). The transcript analyzed in this study is not highly detailed, but it highlights two interactions that have been extracted from a longer problematic episode of approximately ninety minutes. Donna and Sally initiated these two interactions, and Kira responded first to each of them. My work here is consistent with action-implicative discourse analysis in the degree of detail in the transcription, the length of the episode considered, and the extraction of particular conversational moves to make a point.

The texts used in action-implicative discourse analysis capture "routine institutional occasions in which actors experience problems" (Tracy, 1995, p. 207), rather than mundane interactions or public texts, for example. The text analyzed in this study represents an outreach the Speakers' Bureau conducted with youth service providers, in this case, teachers. In this outreach, as was typical in Speakers' Bureau outreaches, each of the three youth speakers told stories about their lives as queer youth in and out of schools and responded to questions posed by those in the class. As usual, throughout the outreach, they encountered heterosexism, or the failure to recognize and/or respect the realities of non-heterosexual people, and homophobia, or the fear and/or hatred of people who are perceived to be non-heterosexual. Thus, the study focuses on the routine occasion of a Speakers' Bureau outreach in which the youth speakers experienced the problems of heterosexism and homophobia.

Action-implicative discourse analysis relies on "relevant contextual information made available through participation, observation, and interviewing to inform an interpretation" (Tracy, 1995, p. 203). From the outset it is assumed a convincing and substantive analysis must go beyond the words used in an interaction, to include additional information that guides the researcher's reading of the interaction. This study is particularly well suited to rely on additional contextual information because I had working relationships with both the speakers and the class in which they were guests. I had worked with Kira for over three years in and beyond an ethnographic study I conducted at *The Attic*, and I was a colleague of both Donna and Sally. My work with these participants informed my analysis of the interactions highlighted here.

Tracy (1995) contrasts the use of relevant contextual information, as in action-implicative discourse analysis, to the use of "historical, social, and political conditions" of the time of the text (p. 207), as in critical discourse analysis. I argue, however, that historical, social, and political conditions of the time are, in fact, relevant contextual information that should be made use of in action-implicative discourse analysis. In order to foreground such conditions in this analysis here, I draw from critical race theory and queer theory.

CRITICAL RACE THEORY AND QUEER THEORY

Critical race theory (CRT), which is interdisciplinary in nature (Tate, 1997), informs this study. The goal of CRT is to eliminate "racial oppression as part of the larger goal of eradicating all forms of oppression" (Tate, 1997, p. 234). Critical race theorists understand that "racism [is] endemic and deeply ingrained in American life" (Ladson-Billings & Tate, 1995, p. 55). This racism is "institutional and structural racism" and is responsible for the lack of success of people of color in schools (Ladson-Billings & Tate, 1995, p. 55). They also recognize the inadequacy of civil rights law, particularly as it has been implemented. The purpose driving the work of CRT is to challenge "claims of neutrality, objectivity, color-blindness, and meritocracy" (Ladson-Billings & Tate, 1995, p. 56) and to challenge ahistoricism (Tate, 1997). CRT pushes me to pay attention to and interrogate power dynamics defined by race, which is particularly important for me as a white researcher analyzing interactions between a biracial youth and one white teacher and one black teacher.

Queer theory also informs this study. According to queer theory (Britzman, 1997; Butler, 1997; Muñoz, 1999; Pinar, 1998), queer is not the lumping together of lesbian, gay, bisexual, and transgender, although it does pay particular attention to sexual and gender identities such as these (Jagose, 1996). Rather, queer is the suspension of these classifications (Pinar, 1998). Queer theorists recognize sexual and gender identities as social, multiple, variable, shifting, and fluid, allowing for movement among such identity categories (Britzman, 1997), but also advocating for movement outside of these categories. For example, queer theorists allow for a shift in identities, like Kira's, from lesbian to gay to dyke; further, they allow for the suspension of such categorization entirely. By rejecting categories of identity, queer theorists interrogate and disrupt notions of normal, with particular respect to sexuality and gender (Tierney & Dilley, 1998), but also to race and class identities as well (Luhmann, 1998). Thus, queer theory works against the oppression that comes with being named, labeled, and tagged (Foucault, 1982). Queer theorists facilitate my analysis by asking me to suspend classifications, such as the categorization of adolescent; to resist dichotomizations, such as the teacher-student dichotomy; and to find discomfort in simplistic explanations of discussions or interactions.

I understand these theories to be compatible. Although critical race theorists focus on racial identities and queer theorists focus on sexual identities, they share some significant commitments: the recognition of the sociocultural nature of identities, languages, and realities more generally speaking; the acknowledgement of multiplicity and the rejection of binaries; the commitment to disrupting norms, including but not limited to racist and heterosexist norms; and the persistence of a political agenda that is characterized by goals of emancipation, transformation, and empowerment of traditionally oppressed people, such as people of color and lesbians, gay men, and people who are bisexual or transgendered.

In fact, McCarthy and Crichlow (1993) assert that the study of race must include the study of other aspects of identities, including sexuality. Similarly, Butler (1997) asserts that "queer studies need to move beyond and against those methodological demands which force separations in the interests of canonization and provisational institutional legitimation" (p. 24). In particular, she names the "analysis of racialization" as the work beyond sexuality that scholars need to do (p. 24).

However, there are ways in which the two theories conflict. For example, CRT highlights a particular identity marker while queer theory works to dismantle identity markers. This tension is evident in my description of the participants. While I recognize that identities are social, multiple, variable, shifting, and fluid, I still use seemingly static identity markers to describe the participants. For example, I identify Donna as white, Sally as black, and Kira as biracial. While this initial move could be understood as in conflict with queer theory, it is in keeping with CRT.

Still, taken together, these theories trouble my analysis. They complicate my positionality within the theoretical conversations, the world, and thus in the study. For example, queer theory positions me, as a queer researcher, inside of that theoretical conversation and on the margins of an often heterosexist and homophobic world. However, by bringing CRT to my theoretical frame, my positionality shifts from insider to outsider and from margins to center. As a white researcher I can be understood as an outsider in the theoretical conversation of CRT, but also as in the center of a racist world. Thus, these theories in conjunction with each other position me to interrogate the power and privilege of others, such as straight people, but also of myself, as a white person.

Teacher/Student Positioning

Donna, Sally, and Kira position themselves and each other in terms of teacher and student identities. As middle-aged women, Donna and

Sally are also positioned as teachers both in the district and in the class, particularly relative to the youth speakers, who were thus implicitly positioned as students. Kira, however, as well as the other speakers, had graduated. Even the two speakers who were in community college were not students of Donna or Sally or anyone else in the room, with the exception of me. I was not a traditional teacher of the speakers, but I was the adult facilitator of the Speakers' Bureau for which Kira and others were youth speakers. Also, because they knew I was a former English teacher, they often asked me to help write, edit, and revise writing for school. However, even my positioning as teacher—particularly relative to Kira—was tenuous. In fact, when youth at *The Attic* interviewed me to determine whether I could spend time there, Kira, immediately upon hearing that I was a former teacher, asked me how I was going to *not* be a teacher in this *youth-run* center. While Donna, Sally, and I positioned ourselves as teachers, we may have, as Enciso (2001) suggests, implicitly positioned Kira as student, though she did not necessarily position herself as such.

Moreover, our positioning was complicated by the particular class context. Kira and the other two speakers were physically located at the front of the room and had prepared and implemented a plan for the class. In these ways they claimed positions more like teachers than students. In contrast, the teachers were physically located among the class and participated in the speakers' plan, more like students than teachers. It is the complicated terrain of teacher and student identities that I examine through the two interactions that follow.

Resistance in Dichotomous Positionalities

To begin, I focus on an interaction between Donna and Kira. Donna framed and asked the second question of the thirteen asked and the first of the three posed by a teacher of the class. She addressed the three speakers:

> I guess several of you said something like my mother wasn't supportive or somebody was supportive or I couldn't find teachers and you used that word supportive. Which is, you know, I mean, on the one hand that's probably a word that we all use a lot of time, but I'm just curious, and I'm most curious about school, um, because that's where I work. But, if, if you were to be at school and you were to feel that teachers were supportive what do you

think, what would that look like or what would that be like or what would it
feel like or what would they do or, do you think?

Here, Donna re-emphasized her position as teacher by stating that she
works at a school, and asking explicitly about supportive teachers.
She implicitly positioned the speakers as students in this question by
locating them in school, when she says, "if you were to be at school,"
and by assuming they were not teachers by asking them to comment
on teachers. This positioning is not surprising. Much of the speakers'
stories included their experiences as students in schools and Donna
was a teacher in the class and in a high school. This positionality is
complicated in that Donna asked a question of the speakers much like
a student would ask a question of teachers. Still, the content of the
question suggested her position as a teacher and assigned the speakers' positions as students. She asked how could teachers support students, "what would that look like or what would that be like or what
would it feel like or what would they do."

I believe that Donna sincerely wanted to support students and for
these speakers, as students, to tell her and others in the class, as teachers, how to do this. In other words, I believe her intentions were good,
but underlying these intentions was a problematic assumption about
students and teachers: students need the support of teachers, or more
specifically queer students need the support of straight teachers. I
would not necessarily argue against this assumption. I believe all
teachers should work to support all of their students, including but
not limited to queer students. Kira, however, troubled this assumption.

Of course, race and perceived sexuality played a significant role in
shaping the interaction between Donna and Kira. Even though I knew
that Donna had a biracial son, Kira did not have that information, and
still, Donna *was* white. Moreover, she was *perceived* to be straight. I
knew that she had been married but was divorced, but again, Kira did
not have this information. Whether she was straight was irrelevant.
She was perceived to be straight because she did not self-identify in
terms of sexuality and she did not match physical stereotypes associated with lesbians. This meant that in the interaction with Donna,
Kira, as a lesbian of color, was asked to represent queer students to
help a presumably straight white teacher to construct ways to support

those students. Not surprisingly, Kira failed to answer Donna's question.

Instead, she debunked both the notion of her student self as a victim and the notion of teachers as supporters of students, particularly queer students. Kira said:

> I found out that my school wasn't supportive not from my own situations just because I had taken it into my own hands to handle any situation that was thrown at me and I. I don't trust people very well, so it was just like I was going to do everything and no one was going to make fun of me because I was going to kick their ass. So, but through the friends I had at school that were out, um, I had a friend who was constantly harassed by other kids in the school and when she did take it to teachers, it was ignored. Or, um, when she did take it, things were said to her like, "well maybe you shouldn't involve yourself in, um, activities that might make people assume you were gay." Um, other things like, um, what else happened. Um, there was this, um, double standard it was always said that, um, people couldn't make out in the hallways or people couldn't hold hands there was none of that but nothing was said to any of the heterosexual couples in the school, only gay couples. Um, and it took her having to file suit against the school, um, for them to do anything.

In her response to Donna's question about how teachers can support lesbian and gay students, Kira first refused to be positioned as a student who needed the support of teachers, or anyone else for that matter. This distrust of support from others and reliance only on self is reflected in Leap's (1999) study of gay adolescent narratives. Leap found that gay adolescents perceived support as "accidental and unplanned occurrences" that are "in no sense reliable," leaving the individual as the only source of "accessible guidance" (p. 265). So rather than positioning herself as a young person requiring the support of adults who are unreliable, she positioned herself as someone who responded to harassment with physical retaliation rather than relying on others to defend her, since she did not trust this to happen.

In fact, rather than affirming her position as a victim, she told about an experience from her own life as if it were from a friend's life. I am referring to the part of the quotation above where Kira described a friend of hers going to a school official for help, only to be blamed for the homophobia she was experiencing, and advised to adapt her extracurricular activities in order to avoid abuse. However, every other time I heard Kira tell about this event, it was about her. She was told that if she did not want to suffer from homophobia then she should not participate in the local AIDS Walk. In short, she lied. It was more important to her not to be positioned as a victim than to tell the truth in this outreach. Here, "language served as a vehicle" for what Bucholtz (1999) calls a "creative respons[e] even as [her] linguistic behavior reflects the stability of social categories" (p. 16). Kira positioned herself as autonomous and powerful and other queer students as victims of homophobia in schools. Thus, she repositioned herself as an independent and strong student rather than as a victimized student who required the support of her teachers.

Kira's account of this experience not only served to position her in a way quite different than the way Donna's question positioned her, her account, along with her other accounts of lesbian and gay students in schools, served to reposition teachers. Rather than characterizing them as supports, like Donna did in her question, Kira revealed teachers as complicit in the discrimination against queer students. According to Kira, teachers ignored homophobia in their schools even when it was brought to their attention by students who were suffering because of it. If teachers did not ignore homophobia, they blamed those who were suffering from it rather than those who were exhibiting it. Thus, Kira repositioned teachers not only as non-supporters of gay and lesbian students but also as practicing homophobes. Donna "work[ed] within" dominant ideologies and Kira "subvert[ed] dominant ideologies" (Bucholtz, 1999, p. 18) as they constructed their identities as teacher and student, respectively.

Production in Shifting Positionalities

Next I focus on an interaction between Sally and Kira. Sally framed and asked her question after a pause long enough for me to ask whether we should conclude the discussion. Her question was the eleventh of the thirteen questions. She said:

> Um, Kira, you, you said something that really struck me. Um, I just think about my own practice in the classroom, um, how much I personally love Langston Hughes, and whenever I teach Langston Hughes I have never mentioned to my students that he was gay, and um and even thinking about doing that now I have to think about a lot of other things in terms of parents,

administrators, and how I would frame that and present it, and what it would mean after, after saying it. But just reflecting on the fact that I have never done that is, is very interesting to me. And, um, I don't know, if you could each say one thing that you would want us to think about as a middle school teacher or a high school teacher, that maybe we can do, other than, now I know, I mean that's something I can think about.

Here, Sally positioned herself relative to Kira in quite a different way than Donna did. Like Donna, Sally positioned herself as a teacher by referring to her "own practice in the classroom" and by talking about *her* students. However, rather than foregrounding her work as a teacher, she foregrounded her work of learning about her teaching by first talking about how what she learned in class, particularly from Kira, influenced her thinking about her own practice and then talking about the details of her teaching. In other words, she positioned herself first as student and then as teacher. More specifically, Sally positioned herself as a student of Kira's by naming what she learned from Kira. Thus, she implicitly positioned Kira as one who teaches. Ultimately, though, she positioned all of the speakers as teachers, and everyone else in the class as students, by asking what do *you*—speakers and teachers—want *us*—teachers and students—to know, to learn from you.

I believe that Donna and Sally were really trying to get at the same kind of information. However, the result of their questions—in terms of positioning effects—was quite different. In asking how teachers can support students, particularly queer students, the assumption is that teachers have power to support their queer students and that queer students lack power so they must rely on their teachers' power to support them, something not very reliable according to Kira. Further, what is at issue in this question is the students' sexual identity—how can teachers help queer students? This is in stark contrast to what is at issue in Sally's questions, which is the heteronormativity of schools and the homophobia of those who inhabit them—what can these queer speakers teach those of us in heteronormative schools about what could be done differently? In the earlier question, queer students are positioned as powerless and in need of support from teachers whom they have come to know as not very supportive. In the later question, queer youth are positioned as educators working to trouble heteronormative practices that have excluded them throughout their schooling.

So, while Donna and Sally may have been trying to get at the same kind of information about how teachers can make schools better places for queer students, Sally's question conjured a very different response. Perhaps this had something to do with the timing of the questions, such that Kira thought of things she could have said to Donna's early question after it had passed and offered those things in response to Sally's later question. However, race and sexuality cannot be ignored in considering the negotiation of positionality among these women. Unlike Donna, Sally is a black woman. Like Donna, she was perceived to be straight. This meant that in the interaction with Sally, Kira was invited by a presumably straight black teacher to name what, in her opinion, teachers need to think about with respect to their queer students, and that invitation was based on a reference to a gay black poet.

Kira responded directly and clearly to what Sally said. First she reacted to what Sally said about the things she had to think about before mentioning to her students that Langston Hughes was gay. She said:

> I think that when we do, I think that when we do read people in school it's, it is constantly mentioned who their partners were except for if their partners were same sex, and so I want you to think about that, and, and I think that it becomes unfair to me, if we're constantly mentioning, you know, all these other people's partners, and then as soon as we get to Langston Hughes, you know, you just like, you totally skip over that portion. It's like a skip in the lesson.

Then, she went on to address Sally's request that each speaker say something that they want middle and high school teachers to know, while continuing to react to Sally's concerns:

> Um, I'm just trying to think of what else would. Um. It, it, it would have been great if we had read um books, just by, about gay people in school. Um, if I had *Heather has two mommies* in kindergarten, I think that would have been great. And I know that when it comes to parents, you got, I continue to hear that it's hard, um, but, I also feel that teachers should think about, um, what their purpose is as a teacher. And um, and, and it would

make it easier for me to learn, if I had images of myself, in my class. Um, I would have been drawn in, I would have been right there. When we had, when we had books about people with AIDS, I was in there. You know. When we had, um, stories about biracial couples or biracial children, I was right there. And I mean, those are the stories and those are the lessons that I remember most from school, because um they reflected me and who I was. Um, women stories were always great because it was about women. I mean, and I was going to read it. Um, and I think it just made it easier for me to learn. And it made me want to [learn].

Here, Kira not only accepted the position of teacher for herself and the position of student for Sally, she also allowed for each of them to be both teacher and student simultaneously. Instead of rejecting the positioning as she had with Donna's positioning, Kira accepted the role of one who teaches by offering Sally feedback on her comment about having a lot to think about in deciding whether to identify Langston Hughes as gay and by directly answering her question about what Kira, as Sally's teacher, wants Sally to know. Throughout, however, she also positioned herself as student and Sally as teacher in her feedback to Sally. She suggested that she understood that *as a teacher* Sally needed to think about parents and administrators, but that *as a teacher* she also needed to think about *students* like Kira. Further, she suggested that if the purpose of teachers, like Sally, was to teach students, like Kira, then they needed to include images of their students in order to facilitate those students' learning. She communicated what Leap (1999) found in his study of gay adolescent narratives: "seeking out information about gay experience is an important part of self-managed socialization" (p. 266). However, she also communicated that she not only needed information about gay experiences, but also experiences with AIDS, being biracial, and being a woman, and she needed access to such information in sanctioned and social settings like school. Thus, this interaction between Sally and Kira allowed them both to assume complicated positions of both teacher and student.

In this interaction, Kira was not only teacher and student, but she was also lesbian, intimately influenced by AIDS, biracial, and a woman, as opposed to just being gay as in the previous interaction. And teachers were not limited to being either supportive or ignorant, as they seemed to be in the first interaction. Instead, they were reflective and thoughtful even if also tentative. In this interaction, when both Sally and Kira allowed each other the space to be complex participants, they seemed to be working together toward making schools better places for queer students and effecting social change.

DISCUSSING DIFFERENCE

I am not arguing that teachers and students need to be alike in one or more significant ways. For example, I do not believe that Kira needed a lesbian teacher, like me, or a teacher of color, like Sally, to engage in educative interactions. And while I do think that Kira was more receptive to Sally's question in part because of her perceived racial identity, I do not believe that Sally and Kira's interaction was more productive than Donna and Kira's interaction solely because both Sally and Kira are people of color and Donna is white. Other differences, including but not limited to perceived age and sexuality, also impact teaching and learning.

Like race, age can be perceived with some degree of accuracy based on appearance, and, in this case, Donna and Sally were accurately perceived as older and Kira as younger. Many times this difference gets interpreted as the older person or people being teachers of the younger person. In other words, in ignorance of each person's experiences and areas of expertise, the older person is expected to take on the role of one who teaches and the younger person is expected to take on the role of one who learns. In this case, the difference in age hindered the educative possibilities of the interactions.

Unlike race and age, sexuality is not as visibly identifiable. Of course when people fail to comply with gender norms, their sexuality is often interpreted as something other than straight, but interpretations based on such information is less than reliable. Still, if one complies with gender norms and does not choose to identify as something other than straight, then one is typically assumed to be straight rather than either LGBT or a less stereotypical identity. Certainly this was the case here: Kira perceived both Donna and Sally as straight. Kira's identity was no less essentialized. She stated her sexual identity as something other than straight much earlier in the outreach. Thus, in this heterosexist and homophobic society, she explicitly located herself in a position of less power and assumed Donna and Sally to be in a position of more power. While she may have positioned herself as having less power than Donna and Sally in terms of sexuality and related oppressions, she positioned herself as having more power than she would have had she elected to conceal her sexual identity or even refused to assume a sexual identity.

In this situation, Kira did not have an option. She was invited to the class to speak about her experience as a queer youth in schools. However, everyone in the class other than the speakers had this option. None of them elected to disrupt the assumption that they were straight, although several of them elected to confirm that assumption. Perhaps all of them were straight, but let's just assume that one of them was not. Let's say that one of them was closeted in this context. I assert that Kira and the speakers had more power than that one hypothetical person who elected to conceal his or her identity because she was able to talk with teachers about her experiences as a queer youth in and out of schools. Even if this hypothetical person engaged in the discussion and talked vehemently against heterosexism and homophobia, she or he still would not have the authority on the topic that Kira and the other speakers did. As a person who experiences oppression, the power of Kira's position obtains from the "authority of experience" (hooks, 1994). Thus by naming and discussing difference, Kira was better positioned to work for change.

So, rather than arguing that teachers and students need to be alike in one or more significant ways, I am arguing that, as educators, we need to work harder at communicating—that is both talking and listening—across differences (Ballenger, 1999; Delpit, 1996; Schultz, 2003). Communicating across differences requires openness to others' ideas without judgment, humility to recognize our own limitations, and trust in one another to "make mistakes, miscommunicate, and even hurt each other sometimes" (Stone, 1995, p. 185). In keeping with CRT, it requires naming and discussing these differences, including but not limited to differences defined by age, race, class, gender, and sexuality, rather than perceiving them and making assumptions based on these perceptions.

Ideally, this would mean talking about our own differences. But to do this in classrooms can be dangerous work. However, teachers and students can prepare together for this work. For example, an English

Language Arts teacher may critically discuss differences and their relevance among characters in a piece of literature or a Social Studies teacher may address and examine differences among various people's perspectives in a particular historical event. In this way, teachers can show students that it is appropriate to talk about differences and facilitate one way of doing it. A teacher can build on this showing by inviting students to assume the role of characters in literature or people in historical events, for example, and engage one another in conversations across differences, although perhaps not their own. The teacher can move these conversations closer to students by using literature that explores issues pertinent to the lives of the students or by focusing on current and perhaps local events. Ultimately, through a developing understanding that it is worthwhile to talk across differences and a strengthening of classroom community, the conversations can be about differences among the people in the lives of the students, as well as among the students themselves.

This is not to suggest important differences that need to be named and discussed are static. Such a suggestion would be in direct conflict with queer theory. In fact, in Ellsworth's (1997) effort at exploring the question of "How should we teach about and across social and cultural differences?" (p. 11), she argues for "pedagogical modes of address that aren't founded on striving for and desiring certainty, continuity, or control," and challenges teachers to address "students in a way that doesn't require them to assume a fixed, singular, unified position within power and social relations in order to read and respond to the address being offered—in order to 'learn' through it" (p. 9). In the classrooms, such as I describe above, students must have opportunities to express their understandings of difference tentatively. They need to be able to try on one way of thinking about difference and then shed that way in order to try on another and another. For example, I am not implying that students and teachers should (or should not) "come out" as queer in classrooms. I am, however, asserting that people in classrooms should be able to talk about sexual identities beyond the heteronormative, as one way of working against heterosexism and homophobia.

Teachers can model trying on a range of ways of thinking about difference by sharing stories from their lives in which they have come to various understandings of a piece of literature or historical event over time as they have learned more about it from their studies and conversations with other people. Teachers can create a context that helps students to be open to changing their thinking about differences by introducing discussions with statements about how we all learn from one another's points of view. It is not only important to share multiple perspectives, it is also important for us to allow one another to change our minds. To do so is not hypocritical but an indication of listening and learning. It is, I believe, a sign of hope. Teachers can provide students with opportunities to learn through discussions across differences by inviting students to document their evolving perspectives on an issue by writing multiple journal entries about a particular topic over the course of a unit exploring this topic. Sharing our perspectives shows differences among us, but documenting our own evolving perspectives illustrates differences within ourselves. Teachers can also document and share their evolving perspectives. This work can be better accomplished when teachers and students do not feel the need to vie for control and power.

Teachers and students need to assume and assign the roles of ones who teach and ones who learn more tentatively and tenuously. Teachers need to be willing to share their roles as the ones who talk, teach, and know, as well as the roles as the ones who listen and learn (Schultz, 2003), just as students need to be willing to exchange their typical roles for alternative ones. Particularly when teachers and students are different in such substantial ways as race, age, and sexuality among the many other ways in which individuals differ from one another, teachers can neither position themselves solely as teachers nor position their students solely as students. Instead teachers and students need to recognize what they know, what they don't know, and what they can learn together from each other. Assuming and imposing monolithic and static identities like "teacher" and "student" hinders the possibilities for educative interactions. While teachers have the power in schools and classrooms to forge ahead, failing to learn from their students, they leave their students behind. This is unacceptable. Teachers need to position their students as ones who teach, particularly about what the teachers know less about (Möller, 2002). Straight teachers need to learn from their queer students, just as I, a white teacher, need to learn from my students of color. We all need to position ourselves and one another as both ones who teach and ones who learn as we interact around issues of difference. As I noted, doing so is dangerous work, but failing to do so is even more perilous. By failing to communicate across differences we not only sacrifice opportunities to teach and learn, we also sacrifice opportunities to talk together for change.

NOTE

1. All identifying names have been replaced by pseudonyms.

REFERENCES

Ballenger, C. (1999). *Teaching other people's children: Literacy and learning in a bilingual classroom*. New York: Teachers College Press.

Britzman, D. P. (1997). What is this thing called love? New discourses for understanding gay and lesbian youth. In S. de Castell & M. Bryson (Eds.), *Radical interventions: Identity, politics, and difference/s on educational praxis* (pp. 183–207). Albany: State University of New York Press.

Bucholtz, M. (1999). Bad examples: Transgression and progress in language and gender studies. In M. Bucholtz, A. C. Liang, & L. A. Sutton (Eds.), *Reinventing identities: The gendered self in discourse* (pp. 3–24). New York: Oxford University Press.

Butler, J. (1997). Against proper objects. In E. Weed & N. Schor (Eds.), *Feminism meets queer theory* (pp. 1–30). Bloomington: Indiana University Press.

Delpit, L. D. (1996). *Other people's children: Cultural conflict in the classroom*. New York: W. W. Norton.

Ellsworth, E. (1997). *Teaching positions: Difference, pedagogy, and the power of address*. New York: Teachers College Press.

Enciso, P. (2001). Taking our seats: The consequences of positioning in reading assessments. *Theory into Practice, 40(3)*, 166–174.

Foucault, M. (1982). The subject and power. *Critical Inquiry, 8(4)*, 777–795.

Holland, D., Lachicotte, W., Jr., Skinner, D., & Cain, C. (1998). *Identity and agency in cultural worlds*. Cambridge, MA: Harvard University Press.

hooks, b. (1994). *Teaching to transgress: Education as the practice of freedom*. New York: Routledge.

Jagose, A. (1996). *Queer theory: An introduction*. New York: New York University Press.

Ladson-Billings, G. & Tate, W. F., IV. (1995). Toward a critical race theory of education. *Teachers College Record, 97(1)*, 47–68.

Leap, W. (1999). Language, socialization, and silence in gay adolescence. In M. Bucholtz, A. C. Liang, & L. A. Sutton (Eds.), *Reinventing identities: The gendered self in discourse* (pp. 259–272). New York: Oxford University Press.

Lesko, N. (2001). *Act your age!: A cultural construction of adolescence.* New York: Routledge Falmer.

Liang, A. C. (1999). Conversationally implicating lesbian and gay identity. In M. Bucholtz, A. C. Liang, & L. A. Sutton (Eds.), *Reinventing identities: The gendered self in discourse* (pp. 293–310). New York: Oxford University Press.

Luhmann, S. (1998). Queering/querying pedagogy? Or, pedagogy is a pretty queer thing. In W. F. Pinar (Ed.), *Queer theory in education* (pp. 141–155). Mahwah, NJ: Lawrence Erlbaum.

McCarthy, C. & Crichlow, C. (1993). *Race identity and representation in education.* New York: Routledge.

Möller, K. J. (2002). Providing support for dialogue in literature circles about social justice. *Language Arts, 79(6),* 467–477.

Muñoz, J. E. (1999). *Disidentifications: Queers of colour and the performance of politics.* Minneapolis: University of Minnesota Press.

Pinar, W. F. (Ed.). (1998). *Queer theory in education.* Mahwah, NJ: Lawrence Erlbaum.

Schultz, K. (2003). *Listening: A framework for teaching across difference.* New York: Teacher College Press.

Stone, L. (1995). Narrative in philosophy of education: A feminist tale of "uncertain" knowledge. In W. Kohli (Ed.), *Critical conversations in philosophy of education* (pp. 173–189). New York: Routledge.

Tate, W. F., IV. (1997). Critical race theory and education: History, theory, and implication. In M. W. Apple (Ed.), *Review of Research in Education, 22* (pp. 195–247). Washington, DC: American Educational Research Association.

Tierney, W. G. & Dilley, P. (1998). Constructing knowledge: Educational research and gay and lesbian studies. In W. F. Pinar (Ed.) *Queer theory in education* (pp. 49–71). Mahwah, NJ: Lawrence Erlbaum.

Tracy, K. (1995). Action-implicative discourse analysis. *Journal of Language and Social Psychology, 14(1–2),* 195–215.

CHAPTER ELEVEN

ReNaming "Adolescence": Subjectivities in Complex Settings

Lisa Patel Stevens

Figure 1. *Who are you?*

In what instances have you encountered texts like the ones layered in Figure 1?[1] The prompting for, and use of, such labels is ubiquitous in contemporary society. We are asked to name ourselves through such categories to enter formal schooling, to gain employment, to be acknowledged as citizens of the nation-state, in essence to be recognised, counted, and known. The prompts for nationality, race, class, and gender identifications are pervasive to the point of occupying a virtually unobjectionable representation of people and how they can be categorised, as seen through the liberal uses of these demographic discourses. However, we are rarely asked to qualify ourselves, demographically via print, into one of three life stages. Instead, these developmental stages are more conversationally pervasive in quotidian exchanges but no less constitutive. Even though demographic discourses typically use specific year brackets, our conversational language more often resorts to three life stages of childhood, adulthood, and adolescence, with adolescence marked as the betwixt and between condition, sequentially predicated upon and defined through the other two stages (see Vadeboncoeur, Chapter 1, this volume; Wyn, this volume).

These age/stage labels are attempting to perform the same functions, in terms of chronologically and biologically hued stages of development, that the labels of African American, Hispanic American, Asian American, and European American are invoked to perform for race and/or ethnicity for some people in the United States. In demarcating essentialised notions about race, class, gender, ethnicity, or development stage, the labels are often offered unproblematically. However, the various chapters in this edited volume have, through differing methodologies and theoretical frameworks, taken up the task of interrogating how the category of adolescence is epistemologically constructed and its epistemological effects. The array of representations and re-constructions of adolescence brings to bear a larger set of questions:

- What does the label of adolescence assume and do?
- How do we interact with these labels and categorical understandings?
- When we use the term, "adolescent," what are we assuming about the people who are meant to be understood by this term and those who are not?
- What physiological, cognitive, and affective characteristics are grafted under conceptions of adolescence?
- What are the material effects of language that delineates and categorises young people?

These questions are concerned with how westernised societies have come to know and continue to know the stage of adolescence. By purposively and pointedly privileging cultural understandings of developmentalist discourses (Lesko, 2001), the researchers in this volume have also questioned the semiotic and communicative significance, baggage, and underpinnings of adolescence.

BRINGING ADOLESCENCE INTO IDENTITY POLITICS

In posing questions about a linguistic category—in this case adolescence—and about its representation, similarity, diversity, and conflation, we are, in a sense, taking up already existing conversations about identity politics. In the latter half of the twentieth century, the politically fueled movements of feminism, civil rights for African Americans, and recognition of nonheterosexual populations, to name but a few, attempted to redress positions of marginalisation, domination, and subjugation. Underpinning these respective movements and the larger social fabric was the implication of a shared identity and/or culturally constructed meaning of what it meant to be African American, transgendered, female, etc. (Young, 1990). While it is beyond the scope and purpose of this chapter to delineate these various agendas and their resultant differences, the instructive point here is how the swirling debates around identity politics have grappled with the tension found in language that attempts to unify difference, the same elision that the term "adolescence" conjures.

One outcropping of the controversy in identity politics is the particular attention drawn to the force of language in society. Reading the world and its components as texts and understanding language as a constitutive force is familiar in contemporary theory. How language coalesces with power and knowledge (Foucault, 1972) has made necessary inquiries into the techniques and tactics used to produce particular subjects of the state. In so prompting us to consider the ubiquitous form of power and knowledge as performed, in part, through language, Foucault drew attention to the use of language and words as having material, felt, and ultimately governmentalised results. This concept, elaborated by theorists and researchers such as Gee (2002), Fairclough (1989), and Luke (1997), has fuelled investigations into the material fruitions of language and discourse, resulting in frameworks and methodologies such as critical discourse analysis, linguistic analysis, and narrative analysis (see Diamondstone, this volume; Patel Stevens, this volume; Rahm & Tracy, this volume). Applied to educational contexts, these approaches shed light upon the constitutive ways that language and texts work to reify constructions and categories such as adolescence.

Along with an understanding of the contextualised consequences of language is a destabilisation of meaning from language. Stemming from the influential work of Derrida (1998), the post-modern perception of language as fluid at once notes that language is a structure, but never an inherently true, architecturally sound, or even just structure. This view of language provides an agentic space within the structural forces of the word. Contradictorily coherent, language can be understood as both constitutive and fluid. In essence, our uses of language constantly support structures, but can also be interrogated of in terms of which structures warrant centrality and support through language. No cleaner demonstration of this exists than in the essentialism resulting from the particular words used to name and categorise.

Among the masses of critiques levelled against the loosely woven umbrella of identity politics is the derision of any particular label as falsely unifying inherently different aspects. In singly naming a group's identity, language works to illegitimately generalise (Heyes, 2000). This illegitimate generalisation contains three planes of dangers. The first danger is that a singular and titular axis of identity is invoked, as though these axiomatic monikers of identity are first separable and able to be ordered. For example, which is my more salient characteristic: my ethnic identity as Asian American, or my gendered identity as female? The second danger rests in the blockage of autonomy that occurs when a particular identity code is invoked as an umbrella term that, in fact, casts silencing shadows across subgroups within a marginalised group. hooks (1994) takes to task this second danger by challenging particular feminist stances as ignoring, sweeping, and ultimately colonizing racialised realities. Lastly and closely related to the second danger, the third danger emanates from waxing generally about a particular identity trait. By metaphysically removing the lived realities of amorphous traits from individuals and their embodied experiences, a Cartesian divide and hierarchy between mind and body is further legitimated (see Hunter, this volume).

For our inquiries into the nominalised stage of adolescence, these three dangerous outcroppings of identity politics are instructive. Even as the authors in this volume read and work with these ideas, the field of education is witnessing renewed and invigorated interest in the middle years of schooling, focussing explicitly and markedly on the "early adolescent" (e.g., Luke et al., 2003). By marking this chronologically and developmentally construed stage, it is constructed as a metacategory, one that supersedes other ways of identifying. In so doing, this politic of identity imbues the traits of the mythic typical early adolescent into all people within an age range. So, then, in terms of "naming to know" the adolescent, which identity are we dangerously privileging?

MOVING FROM IDENTITY TO SUBJECTIVITY

In asking what is most crucial to identity, one can offer, from liberal humanist standpoints, that it is the experience of the individual, the experience of the individual as seen in context of social and cultural structures—the lived experience of the subject. Subjectivity[2] has been defined in marked contrast to traditional psychological view of identity by post-structural feminists such as Grosz (1994) and Butler (1999). Theorists such as these, viewing the self through a powerful Foucauldian lens, present subjectivity as an alternative to internally negotiated, fixed, and positivist constructions of identity. While it is a theoretically dense concept and appropriately elusive of a definitive set of characteristics, using subjectivity here allows us to make two key departures from the territory known through identity.

The first key difference is in explicitly noting our experiences as social, cultural, and historical subjects, and this knowing occurs through our bodies. Grosz (1994) notes that through both violently demonstrable and subtle inscriptions, our bodies and abilities come to be morphologised and categorised into what are seen as socially significant groups. For example, the potential constraining and control of young peoples' movement in chronological and temporal spaces of schools can act as one inscription of age and development. Arguably more subtle, the shared understandings around particular clothes and commercial brands can also work as signs to denote adolescents of certain backgrounds and proclivities (see Moje & van Helden, this volume). By working through the concept of subjectivity instead of identity, we are first moved to strongly contextualise the lived experience of the subject through an embodied understanding of experience. As has been noted, adolescence has been strongly constructed out of biological discourses about developmentalism. By reclaiming and reckoning with the body as a necessarily complex conduit for lived experience, the concept of subjectivity allows us to talk about young people as subjects, but avoid ascribing and morphing neurophysiological traits onto them.

Second, the concept of embodied subjectivity is productively tinged with movement and travel, of fluidity and shift, across contexts (Belsey, 1997; Nelson, 2001). The political potential of viewing the subject as process rather than as fixed serves to include and acknowledge the multiple, competing, and contradictory positions that are both concurrently and disparately invoked within the subject and across subjects. Starting from this theoretical stance at once delegitimates and devalues knowing any person, and moreover, any group as commonly characterised. Working within a frame of fluidity and contestation, ergo an appropriately evasive knowability, subjectivity contains a conceptual saliency previously unknown in academic, research, and educational conversations about young people. Throughout this volume, the terms "young people" and "youth" have been privileged over "adolescence." This is, at once, a symbolic gesture to break with the developmentalist discourses surrounding adolescence, and a linguistic move to more closely bring subjectivities into the foreground.

SITUATING THE SUBJECT IN COMPLEXITY

The epistemological stances of post-modernity have approached the destabilised subject from a variety of tentative positions. To name a few, Anzaldua's (1999) famous self-portrait in hybridity casts her *mestiza* identity in terms of being a Chicana, a lesbian, a feminist, and working class. Spivak (1990) alternately provokes acting as *if* an identity were unilateral, only to achieve specific political aims. However, a reckoning with the subject and the social context has not been addressed even by these post-perspectives. In our case, simply re-naming adolescents as "young people" could be understood to be similarly incomplete, in terms of contextual invocations, refractions, and implications. That is, a shift in moniker may not necessarily ad-dress how the signification is used, how it is viewed by various sub-jects, and the effects of its uses. What is required further is a situating of subjectivities within contexts—a considered return to the collective. However, the concept of a collective is new neither to schooling nor to society. In fact, it has often been through the presence of a collective that individual identity politics have staged struggles for dominance.

By way of explicitly stated purpose, schooling—the most common set of practices explored in this volume—has located the subjectivities of young people within educational contexts but done so in, far too often, unitary approaches to difference, restrictive and controlling practices, and reproductive discourses of dominance and oppression (e.g., Fine, 1991; Oakes, 1985; Thorne, 1993; Sadker & Sadker, 1994). In reifying a dominant white, patriarchal, middle-class, and adultist space, schools have, as one institutional presence in society, stunted the subjective room for young people. What is needed then, is a lens of schooling that purposefully disengages from unitary production of the adolescent to one that is process-focused and recognitive of the embodied, fluid, and situated nature of peoples' subjectivities, in-cluding both the adults and the young people within educational spaces.

Complexity theory offers such a potential. In concert with this re-construction of the young person as embodied is the perspective that complexity theory lends to rethinking how education and schooling attend to its constituents. In short, complexity theory posits two key characteristics to complex systems: one, the systems are composed of necessarily different parts, and two, these systems occur in nested and mutually dependent fashions. The constituent parts are diverse, self-organising, self-regulating, and constantly shifting in unpredictable ways to result in synergistic fruitions, pointedly different to the dispa-rate possibilities of the individual parts (e.g., Bowers, 1995; Capra, 1982). As an example, people are composed of interconnected sets of complex systems: such as cells, tissues, and organs. Each of these systems individually attend to stimuli, or contexts, but do so at once individually and in relation to each other, to form and transform embodied responses and experiences. However, because complex systems defy preconceived hypotheses mapping these responses, they remain inherently and productively elusive of predictions. It is this unpredictability that offers a seminal turn from other models of social, behavioural, and physical sciences. The release from predicting the spontaneous, interrelational, and even fickle behaviours of complex systems renders null questions that attempt to control these behaviours.

While the application of complexity theory has mapped easily onto biologically bounded systems (e.g., cells, tissues, organs, human beings), the next larger nesting of human beings is contextual times and spaces. In this way, people can be first classified as complex systems but then nested with larger complex systems of context, in this example, the ones found in schools such as the classroom.

Put forth in their work that examines the epistemologies of learning normally found in schools, Davis, Sumara, and Luce-Kapler (2000) use complexity theory to reconsider how we structure teaching and learning in the context of productively unpredictable complexity. The authors propose that complexity theory provides a window through which educators might ask what are the enabling constraints and what are the essential limitations within which the complex systems can work, transform, and grow to individual and collective purposes. More typically, teachers use lesson plans and classroom pedagogies to provide learners with discrete, sequential, and often constraining procedures and rules. By contrast, Davis et al. (2000) envisage pedagogy that focuses less on control of predictable behaviour and outcomes and more on facilitating generative structures that allow for multiple pathways and collective symbiosis.

Seen from the lens of complexity, the possible roles afforded to young people and adults are radically transformed and widened. First, there is the expectation that the contexts' participants are different from each other. Whereas pervasive discourses about difference draw from deficit perspectives—urging us to "deal with" diversity—complexity theory engenders us to expect difference, to see it as a crucial and inalienable aspect to being human. Along with the concept of subjectivity, this theoretical stance removes the logic, place, and relevance of unitarily understood definitions and labels, such as "young people," or "early adolescents." Instead, language such as "young people' is used but recontextually understood in light of particular participants within local, institutional, and societal settings. In this way, complexity theory helps to force a recontextualising process of using language, hence mediating its constitutive force with the actual constituents at hand.

Second, complexity theory also redefines settings as complex. The collection of learners is itself a complex and nested set of other systems, the individual learners. However, regarding the collective as a complex system and warranting attention also positions our subjective experiences in a shared context.

With a release from preoccupations with control and subjugation currently governing paradigms around young people combined with a destabilising of the ill-formed focus on predictability of conforming behaviour, the possibility for dynamic interaction becomes forefronted. This dynamic restructuring would be at once embodied, recursive, exploratory, relational, and playful. By making a noted shift from the traditionally adultist views of adolescence, an epistemological stance of subjectivity and complexity yields a qualitatively different set of questions in working with young people (see Table 1).

Table 1. *Adultist vs. complex epistemological questions*

Adultist contexts and purposes	Reconstructing subjectivities within complexity
Not asked—assumed to be known	Who are the participants in the context?
What are the needs of the adolescent?	What are the needs, abilities, and proclivities of these participants in this setting?
What do they need to learn?	What individual and collective learning can occur in this context?
What are the rules?	What are liberating structures that will allow for divergent and productive learning for these people in this setting?

These questions mark wholly new dimensions that need to be opened and explored. Perhaps foremost, the questions are inextricably linked grounded in context. By privileging an ecological view of a learning system, the questions foreground a responsibility to the particular individuals, the collective, and to the interaction therein. The questions entertain subjectivities currently all but impossible in the modernist spaces of education, schooling, and the society, by assuming that they will need to be reposed, reconsidered, and recursively present. Asking who the participants are in the context pointedly casts specific light upon the young people and adults in learning situations. Often assumed to be understood for both entities, asking about the individual entities and their characteristics in a context helps to eradicate preconceived roles and stereotypes of adolescents, adults, teachers, and learners (see Blackburn, this volume; Finders, this volume).

Posing questions around potential learning spaces and liberating constraints (Davis et al., 2000) gives deference to the constituents' capabilities but departs from traditional fascinations with controlling the minutiae of each lesson. Middle schools, junior high schools, and high schools are particularly marked by highly controlled configurations of time, space, and young bodies (see Vadeboncoeur, Chapter 6, this volume). Understanding people, contexts, and learning as generatively complex casts these types of regulations and governmentality as particularly ineffective and antithetical. In this sense, complex views of learning offer a synergistic coupling with the destabilising of deterministic meanings associated with "adolescence." Through a forthright recognition of destabilization, complex views of learners and learning would pose these questions recursively, assuming variant understandings over time, space, and contexts. In this way, this combination of deconstruction and reconstruction offers a potential productive space in which we can actively restructure our epistemological and ontological stances and effects.

The chapters in this volume, while representing an array of theoretical frameworks and methodological precepts, all contribute a voice in an appeal to reconfigure how young people are relegated to liminal spaces. This appeal is multifaceted. It is not to be understood solely through the classroom, the home, the youth centre nor the virtual space of the Internet, to name but a few social spaces. Instead, this appeal attempts to recontextualise, complicate, and purposefully render unknowable any space or single entity that is "adolescent."

NOTES

1. Many thanks to Joy Reynolds for her creative work in designing this image and contributing it to this chapter.
2. In this chapter, "subjectivity" is used to mark the theoretical concept, while "subjectivities" is used in the application of this theory to fluid, multiple, and contested selves.

REFERENCES

Anzaldua, G. (1999). *Borderlands/la frontera: The new mestiza* (Rev. ed.). San Francisco: Aunt Lute.

Belsey, C. (1997). Constructing the subject: Deconstructing the self. In R. R. Warhol & D. P. Herndl (Eds.), *Feminisms: An anthology of literacy theory and criticism* (Rev. ed.) (pp. 220–236). New Brunswick, NJ: Rutgers University Press.

Bowers, C. A. (1995). *Educating for an ecologically sustainable culture: Rethinking moral education, creativity, intelligence, and other modern orthodoxies*. Albany: The State University of New York Press.

Butler, J. (1999). *Gender trouble: Feminism and the subversion of identity*. New York: Routledge.

Capra, F. (1982). *The turning point: Science, society, and the rising culture*. New York: Bantam.

Davis, B., Sumara, D., & Luce-Kapler, R. (2000). *Engaging minds: Learning and teaching in a complex world*. Mahwah, NJ: Lawrence Erlbaum.

Derrida, J. (1998). *Of grammatology* (G. Spivak, Trans.). New York: John Hopkins University Press.

Fairclough, N. (1989). *Language and power*. London: Longman.

Fine, M. (1991). *Framing dropouts: Notes on the politics of an urban public high school*. Albany: The State University of New York Press.

Foucault, M. (1972). The discourse on language. *The archeology of knowledge* (A. M. Sheridan, Trans.). New York: Harper Colophon.

Gee, J. (2002). Millennials and Bobos, *Blue's Clues* and *Sesame Street*: A story for our times. In D. Alvermann (Ed.), *New literacies and digital technologies: A focus on adolescent learners in new times* (pp. 56–68). New York: Peter Lang.

Grosz, E. (1994). *Volatile bodies: Toward a corporeal feminism*. Sydney: Allen & Unwin.

Heyes, C. J. (2000). *Line drawings: Defining women through feminist practice*. Ithaca, NY: Cornell University Press.

hooks, b. (1994). *Outlaw culture: Resisting representations*. New York: Routledge.

Lesko, N. (2001). *Act your age! A cultural construction of adolescence*. New York: Routledge.

Luke, A. (1997) The material effects of the word: Apologies, stolen children and public speech. *Discourse: Studies in the Cultural Politics of Education, 23*(3), 151–180.

Luke, A., Elkins, J., Weir, K., Land, R., Carrington, V., & Dole, S. (2003). *Beyond the middle: A report about literacy and numeracy development of target group students in the middle years of schooling* (191). Brisbane, Australia, The University of Queensland.

Nelson, H. L. (2001). *Damaged identities: Narrative repair.* Ithaca, NY: Cornell University Press.

Oakes, J. (1985). *Keeping track: How schools structure inequality.* New Haven, CT: Yale University Press.

Sadker, M. & Sadker, D. (1994). *Failing at fairness: How our schools cheat girls.* New York: Touchstone.

Spivak, G. C. (1990). The intervention interview. In S. Harasym, (Ed.), *The post-colonial critic: Interviews, strategies, dialogues / Gayatri Chakravorty Spivak* (pp. 113-132). New York: Routledge.

Thorne, B. (1993). *Gender play: Girls and boys in school.* London: Open University Press.

Young, I. M. (1990). *Justice and the politics of difference.* Princeton: Princeton University Press.

CONTRIBUTORS

Mollie Blackburn is an Assistant Professor in Literacy, Language, and Culture in the College of Education at Ohio State University. Her research is critical and activist in nature. It has included exploring privilege through literature with sixth graders, examining discussions of race in college classrooms, studying leadership with urban teachers, and, most recently, exploring the ways in which queer youth use literacies and language to construct identities and work for social change.

Judith V. Diamondstone looks at the relations between learning and identity as they form within classroom and out-of-school activities for young people from diverse, non-middle-class backgrounds. She is working as a Research Associate at Clark University and with local organizations to develop an after-school program in digital media literacies for middle school students in Worcester, Massachusetts.

Margaret J. Finders is Director of Teacher Education and Associate Professor of Education at Washington University in St. Louis. She is the author of *Just Girls: Hidden Literacies and Life in Junior High* and co-author of *Literacy Lessons: Teaching and Learning with Middle School Students.* Her research focuses on adolescents, literacy practices, and on teacher education, specifically in regard to issues of equity and social justice.

Lisa Hunter lectures for The University of Queensland in the Schools of Education and Human Movement Studies. Her primary teaching responsibility is in teacher education in the Middle Years of Schooling Program. Her research includes the role of embodiment in young peoples' learning, in general, with an emphasis on the areas of health and physical education; teachers' embodied subjectivities and the role of preservice teacher education; and young people's engagement and subjectivity construction in "extreme" physical activities.

Elizabeth Birr Moje is an Associate Professor of Literacy, Language, and Culture in Educational Studies at the University of Michigan, Ann Arbor. She teaches undergraduate and graduate courses in secondary and adolescent literacy, cultural theory, and qualitative research methods. Her research interests revolve around the intersection between the literacies and texts youth are asked to learn in formal learning institutions and the literacies and texts they engage outside of school. She also studies how youth make culture and enact identities from their community cultures, popular cultures, school cultures, and home.

Jrene Rahm is an Assistant Professor in educational psychology at the Université de Montréal in Canada. Her research focuses on young people from working-class families and their scientific meaning-making in informal educational contexts such as after-school programs, youth programs, museums, and community gardens. Through qualitative case studies informed by sociocultural theory, she is currently documenting youth access to educational opportunities in science and technology. Her work underlines her interest in representations of, and advocacy for, youth.

Lisa Patel Stevens is an Assistant Professor in Literacy at the Lynch School of Education, Boston College. Her research interests include multiliteracies, critical literacy, policy studies, and cultural constructions of adolescence. She is co-author of *Critical Literacy in the United States* with Thomas W. Bean, forthcoming from Peter Lang.

Karen Tracy is Professor of Communication at the University of Colorado-Boulder. She is the author of *Colloquium: Dilemmas of Academic Discourse, Everyday Talk: Building and Reflecting Identities,* and articles that have appeared in variety of journals, including *Communication Theory, Journal of Applied Communication,* and *Discourse Studies.* She is past editor of the journal *Research on Language and Social*

Interaction and is at work on a book about the interactional challenges of discussion and deliberation in American school board meetings.

Jennifer A. Vadeboncoeur is a Lecturer in Sociocultural Psychology at The University of Queensland. Her research interests lie in applying sociocultural and critical lenses to the study of identity construction, in particular, the social construction of "at risk" identities for young people. Her current research documents the experiences of students and teachers in alternative high school programs. She is co-editor of *Educational Imaginings: On the Play of Texts and Contexts* with Shaun Rawolle published by Australian Academic Press.

Caspar van Helden is a doctoral student in the School of Education at the University of Michigan, Ann Arbor. After completing a masters degree in Discourse Theory and Analysis at the universities of Vienna and Amsterdam, he now studies concepts of adolescence, popular and youth culture, identity, and their relationships to education. Visit www.umich.edu/~cvanhel for more information on his research projects.

Johanna Wyn is Professor of Education at the University of Melbourne. She is Director of the Australian Youth Research Centre and Head of the Department of Education, Policy and Management in the Faculty of Education, The University of Melbourne. She is the author of many reports and articles on youth and of *Rethinking Youth*, with Rob White, and *Youth, Education and Risk: Facing the Future*, with Peter Dwyer.

INDEX

A

M

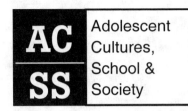

Adolescent
Cultures,
School &
Society

Joseph L. DeVitis & Linda Irwin-DeVitis
GENERAL EDITORS

As schools struggle to redefine and restructure themselves, they need to be cognizant of the new realities of adolescents. Thus, this series of monographs and textbooks is committed to depicting the variety of adolescent cultures that exist in today's post-industrial societies. It is intended to be a primarily qualitative research, practice, and policy series devoted to contextual interpretation and analysis that encompasses a broad range of interdisciplinary critique. In addition, this series will seek to provide a pragmatic, pro-active response to the current backlash of conservatism that continues to dominate political discourse, practice, and policy. This series seeks to address issues of curriculum theory and practice; multicultural education; aggression and violence; the media and arts; school dropouts; homeless and runaway youth; alienated youth; at-risk adolescent populations; family structures and parental involvement; and race, ethnicity, class, and gender studies.

Send proposals and manuscripts to the general editors at:
Joseph L. DeVitis & Linda Irwin-DeVitis
The John H. Lounsbury School of Education
Georgia College & State University
Campus Box 70
Milledgeville, GA 31061-0490

To order other books in this series, please contact our Customer Service Department at:
(800) 770-LANG (within the U.S.)
(212) 647-7706 (outside the U.S.)
(212) 647-7707 FAX

or browse online by series at:
WWW.PETERLANGUSA.COM